Twink

Unzipped!

© Adèle King, 2012

ISBN: 978–0–9566612–0–3

First published in Ireland in 2012

Blackwater Press Ltd.
1–5 North Frederick Street, Dublin 1

The author and publisher gratefully acknowledge the following for permission to reproduce photographs:

RTÉ Stills Library, Michael O'Doherty, Kieran Harnett, Barry McCall,
Colm Henry, Independent Newspapers, Harmonia, Hot Press, Argyll Communications, Irish Heart Foundation, Irish Cancer Society.

Printed in the Republic of Ireland

Foreword

Shy, demure, understated … words that don't seem bespoke when Twink springs to mind (or crashes to mind more like!).

No, that light doesn't cower under a bushel, it lamps you, it blazes at you full on. She's larger than life, that lass. Brash, generous, affectionate, loyal and profane. God, her language is blush-inducing at times! And what a pro … always prepared, words learned, moves rehearsed, antennae honed for improvement and improvisation. When working with younger performers, she's always ready to encourage, suggest ideas, new approaches.

When John Keogh and I were charged with creating *The Live Mike* in the eighties, she was the first cast member to be engaged. Although celebrated as a singer, we knew she could mimic, move and comede. It was a bonus that she could impersonate Mrs Thatcher from the off. The Iron Lady was in her hey-day and with Fran Dempsey's Charlie Haughey in tandem, we had a ball. Then there was Dermot – pre-*Father Ted* – making his debut in television comedy as well. What an impact there was! The show just buzzed. All right, it may look a little retro now, but it got a helluva reaction, and we all hit it off so well!

Photo by: Kieran Harnett

I'm on record about my deep affection for – and admiration of – Twink (Twinkles to me, Adèle to family and friends). And she has a story to tell. Not an ordinary life, you understand. There were uppity ups and very deep downs; there's controversy, fear, love, antipathy, humiliation, rivalry, success and failure.

But has she been noticed? You betcha!

Has she made an impact? That's for sure!

Is she loved and cherished? Is she what?

She's a one-off, that one.

And I'm the daddy of the fan club!

Mike Murphy
November 2012

The Three Rules of the Camera

Rule number one: Look at the camera, Adéle, and not at the action happening behind you.

Rule number two: And for God's sake, Adéle, never get caught picking your nose when in the vicinity of a camera.

'She isn't a woman, she isn't a girl. She's a force of nature.'

Former minister, Justin Keating

Rule number three: And never, ever wear your knickers on your head!.

Dedication

I would like most especially to dedicate this book to my beautiful beloved daughters, Chloë and Naomi.

From the very moment of both of your births, my life changed forever, for the better.

The words in the English language have not been invented to tell, or show you in any way, the depth of my love and admiration for you both.

Thank you for all the joy you have brought to my existence, you are the greatest thing that ever happened my life. I will be with you all the days of your lives …

'Every step you take … Every move you make …
I'll be watching you!' (Thank you Sting!)

I love you unspeakably.

Mama … X

Photo by: Kieran Harnett

Best Run Ever!
I promoted the Milk Run
around Ireland.. Mind you -
just as well I was riding a
bike and not baking a cake
with those nails!!

The Overture

If an autobiography I'm reading starts with the line, 'I was born in …', I immediately find myself resisting the urge to fire the bloody thing at the bedroom wall. Fortunately, I love my house too much (and have fought too hard for it) to risk damaging the paintwork with pages of compressed boredom.

As you will see for yourself, however, this is not your typical autobiography, which is why I feel the need to warn you that if you have either a weak heart or a weak bladder, well, some of the stories in this book certainly won't do them any favours!

I haven't lived a typical life, and so felt it appropriate that my life story should reflect that. From recalling the day I was sent a dead rat by a well-known actress, to the time the depths of depression led to me contemplating the idea of taking the lives of my two daughters and myself, there really isn't anything I have held back on. If I have left out anything, it's because I have either forgotten about it or exceeded my page limit!

For every laugh I have enjoyed, I have shed a dozen tears – but I'm not complaining. While, in some ways, my life has seen more trauma than I would like, it has also had those gilded edges that money can't buy. When I look at my idol, the opera singer Maria Callas, who led a very traumatic life, I wonder if her voice would have possessed such soul and spirit if she had not carried her suffering with her. A great philosophy of my father's was that there's a lesson to be learned from everything that happens in your life – the good times and the bad.

Women have often said to me, 'Ah, but, Twink, you're tough. You're able for it!'

Tough? For God's sake, I'm as weak and as vulnerable as anyone else! I have never been afraid to cry or let off steam ('Zip up your mickey' anyone?). Equally, I have never been afraid to move forward with my life. I have always seen myself as an evolving person. I have had every hairstyle and every hair colour and have been through every fashion phase. I've been fat and I've been thin, but the point is I have always changed. If I were to kill you with something, well, it certainly wouldn't be boredom!

There's a generation of women who have grown up with me. These were the women who sang to the records of Maxi Dick and Twink, and who later danced in the ballrooms when I performed with the likes of Bowyer and the Big 8 and Paddy Cole's Superstars. These same women are now coming to see me perform in theatre shows around the country, but, this time around, they're also bringing their daughters with them.

We've grown up together, we've sung together and, sure fuck it, seeing as we've come this far ladies, we might as well continue on until it's time to start discussing the best brand of Poly-whatsit to keep our false teeth in place!

'Having known of Adèle for most of my life, I got to work with her on the show **Mum's the Word**. She did not disappoint, we got on splendidly and I found her to be mad, warm, funny, and full of stories – always saying 'when I write the book'. It was her birthday during our show and we didn't know what to get her. What do you get the woman who has everything? In a flash, I thought a notebook for all those book ideas, so we got it for her and she was delighted. So my darling, Adèle, I can't wait to see your book in the shops. You had better get started on it because you are bursting with stories that need to be shared.

Love you, Nellie Conroy xx

A little scut in shorts

The whole time we were in the shop, he never shut up talking.

Not once.

Mind you, not a lot changed when he got older. I can still vividly see us standing in Burke's Costumiers on Dame Street as my mother turned to me and said, 'Adèle say hello to Mrs Ryan and her son Gerard …'

He was five years old; I was ten. I remember he was sporting a little quiff and was wearing white shorts, a tiny Fair Isle *geansaí* over a crisp, white, short-sleeved shirt and white sandals. Thinking of myself as a sophisticated ten year old, I initially looked upon Gerry as a little scut, but with both of us being such animated talkers, we soon clicked.

I remember the morning he told the whole nation that very story. Typical man, he also revealed the year it happened without realising that even the biggest thick could do the sums and work out what age I was. Whatever chance I'd had of shaving off a few years were well and truly scuppered there and then. As the years passed, I came to look upon Gerry as a truly great friend, the kind you could phone at three in the morning and without question he would help you bury the body!

We were each other's confidantes and comedians, there to pull the piss or lend a shoulder to cry on. There was no such thing as a bad day when Gerry was around. Even though it has been over two years since he left us, I still talk about him in the present tense, still not quite fully ready to believe he's really gone. I'm sure somewhere in the fabric of time, the grief will heal, but, for now, the pain remains every bit as heartbreaking as it did when I first heard the news.

Like Gerry, I hailed from a very artistic family.

Even though I was as equally academic as sporty, it still doesn't surprise me that my life assumed a more creative path (despite my reluctance to embrace it, I hasten to add). In a way, it was not so much fate that decided my life but a natural progression.

My beloved uncle Jack was a bespoke tailor with a business in Merrion Square. There were a number of tailors in the family, most notably my cousin Louis Copeland. Long before Louis was even in nappies, my uncle Jack was making jodhpurs and riding gear for the gentry, as well as the suits and cloaks for barristers and High Court judges.

My grand-aunt Esther, meanwhile, hand-stitched buttonholes on the most exquisite shirts for a very upmarket menswear shop on Grafton Street called Tyson's. It was from her that I gleaned my stitching skills as a child and, as a result, I now love to indulge in creating fine art tapestries.

My mother, Elizabeth Condron – a most gifted artist with an incredible streak of creativity – designed exquisite wedding dresses for a beautiful shop on Grafton Street. I used to adore looking through her designs. She would create the most elegant slender dresses, a style very reminiscent of the 1940s. She even designed and made her own wedding dress.

Mom was also a remarkable cartoonist. If she was leaving a note to say she had gone out to meet my father, she would draw a tiny matchstick figure cartoon depicting dad waiting with a signature cigarette in his mouth.

L-r: Uncle Paddy, Dad, cousin Hubert, Mom and Aunty Meta.

Me with Dad and my beloved godmother Aunty Meta, Mom's sister. In the background left, my Nana Condron and right my gifted aunt Esther.

I sometimes heard Mom talk about a man called Bertie Collins, whom I believe was a big shot in the ESB. I think she had been in love with Bertie before a certain Leo King swept her off her feet. She adored my father and he, likewise, absolutely idolised her. Army horse riding instructor by day and marquetry lecturer by evening, my Sligo-born father and a plethora of relations in veterinary and dentistry that helped me to develop a lifelong love for horse riding and medicine – not to mention a propensity for devouring medical journals.

As I was born on 4 April, smack bang in the middle of Easter, my dad's nickname for me was 'Bunny'. Indeed, that was the name he always called me *except* for those occasions when he would summon me with a roar of 'Adèle', in which case I knew I was in deep shit.

Another nickname he gave me was 'Now'. Even as a child, I was like a bull at a gate: no patience and always taking to tasks at breakneck speed. The term 'in a minute' was not in my vocabulary, everything had to be 'now', hence the nickname.

My mother, by contrast, was such a gentle creature. In fact, when I was about twenty years of age, I asked her if I had been adopted. I just couldn't figure out how such a quiet ladylike little woman could have given birth to a volcano. If anything, I was more like my father's feisty sister May King (known to us all as Aunty Mamie) who, rather bizarrely, was also born on 4 April! In fact, so alike were we in personality that if I was ever having a temper tantrum as a kid, my father would always throw his eyes up and say, 'Sacred Heart of God, May King will never be dead while you're alive!'

My youngest daughter Naomi is a clone of my mother in every single way, particularly in the way she speaks. It's a very quiet, refined tone and it wouldn't be unusual for her to tell *me* to keep my voice down. Even when she's angry, she won't raise her voice in the slightest which is so infuriating for the person arguing with her, i.e. *me*! At least, my oldest daughter Chloë and I have the bloody manners to roar when we're having a mother-daughter fight. Chloë is a typical Gemini and anyone reading this who has a Gemini belonging to them will know that they are a roller-coaster of emotions with an incredible capacity to swing from laughter to tears in twenty seconds. Overall, the two of them have their fair share of bolshiness, I wonder where they got that from!

❖

Sport also played a huge part in my early years and, if I'm anything like my aunty Kathleen from Sligo, who still enjoyed riding her horse into the village for groceries until she was well into her nineties, it will no doubt be a significant part of my latter years as well.

As a very young child, I lived in London for some time, a city where ballet and dance were almost an automatic part of a child's formative years. Unfortunately, when I returned to Dublin in the 1950s, ballet schools were quite thin on the ground. Eventually, my mother discovered wonderful ballet classes hosted by Jill Margie in Baby Meddlers School of Dance on St Stephen's Green. During this time, I was also taking Irish dancing lessons in Miss Keavney's 'sixpenny hard-reel class', also situated on St Stephen's Green – it was six pence per class, hence the name. In my class was a young boy called John Sullivan, who would later become a lifelong friend, not to mention godfather to my first born. An indescribably brilliant dancer, he went on to star in the first pop television show on RTÉ called *Like Now*, where he was one half of the dance duo John and Olivia.

I, meanwhile, branched out into other areas, developing my dancing skills to include tap, jazz, Latin American and ballroom dancing. I was such a devoted music enthusiast at that age that I can still remember the thrill I felt coming home on the bus with my beloved parents on Christmas Eve. They had just bought my very first guitar (all wrapped-up in brown paper and twine) for the princely sum of eight pounds and ten shillings from Waltons in North Frederick Street, ironically now the home of my publisher. Early in January, my mother brought me to a teacher in Crumlin called Mr Duffy. Prior to taking lessons, I had spent time teaching myself the various chords with the help of a book priced 1/6d from a music shop called Mays on the Green. I can hear some of you sighing at the very mention of Mays on the Green. Be honest now, ladies, how many of you went there to buy your one and sixpenny manuscripts for your music exams? Ah, God be with the days, eh?

Meanwhile when I proudly demonstrated for Mr Duffy the chords I had taught myself, he immediately took the guitar from me and said, 'Well first of all dear … unfortunately for you, we usually hold it the other way around!'

Being a lefty, I had been playing the chords with my right hand and strumming with the left. Of course, the opposite is the norm. I was now facing the chore of having to start all over again by turning the damn thing around and learning how to play it the supposedly 'correct' way.

Mind you, being a left-handed guitarist never affected the career of a certain Mr Paul McCartney – Eh?

My Years of Beloved Irish dancing

1. Loreto Beaufort Champion Dance Team, 1962.

2. Quartet Champions for a shared day.

3. Solo dancing Champion in the costume hand embroidered by my grandmother.

4. Still reeling in the great Irish steps - 30 odd years later.

Ms Eeedel Con-DRON-king

Ireland knows me as Twink, but my family knew me as Adèle Anna Maria Mary Lucia Condron-King. Seeing as how airports don't use hyphens on airline tickets, I have, rather amusingly, become very familiar with being referred to as 'Miss Con-DRON-king' in many an airport around the world.

❖

So how did I come by the name Adèle? Well, before I explain how the name came about, I should tell you that one of my great 'bones of contention' in life is the number of people who mispronounce my name.

Give me a break here folks, it's not Edel.

It's not Eeeeedel.

It's not even Idele.

It's Adèle. And if you can't manage that, Twink will do just fine!

Anyhow, back to the name itself. My father was a devout opera lover and so he and my mother decided to name me after the opera singer Adèle Lee. Mary Lucia was chosen because we were a family with a fixation on all things Italian. (My cousin Gemma Condron even went as far as becoming a dancer with the Rome Ballet.) We were also a family of Elizabeths – with both of my grandmothers, my mother and my cousin having been christened with the name. In a time where everyone was called 'Lourdesy' names like Bernadette, Mary and Frances, here was my family with their Elizabeths, Esthers, Theopholouss, Bartholomews and Huberts!

I can only conclude that the lot of them were a bundle of bloody royalists.

Yes, but can she sing?

School for me was in Rathfarnham, albeit not for long.

When I arrived home in tears one day after being reprimanded for wearing my straw boater at the wrong angle in a Corpus Christie Parade, my father took me by the hand and marched me in to the office of the head nun, who was a right oul' bitch. After politely, yet firmly, giving her a piece of his mind, I was removed from the school, and by the following morning was standing in Sister Madeline's office in St Louis, Rathmines. Sister Mary Herman was also in the office to greet me. I didn't know it at the time, but she was the head of the Young Dublin Singers, a seriously successful choir where the ferocious dedication invested by the students was on a level of its own.

While Sister Madeline was concerned only with my academic qualifications, Sister Herman's sole question to my mother was, 'Can she sing?' I can still remember my mother looking at me unsurely and saying, 'Um … I think she can. Well, she can play the guitar, the harp, the piano and the flute.'

'Can she really?' Sister Herman's eyes lit up. 'The Young Dublin Singers are rehearsing tomorrow. Bring her down!'

We attended the following day and after the initial introductions to the class, I was asked to perform so that Sister Herman could judge my potential. I promptly took my harp out of its case and sang 'By Killarney's Lakes and Fells'. I think it was when I then took my guitar out of its case to sing 'Kitty of Coleraine' that Sister Herman almost had a hernia.

Her response? 'Well, Mrs King … she's in!' She honestly didn't give a fiddler's whether I could read or write; in her eyes, musically speaking, I was of enormous value to her choir.

Almost unbeknownst to myself, I went on to become one of the lead performers within the Young Dublin Singers. The meaning of the words 'perfection' and 'discipline' was instilled in each and every one of us from an early age and not once did we ever stray from it. As a result, the Young Dublin Singers went on to become an established choir, producing some legendary talents in music, including the famous mezzo-soprano Anne Murray, singers Alma Carroll, Colm CT Wilkinson and Judith Wilkinson, Fionnula Hough, Nancy, Bernadette and Celine Cooney and Mary and Frances Black, West End star Siobhan McCarthy, and, of course, Maxi Dick and Twink. On one occasion, a man from EMI in England, Harry Christmas (I kid you not! His wife was even called Mary Christmas), arrived over to hear us perform. Impressed, he signed us to the EMI label and we went on to record several albums. Not a bad career for a kid of no more than nine!

Mixie, Dicksie and Twonksie

During my time in the Young Dublin Singers, I was also involved in the Gaiety Pantos as one of the cute kiddies. Of course, once you developed any sign of boobs, you were forced into early retirement and immediately sent over to Jury's Hotel, which was then located on Dublin's Dame Street, where you could continue your performing career, this time for the American tourist market.

The theatre scene in Dublin was dominated by the luminary that was Eamonn Andrews and even though Eamonn spent most of his time on

MAXIE DICK N' TWINK

Manager : T.J.BYRNE   -   T.J.ARTISTES   21a South Anne Street, Dublin 2.

Telephone : Dublin 779129   Carlow 41322

British television hosting the likes of *This Is Your Life*, he had also opened a formidable theatre and recording empire in Dublin called Eamonn Andrews Studios. This was run by a legendary producer called Fred O'Donovan. Fred and Eamonn were responsible for creating a series of spectacular variety shows in the Gaiety called *Gaels of Laughter*. Somewhere in the midst of organising this event, however, Eamonn decided he wanted to create a girl group, primarily to be the backing singers for their recording studios. In the pre-auditions, they randomly grouped together different girls. For one of the groups, he chose Irene McCoubrey, Barbara Dixon, Mary Cooke and Siobhan Walsh. When they all stood together, however, Fred took one look and suddenly decided to swap Mary and Siobhan with yours truly, or 'young King' as he referred to me then. That one swift decision would actually change my life forever and I have often wondered where I would be today if Fred had left the line up as it was.

Somewhere over the course of the next few days, they decided that a trio of young girls would read very well on the *Gaels of Laughter* poster, and so they announced to us that auditions would take place on the Gaiety stage the following Friday afternoon. The three of us spent the rest of the week religiously rehearsing the piece we planned to perform for the judging panel in the audition. With me also playing the guitar as the accompaniment to our piece, we knew we had the edge over the other groups. Following the audition itself, I sensed that we had done well, as did Irene and Barbara. Our hunch proved to be right and the following day, in between shows, Fred revealed that the judges had named us as the successful trio.

The following Monday after school, we met with Fred in his office on Harcourt Street where he outlined the details of *Gaels of Laughter*, the first of its kind in Ireland, with Maureen Potter lined up as the headlining act. Following the meeting, we were sent off to be coiffured, measured and fitted. By this stage, Irene had become known as 'Maxi', as a result of us referring to her by her initials McC. With Barbara's surname being Dixon, she earned herself the nickname 'Dicko'. My nickname on the other hand had a slightly longer history attached. When I was around six years old, I played the part of Clara in the ballet *Sleeping Beauty*, which was being staged

The first picture of the Young Dublin 3 who went on to become Maxi Dick and Twink.

in the Olympia Theatre. On the final night, the legendary actor Daniel O'Herlihy, who was huge in American movies at the time, had the job of making the closing-night speeches and presenting the bouquets to the principal dancers. Being all of six years of age, I understandably managed to doze off backstage. It had been arranged that Daniel O'Herlihy would present me with a huge teddy bear on stage, however when he came looking for me, he found me asleep in the beautiful broderie anglaise dress my mother had made for me. Scooping me up into his arms, he carried me out on stage where he delivered a very witty speech to the crowd before adding, 'Well, I'm afraid this young sleeping ballerina's name escapes me but I know you will all want to join me in congratulating little Twinkle Toes here on a wonderful job tonight.'

The following day, a newspaper carried a picture of me in Daniel O'Herlihy's arms underneath which it read: 'The young ballerina, Adèle King, made a great impression playing Clara, although I'm sure after Mr O'Herlihy calling her Twinkle Toes, the name will stick in ballet school for a year or two!'

That was over fifty years ago, and I haven't been able to get rid of it yet.

A heart-stoppingly wonderful moment for me occurred at the launch of Maureen Potter's book in the Gaiety Theatre when a lovely young American woman approached me and said, 'I believe my father has a lot to answer for! He followed your career over the decades and constantly reminded us that he was the one who christened you Twinkle Toes!'

She then extended her hand and said, 'I'm Olwyn O'Herlihy, Daniel O'Herlihy's daughter.'

Small world or what?

With every major name in Ireland on the bill, the launch of the *Gaels of Laughter* show attracted major press attention. Prior to the big night, however, Fred arranged for us to do a few small gigs in the Gresham Hotel and other local cabaret slots, just to knock the edges off us before we performed in the main show. During that time, we called ourselves the Young Dublin Three, as a nod to the our association with the Young Dublin Singers. Fred, however, loathed the name and steadfastly refused to put it on the posters, insisting instead that we create something more imaginative.

We sat and wracked our brains for what seemed like forever. We were the Crystalettes, the Gaietyettes, the Graftonettes and every other '-ettes' name you could think of. They were all vile. As our wits' end approached, I remember looking at the other two and saying, 'Girls we're going to have to think of something immediately otherwise we're going to end up calling ourselves something like Dick and Twink and Maxi.'

Suddenly the other two looked at me and, with that, the proverbial penny dropped. After playing around with a few potential variations of our names, we eventually decided on Maxi Dick and Twink.

Somehow it just rolled off the tongue better.

When we told Fred, he was quite amused but had just one concern. Would people remember it? At the time, there was a hugely popular British band called Dave Dee, Dozy, Beaky, Mick and Tich so I argued that if people could remember that mouthful, then they would have no problem remembering ours. Our instincts didn't fail us and Maxi Dick and Twink, the trio in miniskirts and white plastic knee-highs, proved to be the biggest scene-stealing hit of the press launch! Considering it was an era when your decency was measured by how short you wore your mini skirt and when that extra inch of 'shortness' could virtually warrant a lecture from the pulpit, I don't know how some of our outfits escaped controversy. Even though our look was very sixties, I suppose we still had an air of innocence (despite some of our skirts looking more like seat-belts!)

❖

One of the best things that happened to us was meeting a lovely Carlow man called T.J. Byrne, manager of the Royal Showband in Las Vegas. He was way ahead of his time and knew exactly the kind of image that would generate success. He could see that we needed to be 'marketed', so his first duty was to march us into Clery's and buy us fur coats in both black and white. Coney furs were all the rage at the time. We then received a collection of white plastic boots and black travelling cases with our names printed on the front.

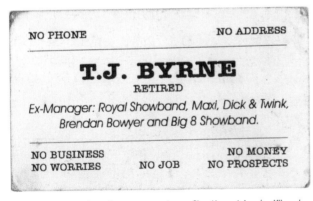

T.J.'s mock business card, reflecting his brilliant sense of humour.

Our transport was a long, pink two-toned Cadillac with a mint-green interior, which T.J. had brought over from America just for us. We arrived at all our gigs in this phenomenal car, each time emerging from it in our white fur coats and plastic boots.

My nicknames

Ireland – Twink

My father – Bunny

Paddy Cole – Gerty

Mike Murphy and Dick – Twinkles

Maxi – Twinkle Toes

Gay Byrne and Dick Hill – Dotey

John McColgan and Bill Whelan – Miss King

Kevin Hough – Dellington

***Mum's the Word* girls (Anna, Neili, Eileen and Flo)** – Delser

Terry Herron – Duracell Bunny

Shay Healy – Twiddles

Noel Kelly – Kiddo

Maureen Potter – Young One!

The actors who played my kids in *Jack and the Beanstalk* and other pantos all call me 'Ma', while the lovely Geraldine O'Callaghan from *The Apprentice* and *Celebrity Head Chef* calls me 'Mammy', Of course, my lifelong friend and colleague Joe Conlon had to take the 'Ma' reference one step further and christen me 'Mudder'!

Maxi Dick and Twink performing on RTÉ's *Steady As She Go-Goes*.

When we performed at gigs in rural Ireland, it must have been like Hollywood itself had arrived!

T.J. always knew how to generate hype – he was a **PR** machine. He would line up local photographers to greet us at whatever venue we were playing. Likewise, if we were launching a boutique, he would always make sure that in the huge crowd outside there were a few 'plants' – by that I mean people he had deliberately positioned to shout out the most complimentary things at the top of their voices to us. Of course, T.J. knew full well that the assembled press would write the

compliments in the newspapers the following day. He would also use only the best photographers to do photo shoots for our handouts. These were cards we would autograph for the fans, and, for us, this was almost as amazing as the Cadillac. Back then, only the biggest acts merited the necessity of 'handout' cards.

The show that truly launched us was RTÉ's *Steady As She Go-Goes*, a phenomenally popular show on which major stars appeared each week. In the show, we were based on a cruise ship that stopped off at different ports around the world.

In reality, however, we never left the RTÉ studios in Donnybrook. On screen, we were sunning ourselves in the Mediterranean, but when the cameras stopped rolling, the set was dismantled and the Med became Montrose!

Our musical director for that show was jazz pianist and general musical genius Jim Doherty. This show was the beginning of a long working relationship with Jim, who would go on to be my musical director for a variety of shows throughout my career, including the magnificent show and TV Special *Hunky Dory* with the legendary Dory Previn.

I certainly knew my life had come full circle when one evening as I was cooking dinner, I heard a very familiar voice on the television. The face and the voice were so recognisable and yet I couldn't fathom how I knew this young man. Suddenly it hit me and I pegged it out to my photo cabinet. Yep, sure enough, there he was in my wedding album! The blond beautiful page boy dressed like little Lord Fauntleroy was in fact the latest Irish comedian to hit British television, the hysterically funny and fabulously popular, David O'Doherty, aka Jim's son. In fact, Jim later informed me that David had used his reference as 'Twink's page boy' in the earlier days of his act. I am so immensely proud of David. Needless to say my daughters and their friends are also huge fans.

As a result of our success on television, an appearance on *The Late Late Show* with Gay Byrne beckoned. While I was thrilled to be on the show, there was no novelty attached to it, simply because I had been on television for years at that point. Mom and Dad had often brought me out to RTÉ after school to record children's television programmes, such as *Seoirse agus Beartlai*, *Junior Concert Hall*, *At Home With O'Reilly*, and the very popular *Cochre Samhraidh*, and so by the time I appeared on *The Late Late Show* with Maxi and Dick, I was a dab oul' hand at it despite being all of twelve years of age.

"You go - brilliant David!"

Old RTÉ Sills promo pic of a 12 year old Adèle.

The after-school job

Ireland loved us. The odd bitchy classmate however – not so much.

We may have enjoyed being chauffeured around in a pink Cadillac each night, but we still had to go to our respective schools each morning.

Stepping out of a fur coat and into a school uniform was not a difficult transition for me; if anything, it felt like the most natural thing in the world. I had been performing all my life and Maxi Dick and Twink was just an extension of that.

Ironically, my daughter Chloë has been through the exact same experience. She would go from starring in Radio City New York with Celtic Woman to returning home into her Alexandra College uniform and studying for her Leaving Cert. While she was on the road working, she studied with tutors, just like I had done. There were some genuinely beautiful girls in her class who welcomed her with open arms and they remain some of her very best friends today, but, as always, there were a few with an attitude.

It had been the same for me. My true friends didn't see any change in me. In fact, they were proud of my achievements. To them, I was still the same girl, just with a different after-school job. The bitches, of course, found it difficult to accept our success, preferring instead to adopt a mantle of arrogance, always to the tune of, 'Ah, you've changed'. The truth was *I* hadn't changed at all, but *their* attitudes towards *me* had.

Unfortunately, there was one other downside to my 'after-school job'.

During the touring days of Maxi Dick and Twink, we would almost always have to visit the parochial house of whatever area we were performing in. One priest in particular, would always deliberately walk into the room while we were changing. This same priest also had a penchant for telling us the kind of adult jokes that would turn the air blue.

One day as we were changing, Maxi was about to step into her dress when he suddenly burst into the room, apparently in need of 'something from the cupboard'. Immediately, Maxi jumped up and covered herself.

He smirked and said, 'Oh, don't worry, dear. I have seen it all before!'

I will never forget Maxi hitting back, 'Well, you're not seeing this one, dear!' before promptly slamming the door in his face.

On another occasion, we were visiting a priest's house in Co. Donegal. It was totally obvious his housekeeper was in love with him and I even remember noticing her toiletries on the dressing table in his bedroom. When the three of us arrived, an air of jealousy was immediately palpable. She absolutely hated us from the moment we set foot inside the house. Anytime the priest paid us a compliment, she would visibly glower at us, before practically throwing the sandwiches on the table. The clerical debauchery we saw around the country during these tours really left me disgusted with religion. Despite what I had seen, I was genuinely stunned when the revelations broke about Fr Michael Cleary, primarily because he had always been such a vocal pillar of moral turpitude. Being the 'Singing Priest', he had been on the same circuit as us, so we got to know him quite well. Considering the morals this man preached, I'm still amazed by the extreme hypocrisy of his life.

The only priest I could say I truly love is Fr Brian D'Arcy. Really, I fancy the pants off him. He married David and me, although, to be frank, if it weren't for that collar of his, I'd have just as happily married Brian himself.

Pay cheques from the pram

A cherubic-faced man, whom I won't name, had convinced us with his entrepreneurial talk that he should be our manager. This guy was so baby-faced that, when I first met him, I remember thinking he would look more at home in a pram than behind a business desk. Unfortunately, we were not long out of the

prams ourselves and so were gullible enough to agree to his offer, a decision for which we would later pay dearly.

Our three mothers – Elizabeth Condron, Helen Dixon and Madge McCoubrey – were our dressmakers and even though they made the costumes for our appearances on *Steady As She Go-Goes*, RTÉ never paid a cent in expenses. The price came straight out of our parents' pockets.

Obviously, it was necessary to have a different costume each week as we had to be in theme with whatever country the 'ship' was anchoring in. We always assured our parents that once we received our cheques, we would hand them straight over as compensation for all the expense they had incurred in creating our costumes. By the second series, however, we still had not seen one pay cheque. Barbara's father, a tough army man by the name of Harry Dixon, phoned RTÉ over the whereabouts of our wages only to be told that we had already been paid. Hearing this, Harry immediately phoned my father, Leo, and Maxi's father, Sam, both of whom confirmed that we had definitely not been paid.

This is why we never knew the colour of dance hall floors!

The following day, the three of us met in Jonathan's Restaurant on Grafton Street. At the time, our 'manager' had been abroad for a few months but we knew he was due back from his travels, so we decided to go to his office and confront him. I can still picture us walking up the stairs towards the big Georgian door that led into his headquarters. As it turned out, the office was empty, and if the number of letters piled high in the mailbox was anything to go by, it had been empty for quite some time.

With no one around, we decided to have a look at some of the unopened mail. Poor Maxi, ever the sensible one, was envisioning us being hauled into a prison cell.

'Oh, God we shouldn't be doing this, girls. We could be arrested! You're not allowed go through someone's mailbox! What if the guards arrest us? Oh my God, if we get arrested we'll be in so much trouble with our parents …'

For once, Dick and I were on the same side. 'Oh for God's sake, Maxi, shut up and stand guard!'

Barbara and I forced open the mailbox and indeed almost every envelope was addressed to 'Maxi Dick and Twink'. Sure enough when we later began tearing them open, we found fees for *Steady As She Go-Goes*, not to mention cheques for a variety of other shows we had appeared on. When he was confronted by our parents, I remember Mr Babyface turning beetroot as he tried to muster some excuse to cover his tracks. When he had been fired, Mick Quinn was appointed as our manager.

We were performing non-stop back then. A typical schedule might include Friday night in Ballyhaunis, Saturday night in Letterkenny, Sunday night in Waterford and then back to school on Monday morning. We had no idea what kind of money our shows were earning.

Our beloved roadie, the late Steven Fitzsimons, tipped us off that the amounts were *more* than significant. He was privy to that side of the business because it was his job to sometimes collect the fees. One particular Monday, we were scheduled to meet with Mick to receive our wages for the previous weekend's shows. Unfortunately, the meeting in question turned out to be rather short and *not* so sweet. 'The bad news girls,' he began, 'is dat dere is no fuckin' readies for yiz.'

'What?'

'Yeah! D'yiz know how expensive dis tourin' lark is? As a matter of fact, youse three owe *me* money after last weekend's shows.'

In tears, we left his office and as we made our way down the stone steps, Mick's accountant Brendan ran out after us. An incredibly sweet man, he felt so sorry for us that he put his hand in his pocket and gave us half a crown each. After I used it to pay my bus fare back to our house in Rathfarnham, I was left with one and threepence. There I was, the biggest young star in Ireland at the time, with just 1/3d in my pocket. That was my week's wage.

❖

Maxi, Dicko and I would always meet after school in the Grafton Street restaurant called Jonathan's before making our way to nearby Hickeys where we would go through the costume patterns.

A row would always ensue.

My dilemma was that I was the chubby one, whereas the other two were enviably thin, and so I would naturally freak at some of the skin-tight outfits they suggested. Granted, I was seen as the multi-talented one of the group, but when you're fifteen years of age and in a girl band, who wouldn't want to be the thin, beautiful one?

Maxi, on the other hand, was always blessed with a great figure and supermodel height. It goes without saying she was the one whom all the boys wanted to have on their arm.

As we were driving from a venue one night, I spotted a sign that said: 'Bridge ahead, maximum height 13ft.'

Immediately I joked, 'Jesus, McCoubrey, you better duck now otherwise we won't get under it!'

Naturally, everyone laughed at my quip because Maxi was always very proud of her height and I knew a joke like that wouldn't offend her in the slightest.

Dick unfortunately was not so tactful. A few yards up the road, she spotted another sign and she laughed, 'Oh look! Maximum weight, 250 tonnes. You'd better get out now, Twinkles.'

Needless to say, her remark was followed by a stony silence from the rest of the crew.

There's a well-known Turkish proverb that reads: 'A knife wound heals, but a tongue wound festers', and I genuinely think that anyone who has been on the receiving end of verbal bullets from a caustic tongue will agree with that. For me, it has always been the smallest comments that cut the deepest; always the seemingly insignificant remarks that linger in the mind years later. I remember back when we were all mad about the boys from a band called The Strangers, who were arguably the biggest pop band in Ireland along with the Bye-Laws. I was going out with the drummer Vic McNamara, Dick was going out with the guitarist Len Guest and Maxi was going out with a bass guitarist who was, rather ironically, called Maxi McEvoy. One Sunday morning, the six of us met in Grafton Street. At the time, Brown Thomas had created a most beautiful window display of mannequins donning the new range of fashion pieces designed by the model Twiggy. Noticing the look of awe on my face as I peered through the window, Dick decided it would be rather amusing to shout, 'Not much point in you admiring those, Twinkles!'

That was forty-odd years ago and while it may seem rather trivial now, for an insecure teenager, the humiliation was on a par with a kick to the teeth. I'm sure Dick is reading this and wracking her memory trying to remember that incident. I, unfortunately, remember all those hurtful remarks like they were yesterday.

❖

When Fianna Fáil held a big gala event in Dublin's Metropole Ballroom, Maxi Dick and Twink were booked as the special guests. On the night we were accompanied by the wonderful Ritchie Burbridge and his band, which meant I was free from playing the guitar and could be more involved in the choreography.

T.J. instantly noticed how the backing band gave us more of a showmanship appearance and so, following that night, we performed our gigs with a band called the Bye-Laws, which consisted of Pat Morris, Jimmy Conway, Paul Holohan and Aidan Scannell. Soon afterwards, Mick Quinn and T.J. Byrne were arranging for us to do a tour of Canada, and it was *here* that we struck it big. The venues that were booking us began to get bigger and bigger, and once we became established on the Toronto scene, our celebrity status exceeded all expectations. That tour should have been the beginning of a worldwide career for us.

Sadly, however, it instead proved to be the beginning of the end.

Bidding farewell to our fans as we boarded the plane to Canada.

Mom and Dad's wedding.

On the beach in Bray. Mom made that exquisite little bonnet from an old broderie anglaise dress of hers - love or what! ...
Sound of Music curtains anyone?

In my handsome daddy's arms, kissing my beloved aunty Meta.

My beautiful mother, Elizabeth. Her bright smile prompted my father to nickname her 'SUNNY'.

Come on, Irene

Dicko and I are 4th of April Aries, but we couldn't be more different. Ariens, by nature, are quite bolshy and, by God, Dicko and I were two of the bolshiest, if there is such a word. Coincidentally, Linda Martin is an Arien as well.

Looking back, it's clear that Dicko and I fought for the supremacy of Maxi. I always felt that Dick, in a way, dominated her. If ever there was an argument, she would begin by saying, 'Irene and I think …' regardless of whether Irene wanted to be involved in the argument or not.

The Bye-Law musicians, like me, were tired of the bickering and it had reached a point where we couldn't agree on anything, not even the music. I had also struck up a relationship with our guitarist, Jimmy Conway, and once this happens in a band, it will almost always cause some dissention in the ranks.

One night prior to a gig in a very prestigious Detroit nightclub called the Top Hat, we were informed that representatives from the world famous William Morris Agency in New York would be in attendance. When they met with us after the gig, they complimented our performance before outlining a few changes that they felt needed to be made. One of them pointed to me.

'You, the little blonde one, you gotta be the lead singer because you are the main vocalist.'

Then, he honed in on Maxi and Dick. 'You two need to be the backing vocals. This is the way it has to be if you wanna go forward.'

Dicko stood up.

'There is no way this is turning into a Diana Ross and the Supremes. I'm not a backing singer, never was and never will be. Come on, Irene!'

With that, she walked out of the room with Maxi in tow.

The people from the William Morris Agency suggested that the girls and I talk it out amongst ourselves, but I could have told them there and then, that there would be no chance of that happening. Rehearsals were already a nightmare, consisting more of rows than music. Things were so bad that The Bye-Law boys were asking me if the band had reached the end of the road. Following the William Morris fiasco, tensions were running high, and, with the girls refusing to talk to me, the shows we performed were terribly strained.

By that point, we had spent almost a year in Canada, and, frankly, I'd had enough of the place. It didn't help that our schedule would sometimes include up to seven shows a week, which was murder on the vocals.

Even though the strict laws meant that anyone under the age of twenty-one was not allowed in a licensed premises, only two members of the entire ensemble, Aidan and Paul, were over twenty-one. I don't think I will ever forget the night we were standing on stage in the middle of singing 'Angel of the Morning' when we suddenly saw two incredibly burly detectives in trench coats enter the room. They were the archetypal police figures you would see in a cartoon. Barging onto the stage, they interrupted our act and ordered us into a room for questioning. It was a terrifying ordeal.

One of them looked at me. 'You! What age are you?'

'I'm … twenty-two.'

'What's your date of birth?'

'The 4th… of April … um … 19 … 1942.'

'Really? Because that makes you thirty-two!'

I had made a complete and utter balls of it. So did the others, mind you. Our passports confiscated,

Here we are performing in a state penitentiary in Canada to an audience of 'lifers', made up mostly of rapists and murderers. Prior to the performance, we had been instructed to cover up as much as possible - our trademark mini-skirts were out of the question. We were also warned against dancing in a way that might be construed as sexual. As you can see from the picture, the movements of the prisoners were also restricted. What you can't see, are the throngs of security guards who were ready to pounce if one of them made a move towards us. For me, the most disturbing element of this picture is that the lifers are all very young men.

we were driven to a jail downtown where we were allowed just one phone call. I decided to call our manager, Mick Quinn. Sobbing my heart out down the phone, I explained to him that we had been arrested and were being held in a jail cell. Mick's reply was not as comforting as we had hoped, 'D'yiz realise … dah it's ten past four in de fuckin' mornin' here in Ireland?'

It didn't make a difference that his young band had been arrested, it was four in the morning and we had interrupted his beauty sleep.

Eventually, we sorted something out and a guy called Bob Hogan signed the relevant forms promising that we would not perform in a bar again.

The following night, we were back on stage.

Legally, we were not allowed to perform in the bar area so it was decided that the band would play on the main stage in the bar and we would set up our microphones in the dining room which could be seen from the main room. The poor audience didn't know which way to look. The drama didn't stop there either. The road conditions were treacherously icy and, as we were driving, the U-Haul trailer carrying our equipment kept jack-knifing behind us. I can still vividly remember us screaming in terror, convinced we were going to crash, as the driver attempted to scale a steep motorway hill. It was one of a number of incidents that made me despise life on the road.

One morning not long after the William Morris meeting, the boys called me aside for a chat. The incessant bickering between Dicko and me had effectively sparked off talks among the lads about the future of the band. They knew things were only going to go from bad to worse, and so

My arrival in Dublin Airport following MDT split.

they made me an offer. They wanted to start a new band and have me as their lead singer. The group would be called Twink and the Bye-Laws.

After I had left the room, I think I walked about five miles in the cold Canadian snow mulling through everything. When I returned to the hotel, I phoned my mother. The poor woman had been beside herself with worry over rumours she had heard about the band breaking up, as there had been a lot of speculation in the Irish media at the time. I explained what had been going on and admitted a break-up was likely, however when I told her about the offer The Bye-Laws had made me, she immediately encouraged me to go for it. She put voice to what I had suspected deep down all along – the aggro and misery within the group was only going to intensify.

As soon as I told the boys of my decision, there was no postponing the inevitable. We phoned Maxi and Dicko and invited them up to the room for a chat. As there was no easy way of saying what needed to be said, I just admitted to them that the previous few days had been hell and that it couldn't continue. The Cadillac days were over. We were becoming women with different ideals, and the backbiting was only in its infancy. I wanted to look back and remember the three little girls brimming with excitement at the press launch as they tried to teach journalists how to say Maxi Dick and Twink; I wanted to remember going to each other's houses rehearsing while our mammies made plates of sandwiches and pots of tea. Those memories were far nicer than the ones being created at that point.

Dicko, true to form, just stood up and said, 'Right, well, that's fine! Irene and I have plans of our own. Come on, Irene.'

Grabbing Maxi by the hand, she stormed out of the room.

If the tensions were high following the William Morris fiasco, I knew they would be at Everest height later that afternoon when we would have to meet to rehearse for a gig that night. The rehearsal was scheduled to begin at four o'clock, so the boys and I hovered around the lobby while we waited for Maxi and Dicko to join us. Forty minutes on, there was still no sign of them. I went to the hotel reception desk and asked if they could be contacted only to be told that they had checked out hours ago. With no warning, they had just upped and left.

I was twelve when I set out on the road with Maxi Dick and Twink and by the time we split up, I was just shy of my eighteenth birthday. Considering how, in those six years, the three of us had achieved amazing heights of fame, it was sad that we were ending the band on such a sour note. When we broke up, I flew back to Ireland on my own. My arrival at Dublin Airport was greeted by a throng of press and sure enough the following day, the band's departure from the music industry had created headlines in every Irish newspaper.

When I returned to Ireland, I performed some very successful gigs with The Bye-Laws. We were really pulling in the crowds everywhere. On one particular night, we were performing in the Embankment in Tallaght when prior to the show, our base player, Paul Holohan came

into my dressing room and said, 'Right, well, I suppose that's the end of this chapter. You could have at least told us who was in the audience.'

I was puzzled. I had no idea who he was talking about, as I had a policy of never going out front before a gig. I was taught from infancy 'that the first time the audience should see a performer is when they appear on the stage'. If you dared break that rule, you would have had the head smacked off you.

It turned out that Brendan Bowyer, Tom Dunphy, T.J. Byrne, Connie Lynch and Bill Fuller were in the audience. What I didn't realise at the time was that Bowyer and Dunphy had recently returned from Las Vegas to source members for their new group Brendan Bowyer and the Big 8, following the break-up of the Royal Showband. They had already recruited Paddy Cole, Michael Keane, Dave Coady and Mickey O'Neill and word had now filtered through that they were auditioning for a female singer. I was barely five minutes off stage when the owner of the Embankment told me Bill Fuller was waiting in the private bar to speak with me.

I walked in and was greeted first by Tom Dunphy.

'My God, you have grown up! What age are you now?'

'Nineteen and a bit.'

'God, I'd hate to be that old!'

Brendan Bowyer stepped in. 'You know why we're here? We have auditioned every singer in Ireland, but we made our decision tonight. We would like to offer you the position of lead singer in the band we want to bring back to Las Vegas.'

'Oh, God … no, thank you. I wouldn't be remotely interested!'

Their faces dropped.

'Lads, I've only just come home from a year in Canada and if I never see the States again, I won't be sorry.'

Dunphy interrupted me.

'No, dear, you were in Canada, not the States. It's a completely different world, and Las Vegas itself is a totally different world from the rest of America!'

I remained adamant. 'No, I still can't go, Tom. Anyway, I'm doing a line with Jimmy Conway and we're quite serious.'

Following that meeting, they phoned me three times a day for two weeks and with each phone call, the money went up, as did the conditions regarding my apartment and perks. The last diamond they dangled in front of me was Jimmy.

They thought Jimmy was a sensational guitarist and singer and asked if I would be tempted into taking the position of lead singer if they brought Jimmy on board. Admittedly, that put a different colour on things. I remember sitting on the steps of my home on Anne Devlin Road and discussing with my parents what I should do. They didn't want to lose me to America again but, God love them, they possessed the most wonderful attitude about it. Sitting down alongside me, they told me they couldn't discourage me from going, as I would never thank them for it in later years. They knew it was too good an opportunity to pass up, and one I would probably regret.

I had their blessing, and with that, Vegas beckoned.

'Elvis, your belt is massive!'

Within weeks, I was out in Las Vegas with my own apartment, an enviable career in showbusiness and Debbie Reynolds as my next-door neighbour. At the pool, she would regale us with stories about working in *Singing in the Rain* and how Gene Kelly was quite the task master. I remember her saying, 'Oh, he's beautiful, but he's a really tough guy. He would make us dance and dance …'

She would recall these memories so nonchalantly while we were there with our jaws practically on the pool floor.

It was such a phenomenal life-transition for anyone to make, let alone a teenager. When I look at *CSI Las Vegas* today, even I am left stunned that I lived there for over five years. I really must have been the cailín bán when I first arrived in the place!

My mother had said to me that evening on the steps, 'Youth is for one thing – burning the

candle at both ends'. Well, let me tell you, I took her advice and burned the two ends until they met in the middle!!!

The whole Vegas scene was truly incredible. In those days, the paparazzi were not as powerful, which meant celebrity sightings were much more commonplace. It wasn't at all unusual to see people like Frank Sinatra, Cher, Tony Bennett and Barbara Streisand playing at the baccarat table in Caesar's Palace following their gigs.

Before we left for Vegas, the boys had told me how popular the Royal Irish Showband had been on the strip, something I just laughed off as self-praising PR talk. I couldn't have been more mistaken. They were more than just big in Vegas, they were absolutely bloody *huge*. One of the first things I noticed when I arrived was the respect that existed between artists who performed on the strip. We were one of the top lounge acts alongside performers such as Kenny Rogers and the First Edition and Gladys Knight and the Pips, and if you were good enough to make it into *that* enclave, you immediately gained the respect of every other artist. They knew that in order for you to have made it there, your talent had to be pretty extraordinary.

Sinatra was known as a grumpy oul' hoor, but, then, I think he probably played up to it in a way. By that stage, he had developed a 'don't-mess-with-the-mob' persona, which he loved. At the same time, he never thought himself too good to mix with the lounge acts. Instead, he would shout across the entire casino, 'Ah, it's Twink from the Irish Showband! I hear you're a great singer. Sing me something, darlin'!'

'To Twink, all my love to a beautiful lady, Wayne.'

Elvis, meanwhile, loved Brendan Bowyer and would sneak into the Stardust Hotel some nights just to hear him sing. Elvis was insanely gorgeous; his face sculpted and tanned, his body the proportions of a Greek Kouros sculpture. You couldn't but feel sorry for any man in his company. I will never forget the night myself and the band's dancers – Angela Larney, Phyllis O'Brien, Rita Houlihan, Jessie Fagan and Maureen Carter – were invited to one of Elvis's spectacular parties, which of course, took up the entire top floor of the Hilton. Phyllis, a Dub through and through, caught the attention of the king himself and said, 'Elvis, your belt is massive!'

'Oh, you like it, Phyllis?' came the distinctively husky drawl.

'Aw, yeah, Elvis. It's lovely!'

Without hesitation, he whipped off the belt and handed it to her as a gift. Pointing at me, Phyllis then added, 'And Twink likes your ring!'

'Do you like it, Twink? Well here have it! I have loads of turquoise rings.'

I have worn some of the most amazing jewellery in my career, but Elvis's ring is up there with the best. I'm only sorry we didn't admire his trousers!

❖

Wayne Newton, the biggest star in Las Vegas, was a bit enchanted with me. For some reason, this really annoyed Brendan Bowyer. In fact, he cornered me one day and said he wanted to talk to me about rumours regarding me and Mr Las Vegas. In no uncertain terms, he told me that he didn't want any of that 'carry on' taking place. Frankly, I felt it was none of Bowyer's business to begin with, but then Bowyer was always of the habit of making *everything* his business. Little did I know then, that my friendship with Wayne was just one of the many bones of contention he would chew to the marrow.

❖

During my first year in Vegas, I found an apartment that was in close proximity of the strip and the Stardust Hotel. It had a swimming pool and the rent was practically pennies. Considering the exorbitant rental rates they were demanding for places on the strip, I couldn't believe that I had found such a cheap place within yards of it. Unfortunately, it wasn't too long before I discovered why.

The apartment was on the ground floor, and, as a result, it was permeated by millions of little geckos. I don't know how, but I lasted about a year in that place. On one occasion, a girlfriend of mine, Katie Reddy, was in Vegas on holiday. Poor Katie had a real phobia of creepy-crawlies, so for pure badness I asked her to phone for a cab. Of course the second she lifted up the phone, she was screaming as a lizard swung from her ear while four more fell from the receiver.

One night, as I was chatting to Phyllis O'Brien, one of the band's dancers, we decided to enquire about a new upscale apartment block situated just outside town. It was absolute luxury, albeit quite pricey, but our naive, youthful optimism had convinced us it would be worth it. About five weeks after we had made our application, we were invited to a tenants' meeting with the couple who owned the building. During the meeting, one of the landlords outlined a problem they had encountered. It seemed an ethnic family had made an application to rent an apartment in the block – a notion that had not gone down too well with the landlords. They went on to explain that unless they had the full permission from the tenants to reject the application, the family in question would be allowed move in. I was shocked, although not half as shocked as I was when I suddenly realised that everyone in the room was agreeing to the proposal.

A sixties Fashion Shoot
for Spotligt Magazine

With guns blazing, I launched into a Twink-style rant about how disgusted I was with their racist attitude. Phyllis likewise voiced her full support. 'I'm the same as hur,' she protested. 'The cheek a'yiz. Dis is disgraceful!'

They responded by explaining that America had experienced certain problems with this particular race and that from experience it might be safer to reject their application.

Phyllis was outraged. 'Don't get me riz! D'youse know where I'm even from? I have friends who would kill youse for saying tings like dah!'

The Ireland that Phyllis and I came from, only ever saw members of this race studying to be doctors in the College of Surgeons, or as pilots in Dublin Airport. Our population was nowhere near as diverse as it is today and, I suppose, a consequence of that was an unfamiliarity with the 'bad eggs' that emerge from every culture. The rest of the tenants in the room were making comments about how I would soon learn the error of my ways, but as far as I was concerned, they were the ones who needed to learn. Phyllis and I steadfastly refused to consent to their rejection plea and, as a result, the family were allowed to move in.

Within three months of their arrival, they had wreaked havoc on the place. They had the original ghetto-blasters, which they would put to good use at four in the morning. They were so out of their heads on every drug imaginable that they would harass and intimidate the tenants. It reached a point where I was forced to ask the security men to accompany me to my apartment every time I entered the complex. I couldn't take the stairs without them roaring abuse at me. 'Hey you Irish mother-fucker. Where you goin'

fuckhead? Think you're too fuckin' good to talk to us you fuckin' Irish nigger?'

Suddenly an apartment full of lizards and creepy-crawlies didn't seem so bad after all.

To think I had accused the opposing residents of being racist and yet here I was being constantly called an Irish nigger by the very people I had defended. Like the rest of the tenants, I was terrified to go home at night. The constant partying ensured no one in the building could get to sleep until exhaustion kicked in. One night, 'the family' even threw a large garden ornament through my window accompanied by a litany of abuse. They would often approach me in the supermarket and roar vulgar racist remarks in my face. I had fought their corner so hard and this was the thanks I got for it.

Of course, the armchair critics will criticise me for placing this story in the book but, you know what? You weren't the one in the firing line of their abuse and intimidation. I'm not making this about race and ethnicity – in fact those two issues have nothing to do with it – it was their behaviour that disgusted me. Eventually, the other tenants couldn't take it, and one by one, they left. They were then replaced with friends of 'the family' and the abuse became even more terrifying. When Phyllis and I left, we lost out *big time* financially, a burn not helped by our landlords saying goodbye with the words, 'We told you so!'

We had signed that family in on a mission of goodwill, but unfortunately our intentions went unnoticed and they made life sheer hell for everyone. To be honest, it was one of many incidents in Vegas that really knocked the *cailín bán* out of me.

Not tonight, Mavis ... we're in Vegas

Vegas is the life of some people and the death of others. A greedy place, it takes your time, your money and your sanity. You really need the strength and resilience of a shire horse to keep the temptations of your inner demons at bay. Believe me, it's no place for someone with any weakness of character, particularly considering that even those with nerves of steel struggle with it. To put it mildly, it's a human zoo. It operates on making gargantuan amounts of money out of gamblers who are overtired and drunk beyond recognition. In fact, it wasn't uncommon for a business junket of thirty-five to return home from a weekend in Vegas with just thirty or so members. They would cram in so much drink and drugs during those two days that their bodies couldn't cope. Sounds extreme, but then it's not called Sin City for nothing. Quite frankly, you don't live there, you survive there!

When I was 'surviving' Las Vegas, I saw two sets of people – 'them' and 'us'. Us, we treated Vegas as both a workplace and a home. Them, well, they played the kind of games that almost always had a tragic ending.

Whenever I think about the dark side of that city, one particular incident springs to mind.

One night, a really suave, handsome man with coiffured hair and a sharp suit was playing at one of the casino tables. Surrounding him was a large crowd of onlookers, which can only mean one thing. He was cleaning up all around him. Sure enough, with every roll of the dice came a loud cheer. I couldn't wait to get off the stage and see the action.

Before I go any further with this story, you should know that Vegas will not let anyone win. Once the house senses a winning streak, it immediately sets about winning its money back. In the case of this particular gentleman, they began plying him with drink and bringing him food. If at any point he became tired, they would offer to hold the table for him while he went upstairs to bed ... with plenty of drink and entertainment. The house would provide him with anything he wanted, even the things he didn't know he wanted. Hospitality for the big customer was the management's priority.

Around this time, my friend Angela and I had decided to spend a couple of days in Indiana with our boyfriends. After we had finished our final show, however, we went out to the table where all the winning seemed to be taking place. The man had stacks of black chips in front of him and was making a fortune. Angela, without even taking her eyes off the table, nudged me, 'Jaysus, would you look at his chips!'

'Never mind looking at his chips darling, look at him!'

It wasn't unusual to see James Bond movies being shot in the area, so when I saw how insanely handsome this man was, my first reaction was to look around for the film cameras. He had that leading-man style about him. A friend of mine, John Lavaroni, worked in what is known as the casino cage, where chips are exchanged for cash. As Angela was admiring the chips and I was admiring the man, I spotted John and joked, 'Hey, Johnny boy, you make sure you get his name and address for us when you're cashing in his chips!'

'Aw don't worry, gals! I don't think he'll be leaving here with much of that!' came the very apt reply.

If it wasn't for the Big 8 poster in the background, you could be forgiven for thinking these were pictures of Chloë and Naomi!

Leaving the casino, Angela and I drove to McCarran Airport to catch our 3 a.m. flight. There was, at most, a handful of people in the airport at the time. One man in particular stood out. Rather small in stature, he was wearing a herringbone tweed coat, scruffy trousers, and a pair of black cowboy boots with the toes barely intact. Our jaws nearly hit the floor when we realised who it was. Liberace, possibly the most famous pianist and entertainer that has ever lived. During his concerts, he would arrive down from the ceiling whilst playing a glass piano and wearing white sequined suits and diamond jewellery. A 'prop' in a Liberace concert was a gold Rolls Royce he would drive on stage. His private life, likewise, was of a chandeliers-and-champagne nature. Here is the man for whom the term 'lavish extravagance' was invented and here he was looking like a penniless pauper! Only for the fact that I recognised him, I would have probably thrown him a few dollars. When we were on the plane, we managed to work up the courage to approach him. Of all the things we could have said, we chose, 'Hello, Mr Liberace!'

I absolutely cringe when I think back on how we referred to him as 'Mr Liberace', although at least my good friend Brendan Grace can't tease me for it, considering how he once met Elton John on a plane and said, 'Hello, Mr John!'

As we were chatting, Liberace asked us why we were in Vegas. As soon as we mentioned the Irish Showband, his face lit up. He was more than just familiar with our group, he was a fan.

When Angela and I arrived in Evansville, Indiana, our boyfriends, Scott Soublé and Rick O'Daniel, drove us out to their dairy farm in the mountains where we spent *the* most fantastic nights smoking dope and listening to Paul McCartney's *Red Rose Speedway*. At around five in the morning, we went skinny dipping in the lake, before riding horses around their estate (and yes,

we did put our clothes back on before we went horse riding!). By lunch-time the following day, however, it was time to fly back to Vegas as we had to be on stage that night.

As I walked into the casino, I noticed a huge crowd gathering around one of the tables. It was now Wednesday evening and the same suave gentleman we had left behind us on Monday night was still at the same table, only this time he looked like a broken man who had aged about twenty years. The polished sophistication was replaced with dishevelled exhaustion. He clearly hadn't slept, showered or shaved. Testament to this was the stubble on his face and the many food and alcohol stains on his shirt, which already looked as though it was stuck to him with twenty-four hours of perspiration. He was distraught. John Lavaroni, our friend from the casino cage, told me the man had lost every penny of the millions he had made. In fact, he now owed the Mafia millions. When his losing streak began to kick in, he gambled away his assets and in doing so, lost his house and two cars. He was now having to gamble to try to earn enough money for a plane ticket home to Chicago. Little did his wife and kids know that his stupidity had left them homeless. Had he quit when he was on his winning streak, he would never have had to work another day in his life. Instead, he succumbed to the overwhelming greed Las Vegas is famous for, and would now be paying back the debt for the rest of his life. For me, that one story sums up how vicious that city can be.

❖

You could always spot the ladies with the facelifts. Back then, facelifts didn't involve cutting into the skin, but rather a procedure whereby the skin was simply tucked behind the ears. If you walked by the slot machines on any given day, it wasn't unusual to see ladies who would have had three or four facelifts, as was evident from the amount of skin folded behind their ears like rows of sausages!

These same women would be sitting there with paper cups full of coins, pulling slot machines for hours on end. Some of them would be wearing over a quarter of a million dollars worth of Tiffany or Van Cleef & Arpels jewellery, yet their hands and nails would be absolutely filthy from handling so many coins. It was all so incongruous. If one of them was on a winning streak, a member of staff would quickly be over plying them with drink and encouraging them to spend even more.

❖

Every place on the planet has some downtime when the shops close, people go to bed and everything goes quiet for a few hours. Not Vegas. Vegas is a twenty-four-hour, no-clocks, non-stop city, which, when you think about it, is not remotely natural. As a result, you have to be completely coherent and absolutely aware of everything, from the people you work *with* to the people you work *for*. When I was in Vegas, I was of the opinion the place was being controlled by the Mafia!

One night, in 1972 myself and a few friends went to an amazing Hawaiian restaurant called the Aku Aku. While there, we ended up chatting with one of the big business bosses we had come to know. His name was Gino and, my God, was he dangerously handsome – you'd have needed dark glasses to look at him on a bright day!

Gino was always impeccably dressed with his sharp suits, cufflinks and expensive Omega watch, and even though he was a big businessman in his own right, his status within the business world was nothing compared to that of his father-in-law. Around this time, there was a beautiful girl called Karen who worked the casino's baccarat table. She was a 'baccarat shill', who would wear a revealing gown to entice men to play the table. She would then serve them drink and encourage them to gamble more and more money, usually hundreds of thousands of dollars. We all suspected there was something developing between Karen and Gino. We used to see her sitting with him during the odd break, however, it reached a point where she seemed to spend more time in Gino's company than she did working.

At the time, we had a dancer from Drimnagh called Angela Larney. You only had to hear her speak to know she was true Dubliner, although Tom Dunphy would regularly announce her on stage as, 'Our charming Angela Larney from Killarney.' To be honest, I don't think Angela ever once set foot in Killarney but, as far as the Americans were concerned, she lived there! She was always amazing fun not to mention a superb dancer. I remember her nudging me at one point and saying, 'I think that pair are havin' it off! There's definitely something goin' on there!'

The thing about Karen was that she was every bit as beautiful in personality as she was in looks. We all loved her. She told me one night that she had arrived in Vegas after having been awarded a scholarship to the University of Nevada where was doing a Masters degree in marine biology. She needed money to pay the bills, so she began working as a cocktail waitress in the casino. Obviously, the boss noticed how gorgeous she looked and probably reckoned that with fewer clothes and some professional coiffuring, she would be a perfect candidate for the baccarat table.

That night in the company of Gino in the Aku Aku restaurant, I, in my complete innocence, happened to say, 'Do you know what? We never see Karen anymore these days. Where is sh—'.

Before I could even complete the sentence, one of my friends landed me with a kick underneath the table that nearly snapped my ankle off. After Gino had left, she explained the reaction. 'Now, here's a lesson for you, darlin' little Twinky. You don't fuck around with the big boys. Karen was fuckin' around with Gino and, because of that, she got the bird.'

'The bird', I was informed, is one of the worst deaths someone could endure in Las Vegas. It was punishment by death whereby they would take a victim out to Lake Mead, in this case a young girl, tie her to a raft and leave her out in the scorching sun with meat strapped all over her face and body. The vultures would then swoop down on her body and peck out her eyes as well as pecking continuously at her flesh, all while she is conscious. Karen was no more than twenty-six years old. Gino's philandering meanwhile probably earned him a slap on the wrist at most. The don wouldn't kill him, after all who would look after his beloved daughter? In his eyes, it was much easier to order a hit on someone else's daughter.

There were so many incidents like that in Vegas where you would notice certain people had just suddenly disappeared. You would later hear that they had 'crossed the boys'. Some of them suffered the cement death. I believe this involved the Mafia bringing them out to the middle of Lake Mead, placing their feet in quick-setting cement before tying their hands behind their back and taping their mouth. They had this routine where they would make the person wait in the boat first so that he or she could feel the cement tightening around their feet, all while knowing that in a matter of minutes they would be thrown over the edge of the boat.

The feeling of terror was the actual punishment, the dreadful death you experienced was just the bonus. Certainly taught the rest of us to mind our manners.

While I never crossed them, on one occasion I did come within a hair's breadth of unwittingly insulting them. During a meeting with two influential people in the business who were reported to be big Mafia bosses, one of them said to me, 'So, Irish, I hear you're a real intellectual. The boys tell me you're always reading. That's not natural for an entertainer! I see you got a book in your bag. What the fuck are you reading?'

Unfortunately for me it was a book called *Real Lace*, which was about the Kennedys involvement in the Cuban Missile Crisis. It was full of Mafia connotations. Here I was about to unknowingly walk myself into one of the most awkward situations with two Mafia bosses. Fortunately, Bill Fuller who was with me, stopped me in my tracks. I used to joke that Bill was so shrewd, he would be out in the fields at six in the morning giving the foxes lessons in cuteness. He had a brilliant attitude and a wicked sense of humour. Recognising Bill's hint, I tried to bury the topic by saying it was just a book about Irish people. Thanks to Bill, the great Kerry businessman, I soon became very well versed in what not to say when around these people.

Beautiful sunny, McCarran Airport, Las Vegas.

For all its faults, Las Vegas gave me a fantastic lifestyle!

Jesus, if my poor mother knew half of what I got up to, she would turn in her grave. One of my boyfriends was the gorgeous Gary Pedano, one of the heirs to the Coca-Cola fortune. We met through his uncle who was a hotel boss in Vegas. Admittedly, the town was like a sweet shop for me, so our 'relationship' lasted about an hour.

One of my most treasured memories of Vegas was my twenty-first birthday when the band brought me to see Johnny Cash who, in turn, ended up singing 'Happy Birthday' to me. He brought me up on stage and made a huge fuss over the fact that it was my twenty-first. It was by far the most incredible way to mark a milestone birthday.

While I was living in Vegas, I worked extremely hard on my performances, however that's not to say I didn't find time for sex, drugs, and rock and roll! I didn't do a lot of drugs in Vegas … well actually that's a bloody lie – I did dabble in cannabis. It was the seventies for Christ's sake, just about everyone was smoking dope! I should add that this was long before the cocaine era. Pill popping, likewise, never interested me. I didn't like the idea of getting into something I couldn't control. One night, I was given Hash Oil Red, an oil that you had to heat and then smoke with a pipe. As far as I'm aware, I went missing for a day – still haven't a clue where I went though. Fortunately, that incident scared me enough to pull the reigns in … a tad.

Celebrating my 21st in Vegas!

'Um... I'm a priest'

The men in Vegas were all gorgeous, not to mention rotten with money. Thanks to the popularity of the band, I was suddenly the hot new thing on the strip and had the pick of the bunch. One of my first boyfriends was Johnny Cochiosi, a real New Jersey boy. On one occasion when I was home from Vegas and playing a gig in the Brandon Hotel in Tralee, I went to visit my aunty Eileen who lived nearby. As I was telling her about my life in America, I mentioned that I was madly in love with a craps dealer called Johnny. Craps is a well-known casino game, unfortunately, Aunty Eileen misheard me. When I left the house, the first thing she said to my cousin Margaret was how disappointed my mother must be that such a well-educated girl would end up going out with a Vegas *scrap dealer!*

Johnny was immense fun to be with. We would often take his boat out on Lake Mead at half three in the morning and water-ski until half six just as the sun was really coming up. Those bright few hours before dawn were ideal for sport. I would take tennis lessons and go horse riding between 4 a.m. and 6 a.m. before enjoying some breakfast in the Chimney Stack or the Flame Bar and then heading home to sleep until midday. Once the sun was up, it wasn't remotely safe to go out on the lake. In fact, you would often hear stories on the news about people being found dead on their boats because they had run out of petrol and were left in the sweltering, dry desert heat.

In the late afternoons, when the heat had abated and it was safe to venture out again, I would cycle to the band's rehearsals in the Stardust. On one particular occasion, as I sped past the local church, I happened to catch a glance of a gorgeous guy sitting on the steps reading a book.

He had tousled blond hair and was wearing a pair of blue jeans and a white shirt. He had a real Californian look about him. I noticed him about the place quite a lot after that, and he obviously seemed to notice me too because he approached me one day for a chat. Following some flirty small-talk, he asked if he could buy me a coffee after my rehearsal. He was far too beautiful to turn down, so I agreed to meet him in a little café just off the strip. We chatted for ages, and with things going quite well between us, we started to arrange to meet up for dinners.

After a strangely prolonged and very odd courtship, one night he ended up back in my apartment. We hadn't done the *bould thing* by that point but let's just say we were about to!

After a passionate session, there we were chatting in the lovely after-glow, me buried deep in his arms half-naked on a beautiful fur pelt in front of an open fire. I happened to ask what he did for a living while he was completing his university studies.

'Um … I'm a priest,' came the awkward reply.

You could almost hear me choke on my beer as our hot and heavy courting sessions returned in the form of flashbacks. Sure enough, at mass a few days later, there he was in the full garb assisting the main priest. In fact, seeing him up on the altar was one of the most bizarre experiences of my life. He had been in Vegas on a training course and as he was leaving for his native California. I asked him if he was really sure about pursuing the career of priesthood. With a smile he replied, 'Maybe not now!'

He had already been having doubts but Vegas had been the ultimate test. (A test he as good as failed I might cheekily add!)

He was so good-looking, it really would have been such a waste to have lost him to a life of celibacy. I don't know what became of him, whether he made it to the altar or if I literally got him 'out of the habit', but all I will say is, Fr Judd, if you're reading this, do get in touch!

❖

When I was twenty-one, I dated a much older man called Tom Parker (no not Elvis's manager!). My Mr Parker had been a parachutist in Vietnam and often regaled me with the most jaw-dropping stories. As well as being a pit boss in the Sands Hotel, Tom was also a diamond jeweller by trade. He would make me the most beautiful diamond necklaces and pendants, which in terms of sentiment, remain on a par with Elvis's ring. Spontaneous, generous and insanely romantic, he was the kind of boyfriend you would find in the script of a Hollywood romance.

On one particular occasion, after the band had finished a run of performances in Indiana, I flew back to McCarran Airport, Las Vegas where Tom was waiting for me on my arrival. We went home to his amazing house in Territory Avenue where after having a cup of coffee, he promptly told me he was taking me on a surprise trip. Typical woman, I had to bring some form of luggage with me, but he wouldn't give me a hint about where we were going so all I could bring was my vanity case. He assured me that everything and anything I needed he would buy for me when we got 'there'. Driving back out to McCarran Airport, he cleverly escorted me through the terminal in a way that I couldn't see a single sign that indicated where we were going.

In the cocktail lounge, he bought me a Mai Tai cocktail that had all the embellishments such as little umbrellas and fruit. It was a hint as to

Flying to Hawaii.

where we were going, but I didn't realise it until I heard the announcement: 'Could all remaining passengers for Hawaiian Airlines to Honolulu please board now.'

Upon hearing that, Tom just stood up and said, 'Well, come on, what are you waiting for?'

We were about to fly to Hawaii. Talk about taking spontaneity to another level. As we were walking up the steps of the plane, me still in shock I might add, he turned to me and said, 'Happy birthday, my Princess!'

We flew to Honolulu before making our way to the island of Maui where his uncle Jack Ackerman owned a black coral shop. We then enjoyed a helicopter trip over the island, flying directly over the location where Steven Spielberg would later film *Jurassic Park*. I remember the turbulent, world-famous 'trade winds' making that flight particularly nerve-wracking, so even though I thoroughly enjoyed it, I did so with a double knot in my knicker elastic. It was the most incredible trip, made all the sweeter by the fact that it was so spontaneous.

Tom and I were quite serious about each other, and even lived together for a while.

My 'brother' Colin

Officially, I am an only child. As far as I'm concerned, however, I had one beautiful darling brother called Colin.

Colin was in fact the son of my aunty Meta and uncle Ronald. Meta and Ronnie had endured several miscarriages before having Colin, so as you can imagine, he was on a pedestal from the moment he was born. Ronnie, son of the British writer Leslie Bailey not to mention a brilliant scientist in his own right, had spent quite some time working on an agricultural powder for cows when, during the course of his work, it managed to creep into his lungs and cause him to develop chronic lung cancer. He never recovered from it and at just thirty-six years of age, much to Meta's devastation, he sadly lost his life. Following Ronnie's death, Meta and Colin moved from London to live with my parents and me.

I absolutely adored Colin and always doted on him like he was my brother. Overnight, he seemed to go from being a gorgeous little boy of two foot six to a dangerously handsome eighteen year old of six foot two. Every young one on the road was in love with him, but he only had eyes for his girlfriend, Shirley. He was mad about fashion so whenever I was out in Vegas I would

While it may sound like a dream, it very nearly turned into the kind of nightmare John Grisham would conjure up when late one night both our lives very nearly changed dramatically. Before that happened however, my world took a turn for the worse.

Colin and I on my Communion day.

pick up different items I knew he would wear with pride. Colin was always the kind of smiley kid everyone loved to be around. He just had a wonderful caring nature paired with a great wit.

On the night of 7 January 1974, as Tom Dunphy was driving me home from our gig in Navan, we were greeted by a throng of cars on Anne Devlin Road. I remember noticing a squad car before then realising that the commotion was taking place outside *my* house. Immediately, I panicked, thinking something had happened to one of my parents. When we got to the door, we were met by a policeman. Behind him, I could see my beloved Aunty Meta screaming crying. My mother came running out and told me that Colin and Shirley had been involved in a dreadful car accident. He had been returning from taking my luggage to Dublin Airport when he skidded on a dangerous wet road and crashed under a parked lorry. Shirley was dead and according to the doctors, there was no hope for Colin, it was just a matter of hours. At 1.55 p.m. the following day, his journey in life ended and my journey into grief began.

I honestly never got over his death. Even to this day, I cannot get my head around the fact that he is dead, not to mention the guilt I still harbour because it was a trip to the airport on my behalf that resulted in his death. I returned to Vegas, but my heart wasn't in it. Nothing seemed to be the same, even the glamour of the Vegas lifestyle had lost its sparkle.

It didn't help that Brendan Bowyer was going from bad to worse. He was snappy and constantly cutting me out of numbers. I was miserable; I didn't care about anything other than wanting to go home. I knew my family were in the midst of grief over Colin's death and I felt incredibly guilty that I was over in Las Vegas rather than at home comforting them. One night, as I was crying in the dressing room after experiencing yet another dose of Brendan's bile, the dancers all rallied around, reassuring me that everything would work out for the best. They knew about Colin and had been an amazing support to me. At one point that night, however, I was on my own in the dressing room. Next thing I knew, I was in a bed in Sunrise Hospital after one of the girls had found me collapsed on the floor. My body had obviously reached breaking point.

Colin in his teens.

It was arranged that I could talk to a psychiatrist and with her, I shared everything. The hassle I was receiving from Bowyer; the devastation I was experiencing over Colin's death; and the yearning I had to return home. At the time, I didn't want to be with my boyfriend Tom, not because I didn't love him, but because I felt I should be on my own for a while. During my stay in hospital, the girls arranged an apartment for me to move into and once I was discharged, I gradually began moving my belongings from Tom's place into mine. I explained my decision to Tom, but he was still understandably very hurt. Relations between us were anything but amicable and cross words were being exchanged more and more frequently.

One particular night after work, the girls asked me if I wanted to go see 'Little Anthony and the Imperials' on the strip. I decided against going because I had wanted to go to Tom's house to pick up more of my things while he was out at work. Unbeknownst to me however, he had decided to leave work early. What happened next still gives me nightmares to this day.

Tom had been out by the pool near the roof when he heard a noise at the front door. Assuming it was a break-in, he immediately turned off all the lights in the hope that he would see the intruder without being spotted himself. As I walked through the hall, under the assumption that I was alone in the house, every hair on my body suddenly stood up at the faint sound of someone walking on the roof. Compounding my terror was the sight of the open pool doors above me.

While Tom was outside the house thinking he was witnessing a burglary, I was inside thinking I was interrupting one.

Without a second thought, I ran down the corridor in the pitch dark and into our bedroom where I opened the drawer beside the bed. It was where Tom kept his gun. I was comfortable around guns because I had learned how to use one at the firing range. With the Smith & Wesson firmly in tow, I snuck back up the corridor. At the time, Tom owned the most beautiful Doberman Pincher dog called Oogee-ray. I remember wondering if they had killed him because I hadn't heard him or seen him. The craziest things went through my head. I even remember contemplating running back out of the house and into the street, but I knew they were on the roof so I was worried that they might see me and shoot. Even with the gun in my hand, I was petrified. I could clearly hear footsteps on the roof, but once I heard the person jump down onto the pool ledge, my fear multiplied.

As the silhouette suddenly stepped into the darkness of the pool doors, I sprang around the corner and warned with a roar that if they made another move, I would shoot. My finger was on the trigger and I was genuinely going to pull it. At that stage, I figured it would be either me or him leaving the house in a box. Suddenly, he flicked the switch and I saw it was Tom. I had, quite literally, been a millisecond away from shooting him dead.

Leaning back against the wall, I slid down to the floor, collapsing in a fit of tears. I was in a dreadful state of shock. Despite having nearly been riddled with bullets, Tom was so wonderfully comforting. In fact, that incident was a turning point for both of us in that the rows stopped and we became much more caring towards each other.

I often find myself wondering what my life would have been like today if this story had taken on a different ending. After all, everyone knew we had been arguing quite a bit, so had I shot him, it would only have been my word that it had been an accident. Let's face it, a jury would more than likely have assumed I deliberately shot him during a domestic row that got out of control. Needless to say, the memories of that night still haunt me to this day.

Not today, Roy Rogers

Paddy Cole's brilliant autobiography has the equally brilliant title, *Tell Roy Rogers I'm Not In*!

In fact, before he brought out that book, nobody ever believed me when I told them the Roy Rogers story. Roy, the legendary movie cowboy that every young fella wanted to be, lived in the same apartment block as us in Vegas. He had taken a big shine to Paddy and would be in his company every chance he got. On one particular occasion, the late Kevin Marron was staying in Paddy's apartment and while the two of them were out on the patio having a drink, the phone rang. Suddenly, Paddy turns around and says to his wife, 'Aw, Jesus, Helen, if that's Roy Rogers, tell him I'm not in!' That's the kind of surreal city Vegas was back then.

We were one of the line-up of star guests opening the MGM Grand. Next thing we knew, Raquel Welch and Cary Grant were being lined up beside us for a photograph. In fact, Raquel was so taken by my hot pants suit that when I informed her it was a creation of my mother's, she immediately asked, 'Would your momma make one for me?' and my mother did!

Now, be honest ladies, how many Irish mammies can say they made a hot pants suit for Raquel Welch?

While it was amazing to be in the company of so many legends, I still maintain that the best thing about the band years was Paddy Cole. Part of the Big 8 show was a slot in which Paddy would have a number of instruments lined up beside him on stage. First, he would play the baritone sax with its deep hornpipe sound, which he would follow up with a tenor sax, a soprano sax, a clarinet and a flute before then taking out a penny whistle from his pocket and playing that! The place would go wild. When we went to modify or change the show in any way, Paddy's instrumental slot was the one thing that the punters insisted remain. People

The official opening of MGM Grande, Las Vegas, with special guests Cary Grant and Raquel Welch.

would return night after night specifically to hear him perform that routine. In fact, when you saw him perform, you knew you were in the presence of true musical brilliance and showmanship.

I can still remember the very first time we met. It was the first day of meetings regarding the Big 8. As I waited for everyone else to arrive, a tall robust man with a great Castleblayney accent walked up to me with his gorgeous little son Pearse, extended his hand with a smile and said, 'How ya doin'? I'm a great admirer of yours. I'm Paddy Cole, you're very welcome to the band!'

From the word go we hit it off. In over forty years, I don't think we have ever exchanged a cross word (nor has he ever *once* called me Adèle or Twink, always Gerty! Don't ask me why!).

Paddy has the most endearing personality of anyone I know, and I sincerely doubt there is one person in Ireland with a bad word to say about him. I don't know how he has managed to go through his whole life without crossing anyone!

A great friend of Paddy's was Bill La Russo, owner of the Flame Bar and Restaurant, the most popular hangout for entertainers in Vegas. It was the type of high-end place where you would see the likes of Sammy Davis Jr and Frank Sinatra drinking late at night.

When word came through from Ireland that Paddy's wife Helen had given birth to their first daughter Katie, Bill La Russo arrived over at Paddy's apartment and filled the bath with ice, cans of beer and bottles of wine. That in itself was a fairly good indication of the night that lay ahead. During the course of the party, one of the lads drove his motorbike through a bush which unfortunately had a cement wall behind it, thus ending up in Sunrise Hospital. A not-so-sober Jimmy Conway, blind as a bat without his glasses, decided the following morning that it was too hot and dived into the swimming pool. Unfortunately for Jimmy, they had been cleaning the pool the previous day and there was not a drop of fuckin' water in it. Sunrise Hospital had yet another casualty from Katie Cole's party.

By the following evening, I think half the band were in the hospital. Injuries aside, it was one of those nights where I can't remember a moment when my ribs weren't aching from all the laughing. I'm fairly sure the staff at Sunrise Hospital still live in dread of any more parties being thrown in Katie Cole's honour!

Performing with my beloved Paddy Cole.

Meeting Martha Fox

There are certain things that science cannot explain; things that even the greatest of minds have to conclude are the works of something greater.

One such experience occurred at a dinner party in Angela Larney's house. Amongst the guests on the night was Martha Fox. Martha also happened to be a psychic and, at Angela's request, agreed to do a reading for us. I have to admit that when we all sat down for the reading, I was paying little heed to what was happening. I was the stereotypical dyed-in-the-wool sceptic, sitting at the edge of the group, half-listening, half-thinking about whether I had enough milk in the fridge for my cats, Puddin and Toulouse.

When she began, Martha turned to Angela and said, 'You have suffered the loss of someone in life. They're not directly attached to you … but you've been upset by a young loss recently.'

When she spoke with Jessie Fagan and Maureen Carter, she sensed she was getting closer to the source of the loss. Next, she clapped eyes on Phyllis O'Brien and remarked, 'Oh wait now, the loss is much closer to you …'

At that point she looked over at me and said, 'Actually, it's you! You had a brother … no wait he's not a brother but he was like a brother to you, and he died recently.'

As she continued going into more detail, I could feel the tears welling up in my eyes. Colin had died just two months earlier and it was clear she was referring to him.

'He was a tall, young, good-looking kid, but he wasn't blond like you, he had very dark hair. It was a motor accident and he died from head injuries …'

She was telling me things that not even Angela and the girls would have known. As Martha was delving into more and more details about Colin, she suddenly said something that almost made my heart stop.

'Tell me, Twink, did you ever find the other clog?'

The thing about Colin was that he was incredibly fashionable and, wherever I went, I always bought him really trendy clothes. I would buy long velvet flares, which were all the rage at the time, and every time he wore them, he stopped the traffic.

It sounds ridiculous now, but patterned clogs were also very much the trend, and Colin loved to wear them with white flares. He was wearing those shoes the night he died, however, when his body was removed from the car, the ambulance men could only find one of the clogs. When Martha asked if we had ever found the other one, I was speechless. There was absolutely no way on earth she could have gleaned that information from the other band members, because only my mother and Aunty Meta knew it. It was also far too specific a detail for her to have even guessed. I had never met the woman before that night, yet she was able to tell me things about Colin that only his immediate family knew.

Later that week, Martha was chatting to us in our dressing room. Just as she was leaving, she pointed to a pair of shoes on the floor and asked who owned them. Dave Coady replied that they belonged to Tom Dunphy. She looked up and said, 'Well the person who owns those shoes is going to be killed in an automobile crash not too long from now.'

Tom wasn't in the room at the time but when we told him what Martha had predicted, he immediately laughed it off. It seemed preposterous, because he was always such a careful driver, a total saint behind the wheel. Subsequently, Tom was killed in a car crash in Drumsna on 29 July 1975. I haven't seen Martha from that day to this, but every time I think of her incredible gift, a shiver runs through me.

Like I said, some experiences just can't be explained.

Another cocktail, Mom?

I was blessed with truly amazing parents. They couldn't possibly have given me a better childhood than the one I had.

As a gesture of gratitude, I decided to bring them out to Las Vegas for their wedding anniversary. When I phoned them to tell them where they would be holidaying, my normally quiet mother literally screamed with delight. They had never been on a proper holiday before and considering Vegas was one of the most exotic places you could think of at the time, it made the trip all the sweeter.

When they arrived, they had the time of their lives. During their trip, they also went to San Francisco and saw Alcatraz, dined on lobster and shrimp at Fisherman's Wharf, and paid a visit to the Redwood Tree Forest. What absolutely titillated my mother most of all, however, was how she and I would sit in the outdoor whirlpool drinking Pina Colada's at four in the morning, the novelty being that she had never taken a drop of alcohol in her life up to that point!

One of the highlights of the trip occurred when we were queuing up to see Debbie Reynolds perform. Mom spotted a nearby slot machine called Big Bertha and begged me to give it a go.

'Ah, go on, put a coin into it. I want to see what it does!'

'No, Mom, I don't gamble. I'm *not* feeding money into a machine,' I insisted.

Handing me a coin she nudged me on, 'Ah, humour me, go on!'

After slipping the coin into the slot, all the bloody lights on the machine suddenly started flashing and bells began ringing. The machine was spewing out so many coins that people were walking over to see what the commotion was. Gino Simorelli, the pit boss who had nicknamed me 'Bernadette Devlin', shouted over, 'Aw, the fuckin' Irish! Leave it to the fuckin' Irish! Bernadette Devlin is after winning the big bucks!'

We had won $1,000 which was an insane amount of money back then. I genuinely don't think my mother heard a word Debbie Reynolds sang that night because she kept turning to me and saying, 'I can't believe we won!'

A few days later, they went to see me perform in the Stardust. I was ecstatic that they were finally getting to see me in action on the big stage in Vegas. I would always tell them about the different shows, but nothing compared to the experience of them actually being there. When I introduced them to the audience, the crowd went crazy. Ironically, Chloë's life has mimicked mine in many ways and as a result, I ended up becoming the proud mom sitting in the audience watching my child perform on stage in America.

This is the exact hot pants suit my mother replicated for Raquel Welch.

Which way are they walkin'?

Paddy Cole and I were always trying to convince Bowyer and Dunphy to change the songs and keep the show fresh.

One night, however, Tom took us aside and said, 'Which way are those people walking? Are they walking *in* or *out* of the show? They're walking *in* to the show! Well, the day they are walking the *other* way is the day you can come up and talk about changing the programme.'

I adored Tom, and to be fair, he had a point, but I still felt we could have gently introduced new songs to the show while still maintaining the general theme that had made it so popular in the first place. Unfortunately, they were adamant that the show would remain the same, which then resulted in a trickle of dissension forming because everyone was beyond bored of playing the same music three shows a night, six nights a week. Anytime we argued the toss, Brendan would always snap back with the line, 'Well your airline tickets are in that drawer so if you don't like it, you know what you can do!'

Around that time, I began to suffer terrible throat problems. This had never happened to me before, so I went to a wonderful woman in the University of Nevada called Dorothy Bokelmann. She went to see me perform that night and we arranged to meet a few days later for a consultation. Dorothy began by asking me if the diamante cross/necklace I was wearing was too tight. It seems she had noticed I was constantly tugging at the neckpiece as though I was psychologically trying to free up something in my throat. Apparently, it's a classic sign of stress and tension. Then she asked me, 'Is that guy's eyes always burning a hole in the back of your head on stage?'

By 'that guy', she meant Bowyer.

'Ah, well, that's the stress!' she continued. 'You can feel his eyes burning into you from behind. Well no one can sing like that, so I'm going to send you to Frank Sinatra's consultant, Dr Abdo.'

She was right, and the next time Bowyer reminded me that my 'airline tickets were in the drawer', I told him to go and get them for me. By the look of shock on his face, that was obviously the last response he had been expecting.

Now that the tables had turned, they all tried in vain to persuade me to stay. At that point however, I had genuinely paid my dues with Brendan and was ready to leave. I'd had enough. I was going home.

Work for the Mafia? No thanks, boys!

It was in Vegas that I learned the meaning of the word 'divorce'. We hadn't even heard of it in Ireland. If a marriage broke up, people would say, 'Oh, he went away'. The terms 'separation' or 'divorce' were not in existence.

In Las Vegas, one of the first divorcees I met was man called Barry McCoy who was the keyboard player with Gary Puckett and the Union Gap.

I absolutely fell for Barry. We met at a musical party in the MGM after Wayne Newton asked me to sing the song 'Killing Me Softly'. Barry had been playing the piano that night and so, after my performance, we got chatting. When he told me his ex-wife was Ginny Polone, my face fell in shock. She was an amazingly gifted performer and the front line singer in the Sands Hotel. I had long been a huge fan of hers. Ginny, however, was no longer a favourite with 'the boys' it seemed. Several times the Mafia 'suits' (who were also major show bosses) would arrive into the Stardust to watch the Big 8 perform, and, on one particular night, they sent me a message asking if I would meet them in another hotel for lunch the following day. I knew they wanted to poach me from the band, but I met with them anyway and listened to their offer. They began by telling me that Ginny, their current performer, was pushing on a bit and that they wanted her out and me in.

'We need a young person … young and vibrant. One month and we could have you fronting the show. I know the Stardust like you to look like the Irish *cailín*, but if we got you the proper grooming, you could look like a Vegas star.'

They then added that they 'didn't give a fuck' about Brendan because he wasn't going to have

his contract renewed with the Stardust. They were right about that. After I left, he didn't get the contract renewed.

When I received the offer from another promoter I distinctly remember thinking, 'You're all a shower of shits'.

Fortunately, I was smart enough not to say it to their faces. Here they were talking about people they had kiss-assed for years as though they were now of no use to them. I absolutely abhorred how they saw me as the new star on the block and my colleagues as disposable commodities.

I admit their offer was tempting, but I couldn't entertain the idea of investing all my time in their show only to be told, just like the previous girls, I was 'past it' when I hit thirty.

I won't lie, I was terrified about turning the offer down. After all, some promoters are famously

Singing with Brendan Bowyer and the Big 8 Showband on RTÉ.

unfamiliar with the word 'no'. When I did reject their offer, their reaction was one of great disbelief. I politely explained that while I enjoyed working in Vegas, I felt I had to live at home for a while because of what had happened to Colin. I also made it quite clear to them that I wasn't even going to continue with Bowyer's show. I had spent five years in Vegas and felt it was time to go home. I assured them I would give their offer plenty of thought in Ireland but the likelihood was that I wouldn't be accepting it. Deep down, I had absolutely no intention of taking up the position. Instead, I hoped that they would find someone else and forget about ever having asked me.

Even though I was very young I had enough cop-on to foresee that one day they would show the same level of disrespect for me as they had already shown for Ginny Polone and the many others who had tread the boards before her, all the while making money for themselves.

I wasn't ever a star-struck young one, thank God. To this day, there are colleagues of mine who would almost do a twenty-minute spot each time they open the fridge door and the light comes on. A number of the younger stars believe in their own hype; they believe they are irreplaceable. If I have learned anything from my years in the business, it's that *everybody* is replaceable and the day you believe otherwise is undoubtedly the egotistical rock you will perish on.

Joining my new band mates in the International Bar! l-r: Wee Louis Dignam, Paddy Cole, Mike 'Bunny' Dalton, Pat Morris, Jimmy Conway, Ray Moore, me and Mickey O'Neill R.I.P.

When I flew back home, I felt like I needed a break from the entertainment business. I underwent an operation on my vocal chords to have some nodules removed, after which I flew over to Dorothy Bokelmann in Vegas who spent a couple of months guiding me through a vocal-training course that has stood to me to this day.

When you have an operation on your chords, you cannot return to singing straight away, otherwise you will ruin your voice. For once in my life, I really *did* shut up. I even carried a slide board everywhere with me which I used to communicate.

When I returned to Ireland, I went back working in my old riding stables, Green Trees, and whenever I wasn't busy mucking out, polishing tack and tending to my beautiful horse, Benefactor, I was studying for a British Horse Riding Instructors exam. All in all, I honestly couldn't have given a toss if I never saw a stage again. While I was out in the yard one evening, Paddy Cole called in. Greeting me with a massive hug and a jovial roar of 'Gerty!', he said he wanted to talk. He went on to explain that things hadn't been the same since I left the band. It turns out Bowyer had brought in a new lead singer to replace me. She was around twenty-one, and from what I was told, the image of his wife, Stella.

To my shock, Paddy explained that the rest of the band were planning to leave Bowyer and Dunphy. He then said that the lads had elected him to seek me out and persuade me to join their new band, The Paddy Cole Superstars. They were all waiting in the International Bar in Dublin's Wicklow Street for Paddy to return with my answer.

No way was I venturing back into the music industry. In fact, the only place I had set my sights on returning to was university. A life of academia awaited me and I wasn't going to turn my back on it *again*. I had always harboured great ambitions of studying medicine, but at that point in my life I was caring for so many animals that I felt veterinary medicine would probably be more beneficial. I wanted nothing more than to escape the vacuous business of entertainment.

Paddy went on to explain that while there would be a few tours in the US, the band would be based primarily in Ireland. At some point during the conversation, his Castleblayney charm must have persuaded me to join because next thing I knew I was in the aforementioned bar celebrating with my old/new band mates, I hadn't even managed to change out of my equestrian gear!

Out for a hold, a grope and a grab!

Admittedly, the years I spent with The Paddy Cole Superstars were far better than those I had experienced with the other bands. We were far more of a rock-pop band and we also enjoyed a lot more freedom on the music front.

Some nights, we would be performing for people who were really only out for a hold, a grope and a grab, but, for the most part, our gigs were held in venues where women met their future husbands – women who, more than likely, are now reading this book!

The only factor that remained the same was my loathing of the road.

It seemed like such a waste of my life, just sitting on a tour bus day in and day out. It got to a point where if I saw the Naas Road one more time, I was going to reach for the razor blades. I had to do things to occupy my mind and distract me from the looming monotony. Back then, however, there wasn't even a Walkman, let alone a bloody iPod. All I had was a Bush radio and one of those singular hearing aids for the deaf which I gaffa-taped to my seat on the touring bus.

We didn't even have my beloved British Classic FM in those days either. How did I live without it?

The next extension to the radio was a little yellow plastic torch with a strong beam which I then taped to the seat and used as a reading light.

At one point, I began studying Italian on the road before subsequently attending tutorial lessons where my beloved Professor Enzo Farinella would

Following Chloë's twenty-first birthday in June 2010, I sent a text to my dear cousin Anne to thank her for driving up from Cork for the party. In the text I wrote: 'Anne you were charming, beautiful, articulate and witty as a little girl, and you're exactly the same as a grown woman.' Her full name is Anne Watkins however to the people who stand before her in the Four Courts, she's known as Judge Watkins. My little baby cousin is a High Court judge! Here she is in a photograph, aged no more than five, standing alongside my cousin Colin and me.

give me exercises to carry out on the coach. I also invested my travel time in completing needlework and tapestries. Looking back, the only thing I am grateful to 'the road' for are those mind-numbing hours I filled with learning.

For Celtic Woman, the group in which my daughter Chloë performs, life on the road has a very different meaning. They practically live in a mobile hotel. The coaches they use were bought from Destiny's Child and contain lounges, gaming machines, plasma screens, stereos, breakfast rooms and every other luxury imaginable. At the press of a button, a lavender scent is emitted to help them sleep! When I saw the style they were travelling in, I couldn't help but laugh at the contrast between my experience of life on the road with my gaffa-taped reading torch and Chloë's life on the road with her luxuries by the dozen.

❖

Paddy and I were the only two members of the band who lived in Dublin, so as soon as he dropped me home in the early hours of the morning following a gig, I would immediately change into my riding gear and take my horse, Benefactor out for a morning jaunt through the fields. I would then cram in a few hours sleep before Paddy would return to take me to the next gig somewhere down the country. Paddy was always very concerned about my career and well-being. In fact he would often say to me, 'Jaysus, Gerty, you shouldn't be in this business at all. You should have become the neuro-surgeon you always wanted to be.'

Paddy knew that my one and only childhood dream was to study medicine. In fact, my father also once said to me in his latter years, 'I know you're regretful about not being a doctor, but look at it this way Bunny, you still get people into

your theatre. They come in with their ills, their ails and the worries of the world, then you come out on stage and in over two hours of making them laugh, you have cured them and sent them out smiling. Now *that's* being a doctor, curing people of their woes – just in a different kind of theatre!'

People assume a performer craves the stage and, for the most part, they do. Not me, however. It's just a job that pays the bills and nothing more. The late Elizabeth Taylor possessed the same outlook. I know from the bottom of my heart that I would have much preferred a career where I could have used my brain rather than my talent. In fact, I would give anything to be walking around hospital wards in a white coat with a stethoscope rather than walking the stages of Ireland in a costume with a microphone.

Colleagues and friends of mine have often described me as successful, but I never have and never will see myself in that light. If anything, I see myself as a failure. In my eyes, the real stars are people like Teresa Lowe, Cynthia Ní Mhurchú, Dr Marian Duane and various friends of mine from the Young Dublin Singers who went on to become barristers, doctors and so on. They returned to the books and used their brains. Even though my family were artistic, they were equally academic. Veterinary medicine, law and psychology are just three of the areas in which my relatives work and so, by comparison, I truly feel like the black sheep, the one who let the side down. I know they are extremely proud of me and my work but I do feel there's an element of, 'Isn't it a pity she didn't use her brain for something better?'

On one occasion, my fellow band member, Dave Coady, was talking about how he would have loved to have become a lexicographer had he not chosen the musical route for his career.

I agreed with him. For those of you who don't know (and to save you the trouble of looking it up in the dictionary) a lexicographer is someone who compiles a dictionary! Following this revelation, Paddy Cole became the third band member to take an interest in the idea, and that very day the three of us bought a big fat tome of a dictionary in a Waterford bookshop. We decided that we would study a page a day and then quiz each other on the way home from our gigs each night. From the meaning of the word to its origin, we would have to know every detail. It was *absolutely* one of the best things I *ever* did in my life. Over the course of a year, we very nearly reached the end of the dictionary. I had to make some bloody use of all the words I had learned and so I became a crossword junkie. It was a perfect challenge for me because I utterly adored learning but, above all, I think it was pretty indicative of how bored shitless I was.

The one thing I possibly hated more than the road were the groupies. They have always been around; I hated them then and I hate them now. They gave new meaning to the word slut. They quite literally had no shame and would blatantly gesture at one of the lads: 'You and me around the back of the dance hall'. Some of the more brazen ones would ask for the keys to the bandwagon. By and large, groupies were rampant in the showband days. There was even a regular few who would turn up at shows, so musicians always knew that if they wanted it, they could have it.

Let's just say, more than a few of the groupie members even returned nine months later …

Admiring Pat

Pat Kenny is one of the sexiest men in Ireland and I once fancied him. I hasten to add that while we're both of the same vintage, I'm pleased to say Pat's a little older! I always felt he should have upped and left for America the moment the Irish press started sniping at him. The American viewers would have loved his cultured Irish accent and drop dead gorgeous looks, and I guarantee if he were over there today, they would consider him a heartthrob. There is nothing the man can't talk about and I know that anyone who has ever met him will nod in agreement when I say he is very engaging company. You would never run out of conversation with him; he's just so articulate and well read. Contrary to what people think, he also has a wonderful sense of humour.

The Late Late Show was never his forte, a point made more obvious when you see the remarkable job he is doing on *The Frontline*. It's just a shame RTÉ didn't have the cop-on to use Pat as a political intellectual much sooner than they did.

I remember watching him interview Gordon Ramsay's alleged mistress when she appeared on *The Late Late Show* to plug her new book on how to catch a married man. In my opinion, he looked desperately uncomfortable. Put him in front of Bill Clinton or Barrack Obama, however, and he would give them the interviews of their lives.

Tom

In the film *Singing in the Rain*, Cosmo Brown says, 'What's the first thing an actor learns? The show must go on! Come rain, come shine, come snow, come sleet, the show *must* go on!'

A cliché it may be, but it's one that is most certainly wrapped in truth.

When it comes to showbusiness, any sorrows lurking in the performer's private life are of absolutely no significance, nor should they be. After all, the audience have paid to see a performance; it's not their problem if the performer is having a bad day. The show must always go on and the star must always smile and shine. As an actor, you learn to zone out of your own life and immerse yourself in the character you're portraying. My theatre training always really stood to me in that regard. On occasion, however, even the most disciplined of actors can struggle with this.

With one of the greatest loves of my life, Tom Dunphy.

I will never forget 29 July 1975, the night we were playing in Castleisland, County Kerry. Just moments before the show, news filtered through that Tom Dunphy and his keyboard player Noel Ryan had been in a car crash in Drumsna, near Carrick-on-Shannon. It transpired that they had been on their way to perform at the Mary from Dungloe Festival in Donegal when their car collided with a lorry. Noel escaped, albeit with serious injuries, but Tom was killed instantly.

I wholeheartedly loved Tom and his death absolutely devastated me. I still don't know how we finished the show that night. All I can say is our hearts weren't in it. We went through the motions, with great difficulty. It was just so hard to believe our beloved Tom was gone. When I heard he had died, one of the things that crossed my mind was the reading conducted by the psychic Martha Fox regarding the owner of *those shoes*, six months earlier.

Sadly, her prediction had come true.

The Vision

My wonderful friend Alma Carroll was, and still is, insanely gorgeous. In fact, her incredible elegance and ladylike nature earned her the nickname 'Princess Grace'.

We first met through the Young Dublin Singers, where the nuns branded us both as gifted singers and effectively pitted us against each other, thus quickly turning us into rivals. It was only in later years that we realised we actually quite liked and admired each other. She remains one of my dearest friends to this day and both she and her husband, Arthur Ryan, are godparents to my Naomi.

Back when we were in the choir, however, we were often sent out to perform in RTÉ. Whenever we were in the canteen having lunch, the same gorgeous boy always caught our eye.

The vision, John McColgan.

With his black clothes and slick black hair, he was the image of the film star Fabian. Alma knew him quite well and so whenever he walked in, he would always say hello to her, leaving the rest of us absolutely sickened with envy. He was only around eighteen years old at the time and my God, we could have just sat and stared at him for hours. He was working as a vision mixer so we appropriately referred to him as 'the vision' because that's exactly what he was, a beautiful vision. Oh and, by the way, his name was John McColgan, only the man who would later go on to become known as Mr Riverdance! During his career, he has been a vision mixer, floor manager, cameraman, producer and director. The man was, and still is, bloody diseased with talent.

John was a wonderful ideas man and I had the good fortune of working with him on many occasions. We got to know each other quite well, although admittedly nothing happened between us at first because our lives and careers took us in two different directions. I went to live in America while he married an actress called Virginia Cole with whom he went on to have two beautiful children, Justin and Lucy.

On one of the occasions I was home from the USA, we had arranged to meet up for a drink and a catch up in Sachs Hotel on Morehampton Road. During the course of conversation, I made reference to himself and his wife Virginia, at which point John interrupted and explained that they had been separated for quite some time. I expressed my sadness at this to him as I was genuinely sorry to hear their marriage had ended.

Following my return from the band's England tour, we met up again for lunch and spent ages just chatting and reminiscing. I suppose it was the age-old story of one thing leading to another before gradually developing into head-over-heels love. We were really serious about each other, in fact, we lived together for five years. We also worked together on different productions such as *Castle Backtax* and my own Christmas television show *The Twink Special*, to name but two. Relationship aside, I always loved working with John primarily because the standards he introduced to a job were above and beyond phenomenal. He always produced the best shows and when *you* work with someone like that, they always tend to get the best out of *you*.

Would you believe that when I was going out with John, his car was such a banger it was actually up on four blocks in the RTÉ car park? I don't think I will ever forget the Director General approaching me at one point and asking me if I could 'talk my partner into removing the heap of rubbish that was parked outside Montrose House'!

With my then partner, John McColgan, in the RTÉ make-up room before **The Live Mike**.

Gabriel Byrne

The actor Gabriel Byrne has an amazingly dry wit, a trait perfectly summed up in a response he once gave to an interviewer.

'I would like to break out of this "dark, brooding" image, because I'm actually not like that at all. In Ireland, brooding is a term we use for hens. A brooding hen is supposed to lay eggs. Every time somebody says, "He's dark and brooding", I immediately think, "He's about to lay an egg!"'

John and I would often go out for dinner with Gabriel and his then girlfriend, the late broadcaster, Áine O'Connor, our favourite place being a little Italian restaurant on the main road to Dún Laoghaire called Pavannis. Afterwards, we would almost always end up going back to Gabriel's place in Ballsbridge where we would chat and laugh into the small hours. Admittedly, Gabriel and I were the ones doing most of the

laughing. I remember one night when he and I were behind the couch in hysterics smoking a joint between us, Áine and John were having the most intense discussion about broadcasting and television. We laughingly joked that the four of us needed to be re-matched.

One occasion about three years ago, I was in the car with an American friend who was in Ireland for a few days, and as we were driving through Rathmines, he suddenly remarked, 'Am I seeing things or is that the film star Gabriel Byrne?'

He had no idea I knew Gabriel, so I rolled down the window and roared, 'Oi, Byrne! Get up the yard, there's a smell of Benji off ya!'

Realising it was me, he laughed and immediately waved back. Shocked my friend turned and said to me, 'Well … I take it you know him then!'

'Please Return Immediately'

When people look back on 1980, they remember listening to **ABBA** and Eric Clapton, they remember tuning in to *Dallas* to find out who shot JR, or tuning into the news to find out who shot John Lennon.

For me, however, 1980 saw me spend more time in the air than on the ground. When I was preparing for my 1980 RTÉ *Twink Special*, I was constantly flying back and forth to London. As well as helping to audition dancers in the famous Pineapple Studios, I also had to travel to Seymour Place for various wig and costume fittings.

At some stage during that year, I also became the face of Polaroid cameras, which meant my photograph was on almost every billboard in Ireland. When I travelled to London to film a cinema ad for them, I met up with my best friend John Sullivan and his partner Tony, who worked for Joker Costume Hire in Chiswick, a shop that stocked the most amazing showgirl headpieces. As the three of us were leaving a restaurant one night, I spotted a woman wearing the most beautiful blue fox fur coat, which was all the rage at the time. The following day, I made a beeline for Swan & Edgar in Piccadilly Circus where blue fox furs were sold. The moment I tried one on, I fell in love with it. Unfortunately, the price tag was nowhere near as lovable. It cost £600, which even *now* is still a bloody expensive price for a coat, but back then it was particularly humongous. No matter how much I tried to convince myself I deserved it, in the end I just couldn't bring myself to pay that much.

As I walked up Oxford Street, I turned a corner and walked along by the railings where a woman was chatting with her friend. As she looked over her shoulder to say goodbye, she stepped off the pavement and out onto the road where I could clearly see a black taxi was within seconds of hitting her. With as much strength as I could muster, I grabbed her by the arms and pulled her back on to the pavement. She knew immediately that her momentary lapse of concentration had very nearly resulted in her ending up underneath the car, and when she realised just how close she had come to being killed, she was shaking with fright. So eventually, to help calm her nerves, I brought her for a coffee, and, as we were chatting, she asked why I was in the area. I explained that I had been to Swan & Edgar to try on a fantastic fur coat but had decided at last minute not to buy it. I then laughed at how fate had clearly put me in the right place at the right time because had I bought the coat, I would more than likely have still been in the shop as she was stepping on to the road. She then came out with a revelation that I certainly wasn't expecting to hear. 'Adèle … *I'm* the general manager of Swan & Edgar!'

She brought me back to the store and, as a show of gratitude, sold me the coat for a fraction of the original price. Even when I think about that story today, I still can't get my head around the fact that out of all the people on the streets of lunchtime London, what are the odds of me saving the life of the manager of the very shop I had just been in?

Clearly that coat was meant for me! Well hold that thought folks!

The following day, John Sullivan had arranged to bring me to the aforementioned Joker Costume Hire to try on the headpieces. Arriving out to John's car decked out in my new fur, I was greeted with a gasp and a wolf whistle, followed

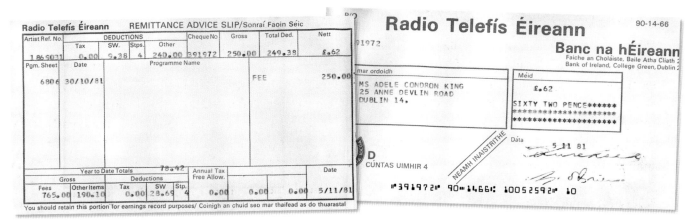

For anyone who thought I made millions from RTÉ, take a look at this! A cheque for 62 pence! It was originally £250, however I was left with the princely sum of 62p after taxes! Before any of the station's suits argue that the amount in question was a big sum back then, don't kid yourselves, dears; if it was that bloody big, I wouldn't have kept it!

by the most appropriate response for such an extravagant item, 'Well, get *you*, girl!'

When we arrived at the shop, I took off my precious coat and left it on the counter while Tony brought us upstairs to what can only be described as a goldmine of show-stopping headgear and costumes. Charles Self, the set designer and overall costume co-ordinator for my television special, later joined us to see the pieces I had chosen. Following his stamp of approval, our work was done. The next morning, Rita Hayworth herself would have been hard pushed to have matched my swagger as I made my way through Heathrow Airport in my blue fox fur. Like anyone who owned one of these babies, I really thought I was *the business*. When I took my seat on the plane, who was sitting next to me with only an empty seat between us, but Lady Miranda Guinness. With great flourish, I took off my coat and placed it on the vacant seat hoping and praying she would notice the famously swish Swan & Edgar label. As we were

chatting, I could see her eyes glancing at the coat and at one point, I noticed a change in her expression as she caught sight of the label – in fact, I actually thought I saw her wince a little. Regardless, we continued with the polite small-talk until we arrived in Dublin at which point we said goodbye and wished each other well. The moment I was home, I showed the coat to my mother and my aunty Meta.

Meta immediately wanted to try it on and as I was about to put it on her, something caught my eye. Suddenly Lady Miranda's wincing expression began to make sense. When I left my coat on the counter of the shop, John and Tony had taken it, and for the craic, had lightly stitched over the Swan & Edgar label with one that read:

'ON LOAN FROM JOKER COSTUME HIRE, CHISWICK – PLEASE RETURN IMMEDIATELY.'

Of course, John was twisted laughing when I told him that I had all but pushed the bloody label in Lady Miranda's face hoping she was getting a good look at the Swan & Edgar name, when instead she probably left the plane thinking I was a cheap bitch who had stolen a hired costume!

My set designer Charles Self was a great friend of Vincent Hanley. In fact, the two of them were like a double act when they got together, one always trying to be even funnier than the other. We would often meet up for lunch when we were all in London, during which Vinny and Charles would always try to 'out-queen' each other, making me laugh until my jaws ached and the tears practically streamed down my face.

Apart from sharing an amazing sense of humour, both were also insanely talented in their respective fields. At the height of Vinny's fame, there was nothing he couldn't turn to gold. His effervescent spirit relayed through his broadcasting, making him an instant hit with the Irish public.

I even remember Vincent telling myself and David that he was in talks about 'something very exciting that would revolutionise television and the music industry'.

He was talking about *MT USA* and he was certainly right in his prediction.

Charles meanwhile had been involved in the design of *The Late Late Show*, not to mention countless other productions. He had a wonderful mind and his creative flair made him a brilliant set designer. Like Vinny, Charles was loved by everyone who had the pleasure of working with him. He had absolutely everything to live for but, unfortunately, life was just too cruel to let him. On the morning of 22 January 1982, I was working in a radio station when John McColgan phoned me. To my absolute horror, he told me that Charles Self had been found the previous night brutally murdered in his Monkstown apartment. He had suffered thirty-seven stab wounds to his body. Vincent was utterly distraught by Charles's death; we all were. No charges were ever made, although early in 2011, there was talk of the case being reopened following the discovery of a new lead in the form of fingerprints. I can only hope and pray that after all this time, the bastard that took the life of my beautiful and talented friend will finally be put behind bars.

'That is our Dermot!'

I actually considered naming the book *That Is Our Dermot!* as an homage to one of my favourite stories (and also to have you all wondering who the hell Dermot is!). When I was in London, fabric shopping for panto costumes, I met up with my good friend John Sullivan. As we were walking down Berwick Street, he began telling me how they were having awful problems with his younger brother Dermot. In fact, the family were really worried about him as he had gone off the rails and no one could control him. While we were chatting, I was reassuring John that things would work out and that it was probably just a phase. In fact, I honestly couldn't imagine it being as bad as he was describing because I knew the Sullivans so well – they were a rock-solid family, salt of the earth.

Just as I was saying the words, 'Don't be ridiculous, John, it's only youth, you have to let the phase pass', a tsunami of very punk-looking lads began walking towards us. The worst of them was this fella positioned smack bang at the front, with a huge red Mohican, not to mention rings and *actual* safety pins covering every inch of his skin. As the gang was walking menacingly up the street, people were moving out of their way, a true testament to their intimidating appearance. The moment I saw them, I immediately nudged John and remarked, 'Oh my Jesus, would you look at that lot! There you are now, *that's* problems! I mean seriously, look at that fucker in the middle! Imagine if that was your Dermot!'

'Adèle …' John replied, 'that *is* our Dermot!'

Fast forward a few years and Dermot is now a pillar of society in Clonakilty, Co. Cork! He's also an award-winning photographer and restaurant owner married with two beautiful daughters, and not a pin or a chain to be seen on him!

The ex

An ex-partner of John McColgan's was creating a lot of problems for us at the time. She loathed me for being with him, and made this obvious on more than one occasion. Being quite young, I found the situation very difficult to deal with.

One Christmas Eve, she arrived at my parents' door. Knowing that John and I were inside, she threw a brick at the house before proceeding to call me every vulgar name imaginable. Despite the fact that she and John had not been together for about seven years, she did her level best to run my name into the gutter and make our lives hell. Looking back now, I can see it was the behaviour of a woman pained and I can only assume it stemmed from her still being hopelessly in love with him. In the end, unfortunately, her behaviour put so much stress and strain on our relationship that it began to break us up.

After almost five years together, we both knew it was over. I can still remember that day in the car park of Network 2 in Ballsbridge when we decided to call it quits. We had been invited to an event that night, however I couldn't go because of work commitments, so I suggested to John that he ask out 'that lovely sweet production assistant' that Brendan Balfe had brought in from radio to work with us.

She was a shy girl from Donegal, but armed with a determined attitude.

Her name? Moya Doherty! He did as I suggested and sure enough they promptly fell in love, got married and had two amazing children. Moya and I are now determined that the two McColgan boys will marry the two Agnew girls!

Years later, that same ex who had caused all those problems for John and me, ended up becoming a regular face on a show I used to work on. I'm a great believer in moving on and getting over things; harbouring bitter grudges will do nothing other than ravage your sanity like a cancer. She and I acknowledged that there had been a lot of bad blood between us, but John was in neither of our lives at that point, so there was no reason why we both couldn't put the past behind us.

Love post

Despite the tumultuous latter years of our relationship, David Agnew and I enjoyed the kind of love affair that would have made even Lord Byron and Lady Caroline blush. He wrote like a poet, sending me the most incredibly romantic notes and letters imaginable. For the most part, it was a dreamy bohemian relationship, but sadly there was always someone waiting in the wings with the proverbial vial of poison. Unfortunately, while David has many qualities, self-control and fidelity were never amongst them.

I first laid eyes on David in November 1979 not long after breaking up with John McColgan. Noel Pearson had brought the London production of *Oliver* to Dublin, with him as principle oboist and me in the wonderful role of Nancy.

Dearest Adèle,
I love you, David
xxx

While the orchestra were rehearsing in the downstairs hall of a premises on Mountjoy Square, I would sometimes work on my music in the pianist's room upstairs. One freezing-cold November night as I was about to leave the hall, Don King, the bass player, was on his way in. During our quick chat, I asked him who was in the orchestra to which he replied, 'Aw, the usual suspects and one or two new faces'.

We shared a few laughs and after he went inside, I wiped the haw from the glass and looked in to see who was playing. I spotted a number of musicians I had known for years, but sitting in amongst them was a terribly good-looking boy. Actually no, the term 'good-looking' didn't do him justice – he was above and beyond gorgeous.

When I saw him pick up my favourite instrument, the oboe, well that was it, I was smitten. There I was, standing outside the window thinking, 'I'm going to marry you', when he suddenly looked up and gave me a heart-stopping smile followed by a tip-of-the-finger wave. Any time I rehearsed with the orchestra after that, I would catch him giving me the glad eye, a look I only too happily returned. I still didn't know anything about him, but that soon changed when one night I spotted the wonderful oboist, Peter Healy, on his way into rehearsals with the orchestra.

'Oi, Healy! Get over here a minute!'

I could tell by the look on his face that he knew exactly the topic I was going to broach.

'Who's your man?' I enquired with a smile.

'Aw he's a bit of a dark horse actually! He's in UCD studying to be a doctor of botany.'

'You're kidding?'

'Seriously! He's a scientist as well as a brilliant oboist. You know he won the gold in the Paris Conservatoire for oboe? He's one of the new talents.'

'What age is he?'

'I dunno, about twenty-two or something around that.'

'What's his name?

'David'

'David what?'

'David … em … oh God, what is it? It's an unusual name … kind of French or Breton … I'll find out for you.'

Ever the bull at the gate, I didn't wait for Peter to get back to me.

Instead I sent a note to Mr Scientist/Oboist and asked him myself.

'David. We have bets going on here as to what your name is.'

'Agnew' came the returning note.

'Is that a Breton name?'

'Well sort of, it comes from the Breton Normandy name D'Agnew. By the way, how did you find out my name was David?'

'A little bird told me!'

'Would this little bird be called Peter Healy by any chance?'

By this point our poor stage director Yvette Hally was exhausted from couriering our 'feckin love notes' back and forth but, God love her, she still did it.

At some point during the flirtation, I realised I had seen David before, back when he was a teenager and performing with the youth orchestra. He stood out at the time because he was the only kid with big hair and sideburns. I also discovered that David's father was the legendary tenor Arthur Agnew, a man who was on a par with some of the world's finest tenors. As a soloist with the Young Dublin Singers, I often stood on the same stage as Arthur Agnew in O'Connell Hall, completely unaware that I was actually looking at my future father-in-law. Even as a child, I used to love to hear him sing. Ironically, Arthur also used to sing with my cousin Monica Condron, who was the secretary general with the Dublin Grand Opera Society (DGOS) for years.

❖

As anyone who has seen *Oliver* will know, it begins with a thundering-loud overture followed by a short beautiful piece performed by an oboist. I would always hear this introduction when up in my dressing room and from the first seven notes, I would be able to tell whether or not it was David who was playing. His style of performance always possessed such an exquisitely sweet melodic tone. Poor Yvette was still on love-post duty at this point and would regularly knock on my dressing room door with the words, 'Juliet, I've another note from Romeo!'

One night, however, Romeo sent a note back asking if I wanted to go for a drink after the show. When I walked into the bar, I vividly remember it being somewhat awkward between us at first, almost like we didn't know what to say to each other. There had always been a safety with the notes in that we could be a little cheekier than we would face to face. Fortunately, we hit it off and things went from good to great. Almost from the start, we were besotted with each other. Whenever I was on stage, David would always wink at me and blow little kisses up at me. One night, as the curtain went up, he gave me one of his trademark smiles. Noticing how infatuated I was, my fellow actor Aidan Grennell, a terribly elegant gentleman who at that stage was probably in his late seventies, very wittily remarked, 'Oh dear, dear, dear, if only I were two or three years younger!'

Don't kick the bucket, Red

In my opinion, Red Hurley is the greatest singer this country has ever turned out. I have duetted with him in the past and I swear to God, a word has yet to be invented to describe the immense privilege it was to sing with that man. In fact,

I have stipulated in my will that I want Red Hurley to sing 'When' at my funeral. I've already told him he's got the gig, now all I have to do is make sure he doesn't kick the bloody bucket before me!

Lovestruck

David and I were so in love; crazy about each other.

On the final night of *Oliver*, he sent me a beautiful love letter written on the back of the music sheet that contained the notes of that distinctive overture music I had come to know so well. He would declare his love by whatever means possible.

On the many occasions we lay in the long grass in Enniskerry, he would write tiny 'I love you' messages on the wooden corks from the copious

amounts of Codorníu we enjoyed on our dates. Whatever form the note arrived in, I have treasured them all to this day. In fact, I can always remember exactly where and when I received each one. Some of them, however, held much deeper stories than just tokens of undying love.

For instance, one little message read:

'This is just a quick note to remind you that I love you very much. It's been a nerve-wracking time, please forgive me.'

His reference to 'a nerve-wracking time' relates to an incredibly difficult decision he had to make. As well as having been invited to audition for the RTÉ Symphony Orchestra, David had also been conducting pioneering work in the area of botany. Earlier that year, he had devised a computer programme to demonstrate the growth of Fagus sylvatica (the common beech tree). As a result of his remarkable formula, not to mention his phenomenal exam results, he had been awarded a French government scholarship to pursue his studies in Montpellier in the south of France as well as in the tropical rainforests of Indonesia. This coincided with an invitation to study for a PhD in the Fairchild Tropical Botanic Gardens in Florida.

While I was writing this piece, I had to text David for the correct spelling of some botanical terms. During our texts, I asked him why he didn't take up some of these amazing offers. When he texted me back, I couldn't help but laugh as his wry musician wit came to the fore as always:

'Half an hour before I was to get on the plane to France, I decided I was in love and wanted to be a musician … and it was all downhill from there! lol! D x'

The decision was one he had reached himself. I was delighted because I didn't want him to ever feel as though I had stopped him from chasing his dreams. Later that year, he wrote me the following note:

Dearest Adèle, after a long and difficult year, it's nice to say I wouldn't do anything differently. I hope that every year for the rest of our lives will be as happy as this one has been. Adèle, I love you always, you are the most gorgeous woman I have ever met.

I love you, I love you, I love you

David x

Almost good enough

In the autumn of 1980, David and I took a trip to a beach in West Cork. We were almost a year together at that stage and while I can't remember if I was deliberately hinting towards a proposal, I do recall talking about the general pressure people imposed on couples to tie the knot, not to mention the number of times we ourselves had been asked if we were getting married.

It was a fairly casual chat until David turned and asked, 'Well … will you marry me?'

'What?'

'Will you marry me?'

'Are you really asking?'

'Yeah!'

'Oh, God! Yeah! OK!'

At that point, the two of us just burst out laughing.

We decided we would officially get engaged on Christmas Eve. In the meantime, I had looked everywhere for a ring but nothing I saw was 'the one' that I wanted to wear proudly for the rest of my life. Despite not having the diamond, we still decided to press ahead with our original plan to reveal the engagement on Christmas Eve. That evening, before visiting David's parents, we stopped off at Stillorgan Shopping Centre where I had to pick up a number of items for my mother. As you can imagine, the last-minute Christmas shoppers were out in force and the only parking space we could find was directly outside a jewellery shop called Rocks. While I was waiting for David, I walked over to the window for a casual browse and as I was looking at their selection of rings, I immediately spotted the one that belonged on my hand! There, sitting in the window, was a gorgeous ring with a sapphire stone surrounded by diamonds. Once it went on my finger, I had to prize my eyes away from it.

We were absolutely buzzing that evening when we arrived at the house of Bernadette and Arthur Agnew. Unfortunately, I don't think they shared our joy. They were more than shocked by the announcement and I always got the distinct impression that they were not exactly keen on me being David's wife. My suspicion was certainly cemented when Bernadette remarked, 'Well I suppose you're *almost* good enough for my son'.

The memory of that moment stings every bit as much now twenty-nine years later, as it did back then. To make matters worse, she then proceeded to tell me how to iron David's shirts. At that point, I had never in my life even so much as held an iron, and I certainly harboured no desire to begin doing so either. I loved cleaning, but my Achilles heel has and always will be washing and ironing clothes.

'Now when you're ironing his shirts for the orchestra,' Bernadette began, 'be careful not to put too much starch on his wing collars because it will be very hard on his neck when he's playing the oboe.'

When she was finished with the instructions, I politely explained that I was marrying David because I loved him, not because I wanted to become his cleaning lady.

'If he wants his clothes washed and ironed Bernadette, there's nothing stopping him from doing it himself,' I pointed out, much to her horror.

'But David wouldn't know how to turn on a washing machine!' she replied.

'Well the bad news is, I don't know how to either! So I guess we're both rightly scuppered now!'

I always knew David was his mother's boy, but I don't think I realised the extent of it until that night when Bernadette informed me that she would also be giving me recipes suitable for David's coeliac condition.

Ladies, take my advice, don't marry a mammy's boy!

Chya-aracters from Chya-astleblayney

I love Mike Murphy, and I always flatter myself that Mike loves me. He is an intellectual with an incredible flair for the arts. Like Paddy Cole, there isn't anyone with a bad word to say about him, despite his popularity, Mike was never comfortable with being in the public eye. He's the craic personified when you get to know him, but at the same time, he is a very reserved gentleman and finds the publicity that accompanies being a television personality a relatively high price to pay. He likes his privacy and I think that's why he loves living in America so much.

He and I first ended up working together as a result of a radio show I had been involved in. My ability to read music made me a popular choice when it came to jobs for ads, jingles and

voiceovers and, looking back, it inadvertently led to me working in a whole new spectrum of entertainment, one I never even realised I was capable of doing professionally – impersonations.

Almost from the time I could talk, I was mimicking people. My mother would often recount how even as a child of just four years old, I would return home from a weekend with my aunty Maura and uncle Jack and begin impersonating them both to a tee. Even to this day, I automatically take on the accent of the person I'm talking about whenever I am relaying a story. Some people really enjoy it while others find it highly annoying, but, to be honest, most of the time I don't even realise I'm doing it because it has become such an ingrained habit.

I always insist that the man who brought out the humour in me was Paddy Cole. Honestly, he's one of the funniest people I have ever met. Paddy was the best raconteur and would regale us with stories on the tour bus about chya-aracters from Chya-astleblayney. I think I really picked up on his comedic timing and delivery and, in doing so, began to develop the courage to trade stories with him. Of course, there's absolutely no doubt that the Monaghan accent really does accentuate the humour of a story, and so my ability to copy accents really helped me to get one over on Paddy for a change.

It happened one night in the Stardust restaurant when I spotted Paddy chatting to a group of stunning six-foot showgirls. As there were telephones on all the tables, the dancers with the Big 8 dared me to have Paddy paged. When he answered, I immediately adopted the voice of his wife, Helen. I tore into him for his carry on, giving out about how I had never been so mortified in all my life and that I was heading back to Ireland. He fell for it – hook, line and sinker – and was completely taken aback. As he became more and more flustered, I could see him looking around the restaurant frantic to see where his wife was

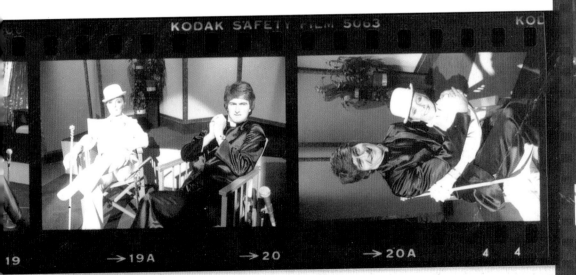

calling from. The whole ruse was going well until Angela actually screamed with laughter, leaving all five of us in a state of hysterics. I knew he wanted to throttle us but fortunately he saw the funny side, as did Helen herself, and that story is still doing the rounds of many a dinner table to this day.

Impersonating people *professionally* only came about when Dick Keating, the owner of a popular voiceover studio in Ballinteer, Dublin, recommended me to two brilliant copywriters called Frank Sheerin and Catherine Donnelly. When we met, Frank told me about a project he was working on – a new radio series that was to replace Rosaleen Linehan and Des Keogh's programme *Get an Earful of This*. He then asked if I would be interested in participating, to which I immediately said yes, without thinking to ask exactly what kind of role he had in mind for me. I think I presumed it was a singing part.

The following week, I joined the other actors in RTÉ's Studio 8 for a dummy run of the script, however when it came to my turn, Frank looked at me and said, 'OK, Adèle, so who do you feel you *do* best?'

'Eh … excuse me, Frank?'

'Who would be the easiest for you to do?'

'Frank, unless I'm reading into a very bad connotation here, I don't quite understand what are you asking me?'

'Who can you impersonate best?'

'Impersonate? On the radio? Oh God, no! I couldn't do that. No way! It's not what I do. I'm a singer!'

'Yeah I know, but how about singing in the voice of Maggie Thatcher, Dana, Shirley Bassey …?'

'Oh no way! Someone has their wires crossed here. I only do that kind of thing for the craic, not in a professional capacity!'

'Well sure why not do it for a bit of craic and get paid for it?'

I honestly thought the whole idea was preposterous!

I soon discovered that Frank's power of persuasion was as brilliant as his writing, and sure enough, two days later, I was meeting with him to run through some fantastic parodies he'd written. The radio show turned out to be a huge hit, even receiving a great review in *The Irish Times* with the reviewer remarking: 'Somebody pinch me, surely this is not the same Adèle King who was Twink in Maxi Dick and Twink doing this sensational comedy?'

Gradually, my phone began to ring with journalists enquiring if I was *her* – if the woman who was now impersonating Maggie Thatcher was the same girl who had stepped out of the pink Cadillac in a fur coat all those years earlier. Word soon filtered through the media and it quickly became a talking point. I always say Paddy Cole inspired the comedian in me, but Frank unleashed it.

❖

One day, Mike Murphy and Tom McGrath approached me in the RTÉ radio centre and asked if I would join them for coffee to discuss the possibility of being involved in their new television programme, *The Live Mike*. The idea was a variety show that would contain parodies and comedy sketches as well as interviews. In my head, I was still telling myself that impersonations were not my forte and so I genuinely couldn't envisage being able to carry it off for television. Impersonating people on a television show meant so much more than just mimicking their voices. The visuals would have to be equally as amazing. I would now have to *look* like them, mimic their gestures and adopt their every mannerism.

'No way, not possible,' I concluded.

as Dolly Parton

as Shirley Bassey

as Nana Mouskouri

Clearly, they had been taking lessons from Frank in the art of persuasion, because I soon found myself travelling to London for costume and wig fittings. Not one detail was left to chance when we set about emulating a look. We even had the eminent optician Dr Gerard Brady make me a variety of different colour contact lenses to match the eye colour of the star I was impersonating, whether it was Shirley Bassey, Dolly Parton or Cher. I was then given reels of footage to study so I could learn their signature moves and accents. Stella Bowan, the head of make-up, would then work on my face, making sure to use the exact colours and shades of whatever star I was to portray that night.

In the end, the union of comedy sketches and entertaining talk proved tailor-made for success, and every Friday night following the news, *The Live Mike* was broadcast to hundreds of thousands of viewers. There was no autocue; everything we said, we had learned to within an inch of our lives. The pressure was often crazy because sometimes a rewrite would be taking place while the news was on air, leaving us with just minutes to learn the new lines.

❖

Mike also came up with a great idea of having me talk to school kids around the country. It became a hugely popular slot, primarily because children by their very nature will opine on absolutely anything you put to them. We would speak to children from all backgrounds – country kids, inner-city kids, posh kids, poor kids – and ask them a litany of questions on the same topic. The different inflections they offered were always incredibly witty and insightful, and, on a few occasions, even quite sad. On one particular occasion, every service in Ireland seemed to be on strike, so I decided to ask a child from a school in Dublin's Brunswick Street how the strike had affected his family. He so innocently replied, 'Well, my mammy works as a cleaner in the hospital and if there's no money coming in, I'm gonna have to go out and rob stuff because there'll be no bread on the table.'

God love him, he didn't mean it in a delinquent way, just in an earnest robbing-to-survive way. Later that evening, however, we went to Our Lady's in Templeogue where we spoke to a child who clearly hailed from an affluent background. Asking her the same question, she confidently replied, 'Well, you know, the last time there was a strike, the bin men didn't come and it was the day of the party. Some dogs or some bold people upset the bins and they were absolutely all over the place and Mom was *furious* because she couldn't get anyone to clean them up and it absolutely ruined the party!'

That was the extent of the worry in her young life.

I always noticed a vast difference between the opinions of the country kids and those of the city kids. The country kids would say things like, 'But the politicians *do* work for the good of the country! Sure that's why we elect them and put them there in the first place!'

Of course, we would then edit the video so that the next scene was of an inner-city Dublin child saying,

'AH, DEM POLITICIANS ARE ALL DE FUCKIN' SAME AND MY MA SEZ DERE ALL FUCKIN' USELESS!'

It was wonderful entertainment, but it also managed to be a very poignant social statement. The kids we interviewed were liable to say anything that entered their heads, literally anything at all! There was just no way of knowing what kind of an answer a child was going to offer and people truly loved the humour of that.

A live wire on *The Live Mike* WITHDRAWN

One Christmas recently, Mike treated everyone who had been involved in *The Live Mike* production to a reunion party on a barge. I don't even know how we managed to get off the flippin' boat in one piece what with the 9,000 bottles of wine and Christmas spirit inside us. On the night, we toasted the members of the team that were no longer with us.

One of these was Dermot Morgan.

I first met Dermot through Mike. Dermot was a loose cannon with a screaming energy that couldn't be tamed – a real live wire so to speak. I was always more of a disciplinarian, thanks to my theatre training, and this often pissed off Dermot because he felt comedy should be free, loose and wild – live television, however, doesn't work like that. It's OK for solo stand-up pieces, but disastrous for team sketches. Ironically, when he did discipline himself, his delivery was impeccable.

We had our arguments, but the one thing we always agreed on was the importance of a quality script. Whenever we pointed out that a sketch just wasn't up to par, the attitude we were faced with was typical RTÉ. 'Sure once you have the costume on, it will be brilliant'. Dermot and I were always of the belief that if didn't 'read funny', then it wouldn't be any funnier when dressed up in a costume. If anything, it would look even more ridiculous. As time went on, Dermot became more vociferous about the script; he wouldn't hold back in a sketch meeting if he thought something was a load of shite. However, getting him to sit down and restructure it was nearly impossible. I would find myself trying to discipline him, trying to encourage him to create a starting point from which to progress. Dermot would begin a sketch so manically that the opening scene would be gargantuan, whereas I was always trying to show him that he would be better off with a calm introduction and then building up the momentum from there.

There was absolutely no doubting that the man was gifted, it was just a matter of convincing him to change his style of delivery. When I was top of the bill for the Boat Show in the RDS, I asked for Dermot to be my support act. When he was on stage however, his wild and rambling act cleared the room. While a lot of comedians are known for giving their acts a 'rambling style', believe me when I tell you that it's very deliberate. It's true what they say, 'there's no ad-lib like a well rehearsed one'. It was only when Dermot went over to London to perform in *Father Ted* that he picked up the good old "British television

discipline". When David and I went to see him perform in the Olympia a year later, honest to God, his act was unrecognisable from the one at the Boat Show.

This time, his show had shape and format and, as a result, it was hysterically funny. Ironically, when we were on *The Live Mike*, Dermot was desperate to get rid of his Fr Trendy character. I, on the other hand, felt that that would have been absolutely detrimental, not to mention daft, considering it was his strongest act. Who knew then that he would end up becoming a huge star in Britain as a result of playing a priest not too dissimilar to the Fr Trendy one he had become so fed up with?

I don't normally entertain regrets but I have to admit, one of my biggest grievances of all time was not being able to accept an offer to appear in *Father Ted*. Graham Linehan and Arthur Matthews had asked me if I would be interested in auditioning for the part of a popular character who appeared sporadically throughout the series. I was ecstatic to say the least when they subsequently phoned to offer me the role. Unfortunately, however, I was contracted to the panto in the Olympia. In fairness to Gerry Sinnott, the man did absolutely everything within his power to try to facilitate my request, but in the end nothing could be done to change the date and I had to forgo a role in *Father Ted*. Anytime I see it on television now, I always think about how incredible it would have been to have worked with Dermot in that capacity and be part of that legendary show.

The last chat I enjoyed with Dermot was outside Patrick Guilbaud's restaurant about a week before he died. He was telling me all about how he was due to fly back to London to film the final few scenes of *Father Ted* and how he was so looking forward to taking a break following the wrap party. Someone took a picture of us that night and when I look at it now, I still can't quite believe that only a week later, he was gone. When I heard of Dermot's death, it was like one of those surreal flashes you never forget. I remember arriving home and turning on the ITV news while I went about the housework. As I returned from the kitchen with fresh water for the birds, I suddenly heard the newsreader say, 'Tributes are pouring in today from entertainers and fans following the sudden and very sad death of Irish actor Dermot Morgan'.

Immediately, I phoned my friends Ros and John Hubbard, the casting agents for *Father Ted*.

I spoke to their daughter Amy who confirmed it was true. I immediately phoned my then manager Margo Tracey, who had been a great friend of Dermot's. Neither of us could quite believe it. Everything he had dreamed about was only just beginning to come true when he was cruelly taken from us.

Only recently I had a wonderful night out in the beautiful Residence Club with the aforementioned Margo, Dermot's partner Fiona and his divine sister, Denny Morgan and great friend, Martha Ward, where we reminisced endlessly about Dermot.

I have such great memories of Dermot both on and off the stage. We did a number of sketches in which he played Garret FitzGerald and I was Maggie Thatcher. Dermot would mimic him brilliantly. If you closed your eyes, you would genuinely think it was Garret talking. Likewise with Charlie Haughey: Dermot had his every mannerism, right down to those facial expressions!

To dear Adèle

Just to say

I love you

David

XXX

Thur. 12ᵗʰ Jan '84

I wasn't a bridezilla, in fact, that word hadn't even been invented at the time! Actually, I was surprisingly calm. At the time, I was performing at the Gaiety Theatre as the narrator in the production of *Joseph and the Technicolor Dreamcoat*. Also starring was Johnny Logan as Joseph, and Ronnie Drew as Jacob.

On the closing night of the show (which was the Saturday night before my wedding the following Thursday), I arrived out on stage to the overture music to begin singing my piece. Suddenly, Earl Gill and his orchestra went from performing the overture, to playing the tune of the bridal march. It was done so seamlessly that it took me by complete surprise. I later found out that the entire crew had been in on it. Everyone in the country knew I was getting married so, of course, the whole audience roared and applauded when the tune began. It was about five minutes before I could begin my narration and about twenty years before I could stop smiling at the thought of it!

❖

During the run-up to the wedding, I received a letter from an eleven-year-old girl called Tracy Sheehan – the sweetest kind of letter that only a child could write: 'Dear Twink, I'm your biggest fan and I have been to all your shows since I was two years old. Would there be any way please that I could be your bridesmaid?'

I just felt it would make a little girl's dream come true, so Mom and I contacted Tracy's mother and asked to bring her to the house to meet us. When she arrived out, she was the sweetest little girl imaginable.

I sat her down and said, 'You see Tracy, I have already picked my flower girls and bridesmaids'.

As I was talking, I could see her lower lip begin to quiver as her poor little face fell.

'In the end, we just decided there was no way …'

By now her eyes were about to fill with tears.

'… that we could do the wedding … without having you as my bridesmaid!'

Immediately, the tears were replaced with ecstatic smiles as we told her about the dress fittings she would have to attend. We stayed in touch for years and I do hope that if she is reading this she will get in touch with me again.

As much as I try to steer it in a different direction, my life always tends to gravitate towards drama.

The week of my wedding (and the weeks afterwards) were no exception.

Not long before my big day, I had been hired to do promotional work for the Pimm's drink at the Horse Show in the RDS. As I was going about my business, PR man Michael Hutchinson, whom I considered to be a friend, shouted across the Pimm's enclosure, 'Miss King, I hope I'm getting the PR job on your wedding!'

Annoyed by his remark, I abruptly reminded him it was *my* wedding, not *his* PR event. Margo Tracey, my manager at the time, was equally as disgusted by his behaviour as were a number of other people who had witnessed the incident. It just seemed like a demeaning, blasé way to talk about what would be one of the most important days of my life. Unfortunately, his remark was just the tip of the sting.

Being the narrator on *Joseph and the Technicolor Dreamcoat*, I was never off stage and as you can imagine, it became vocally very taxing. I was trying to do everything, from the shows at night to matinées during the day, as well as oversee all the wedding preparations. Towards the final week, however, my throat was exhausted and my body was following suit. My manager Margo relieved some of my workload by helping me with a variety of wedding-related chores as did my good friend Gerry Lundberg, the PR man for *Joseph* in the Gaiety. Neither of them were doing it in a professional capacity, I hasten to add, they were just helping out as friends.

The morning of the wedding was almost as incredible as the event itself thanks to the great buzz of excitement around the house.

I wouldn't do anything without my dogs, not even my wedding day! All the animals around the house were dressed in white satin bows, but we couldn't bring them all to the reception so

my parents brought my favourite dog, Jayne. My wedding morning started with receiving a phone call from the *Gay Byrne Radio Show* asking me if I would go on air and have a chat with Gay. I love that man so much that I would probably have agreed to take a call from him during the wedding mass if he had asked! I'll never forget as the opening theme tune of the show trailed off, his first words to me were, 'It's not too late now, my dear, it's not too late to turn back. You can still change your mind! The nation is waiting with bated breath to know will she go through with it! Will David actually snare the biggest catch?'

I remember that interview with Gay being so much fun; it was a really wonderful way to start my wedding day.

I used two ancient layers of lace handmade by my Aunt Esther c. 1940 on the neckline.

With my beautiful bridesmaid, Tracy Sheehan.

Chloë Buswell, after whom I would later name my first born, was my little flower girl. She was joined by two more beautiful little flower girls Amy and Vicky, daughters of my good friend, the singer Rita Madigan. All three wore white dresses with pink cummerbunds while the page boys wore black velvet bloomers and white shirts. My bridesmaids consisted of my soon-to-be sister-in-law Brenda Agnew, my cousin Shirley Andreuchetti, and of course little Tracy Sheehan.

My wedding dress had been designed by Taffy Miller, a brilliant costumier for the band Sheeba and practically everyone else in the business at the time. It was made from layers of satin and chiffon material and consisted of hand-beaded pearls cascading from the sweetheart neckline to the waist. The full sleeves and lower half of the dress were lined with silk and ornamental lace trimming that contained the most beautiful floral accents. In my hair, I wore a crystal crown that had belonged to my grandmother. This look

was then completed with a veil and bouquet both long enough to challenge that of Princess Di's!

We had arranged for a horse and carriage to take my dad and me to the church, but when we got as far as the Garda barracks in Rathfarnham, there were thousands of people on the road causing a major jam. I was beginning to panic.

'What's going on? On my wedding day of all days!'

Without missing a beat, the horseman turned and replied, 'I think what's going on *is* your wedding day!'

It took Rathfarnham Gardaí around twenty minutes to escort the horse and carriage through the crowd. Gay Byrne had memorably dubbed our day 'the Irish royal wedding' and if the crowds that lined the roads that morning were anything to go by, it was certainly the closest thing to one. There were people everywhere, on the road, on the railings, on the walls, hanging out of windows, all waving and shouting the most beautiful things. It was the most uplifting experience – a truly superb sight as I made my way to the church.

The ceremony itself was so beautiful. Tragically, we have no video recording of it. A bloke called Pearse Butler was booked to video the day. We later found out that he got pushed in the crowd and was so precious about his bloody camera that he decided there and then to go home without letting any of us know. The only footage we had of the church was what appeared on the nine o'clock news that night, which they scrapped immediately after broadcast. Fortunately, I managed to arrange another cameraman to record the reception. Apart from that hiccup, everything about the day was perfect, even the weather. When we left the church, the sun was absolutely beaming, allowing us to enjoy the drive to the reception in the Summerhill Lodge in Enniskerry in a vintage open-top car.

My mother looked so beautiful that day. She always loved simplicity so her mother-of-the-bride attire consisted of white ruffled *crêpe de Chine* blouse paired with a black velvet skirt and matching hat. Dad, likewise, looked so handsome in his suit and relished his role as father-of-the-bride.

1. John McColgan and Moya Doherty.
2. The newlyweds.
3. Dermot Morgan with his wife Suzanne, left, and Taffy Miller, costumier and maker of my wedding dress.
4. A kiss from Ronnie Drew!
5. Mike (signing autographs!) and Eileen Murphy.
6. The cake!
7. My darling Brendan Grace.
8. David and Shay Healy.

While we were posing for the obligatory wedding photographs, our guests remained out on the lawn enjoying their champagne, not one of them in a rush to go inside. At one point, I spotted the PR man Michael Hutchinson on the phone in the lobby. It was very obvious he was relaying details of the wedding to a journalist as he was looking out the door and naming the various people he could see. He got the shock of his life when I confronted him. Immediately, he began fumbling with the phone and stumbling over his words, all the classic signs of guilt. I thought that would be the end of his backstabbing, but how wrong I turned out to be. I had made it very clear to the press that they could take all the photos they wanted at the church but that the reception was private. We wanted our guests to be able to enjoy a few drinks without worrying about being photographed or monitored by the media.

The meal was truly amazing and the man responsible for creating the phenomenal spread was Jimmy Harkin, a very good friend of mine who worked as a prop buyer and set dresser for the film industry. What I hadn't known was that he also owned the beautiful bistro in Ranelagh whose Michelin star-worthy dishes I had forever been praising. Six months before my wedding, I had been dining there with my mother when Jimmy suddenly walked out in his chef's hat. There was seriously no end to this man's talents. When I saw his partner Ian Fox in the radio centre the following day, I asked him if Jimmy catered for big events. 'You mean big like the size of your wedding?' he laughed. 'Absolutely! He'd pull all the stops out for you dear!'

And with that I had found my wedding caterer.

The display of food Jimmy created for my wedding was like nothing I had or have to this day ever seen before. It was incredible, like a royal banquet. One of the platters consisted of salmon which he had placed on mirrors and surrounded with water cress and lemons. It was presented in a way that it looked like the water cress was growing around the salmon. He also provided pink champagne which, in 1983, was considered very exotic. To match the colour scheme, he hired pale pink napkins and tablecloths from the Shelbourne Hotel. The heavy-solid silver cutlery also came from the Shelbourne. Unfortunately, we ended up having to pay them in the region of £600 to replace the cutlery and napkins that had been taken by guests. I'm willing to forgive, however, on the basis that people with drink think nothing of wrapping a piece of cake along with a fork in a napkin and shoving it in their bag.

My wedding day was by far the best day of my life, topped only by the births of my children. The following day, my going-away outfit consisted of deep purple trousers with a cream cape and a purple hat all made by the late great Peter Fitzsimons. David and I had planned to go to Rome for our honeymoon but we began our trip by spending the night in London with one of my best friends, John Sullivan.

There are two people whose company I absolutely hate being in only because I always end up aging about twenty years from all the laughter they incite. One is Bill Hughes, the other is John Sullivan. That particular Saturday, however, I think I was at risk of ageing about forty years with all the laughter lines caused by John and his then partner Tony. Unfortunately, our fun was short-lived.

When the four of us arrived back at John's house after dinner, I got a phone call from our solicitor

Elio Malocco. When your solicitor phones you late at night and begins his call with the sentence, 'I presume you haven't seen the papers', it's fair to say a slight sense of panic hits.

All the newspapers had been fantastic at the time of our wedding. They used beautiful pictures and fully respected our wishes to keep the reception private – all except the *Sunday Independent*.

They created the most disgusting story in which they said the wedding had been paid for by a company sponsor. Believe me, no one other than David and me paid for that wedding. In fact, we were probably still paying it off ten years later. The article also went on to state that Margo Tracey and Gerry Lundberg had been phoning different businesses looking for freebies and that my dog, Jayne, had been fed steak at the top table. It was a scurrilous piece of press and completely fabricated.

A derogatory spin was put on everything. For instance, there was reference made to us keeping the guests waiting while photographs were being taken. It was a wedding for crying out loud! At absolutely every wedding that takes place, the norm is for guests to go to the hotel and enjoy a few drinks while they wait for the bride and groom to have their photographs taken. Our wedding was no different. To be quite honest, I don't think any of our guests wanted to go back inside for the reception as they were having a great time on the lawn enjoying the sunshine and the endless supply of champagne.

As Elio read the article to me, the penny dropped. I immediately knew who had been the Judas in the crowd. Michael bloody Hutchinson on the phone in the lobby. The author of the article was Tony Hennigan, but it couldn't have been more obvious who supplied him with the details. I can only assume Michael's motive was that he had obviously thought I had given the PR job to Gerry Lundberg when in fact, there was no PR job to begin with. Gerry had helped out as a friend and at no point did he or Margo ask shops for freebies, which the article had implied. As for Tony Hennigan, his father, the late Tom Hennigan, had lived ten doors up from us on Anne Devlin Road and in his time as a journalist, had written some of the most complimentary articles about me. On the day the *Sunday Independent* article was published, Tom's wife visited my mother in tears over what her son Tony had written. The poor woman was so ashamed of the article that she completely broke down. My mother, who herself was in bits, ended up consoling the mother of the journalist who had written it!

Elio advised me to act on it immediately and told me he was going to draw up the relevant paperwork so that we could sue the *Sunday Independent* over the defamatory rubbish they had written. We were meant to be flying out to Rome the following morning to begin our honeymoon, instead we were flying back to Dublin to begin legal proceedings. We were absolutely broken-hearted. After all, it was such a bitter outcome from what had been such a beautiful day.

Eventually, the court case rolled around and I don't think I will ever forget standing in the lobby of the Four Courts with Elio and our barrister Harry Whelehan while the jury selection was taking place. As we were talking, I suddenly spotted the then *Sunday Independent* editor-in-chief standing alongside Tony Hennigan and Michael Hutchinson. 'There's that son of a bitch,' I said to Elio. Against his stern advice, I walked over and said, 'I've done every walkathon, marathon, charity do and ribbon cutting event for the Independent Newspapers for the best part of my life, I would have expected a bit more respect for my wedding day. I intend to wipe that courtroom floor with your asses. Good afternoon gentlemen – see you in court!' I knew by the expressions on their faces that they could feel the case crumbling beneath them before they had even set foot inside the courtroom.

At one stage, the judge took a break for an hour and it was during that time that a settlement offer was made to our legal team. We accepted it and when we returned to the courtroom, the judge was told that an agreement had been reached. The judge was surprisingly very sweet and in his closing speech, he turned to us and said, 'Miss King, Mr Agnew, or should that be Mr and Mrs Agnew! May I just say that I think what happened to you was an absolute disgrace!'

He then turned to the *Sunday Independent* party and remarked rather furiously, 'You should be ashamed of yourselves for doing this to two young decent hard-working newlyweds. Miss King, Mr Agnew, if this paper ever offends you again, feel free to bring it back into my court and I will deal with it personally. Case closed!'

Most of the money we received in the settlement went towards various women's shelters and animal welfare organisations. A large apology was also printed in the newspaper. On the night of the court case, I was scheduled to appear in Dobbins as part of a show devised by my good friend Alma Carroll in which I played the American legend, Connie Francis. The place was stuffed with people. Even Elio came along on the night. Everyone knew I had been in court all day and a rapturous applause erupted. First on his feet was Gay Byrne who shouted up at me, 'Fair play to you! You beat the *Indo*!'

Gay hated to see the media do something like that to one of us.

The place was electric. The crowd had an infectious kind of energy that made the hairs on your skin stand on end. It really was the sort of night that every performer dreams about.

Within eighteen months of the court case, Michael Hutchinson had passed away from cancer. A few months after that, in November 1984, Tony Hennigan died in the Eastbourne plane crash during the Dobbins wine run. It was a succession of tragic events but even the biggest sceptic has to admit it's terribly odd that within two years of the court case, the person who gave the story and the one who wrote it, were both dead.

About three days before the plane crash that killed Tony, I had been hired by my wonderful friend Pat Gibbons to open an air-display show. He owned the Sands Hotel in Portmarnock at the time and, following the launch, asked me to come out to the hotel for dinner so he could get the low-down on the court case. We talked and talked, and when we were finished, we brought a bottle of wine down to the beach and watched the sun come up. We had quite literally talked until the sun rose. It was such a lovely night of banter and laughter. Once the bottle of wine had been polished off, we managed to talk ourselves sober and went inside to enjoy some breakfast. It was then that Pat mentioned that he was going to be taking part in the Dobbins wine run, a well-known race to bring back the first Beaujolais Nouveau wine from France to *The Late Late Show*. I immediately wished him luck with it.

I had done the wine run the previous year and it was something I swore I would never do again. It was such a light plane that when the lads all started jumping around drunkenly, it began to sway very violently. It became a truly terrifying experience, one not helped by the fact that I was already a nervous flyer to begin with. In the early hours of 13 November, I was woken by a phone call from my friend and then-hairstylist Colin Connaughton.

'Adèle I have some terrible news for you,' he began. 'The wine run plane has crashed in Eastbourne, off the coast of England.'

As I shook off my sleepy stupor and tried to absorb the shocking news I had just been confronted with, my heart sank as I suddenly realised that Pat had been on board the plane.

I will never forget going out to Dublin Airport as the bodies were being brought home and seeing poor Paddy Cole who was beside himself with grief. The *Sunday World* editor, Kevin Marron, who also perished in the crash, had been one of his best friends. The other men aboard the plane that night included Tony Hennigan, Niall Hanley, editor of *The Evening Herald* and John Feeney, a *Herald* columnist.

A seat on the couch, a hand on the leg

By the time English television beckoned in the early 1980s, I felt I had pretty much exhausted every avenue of Irish television. It seemed like the perfect time to leave secure pastures for tougher challenges as a variety of opportunities were already presenting themselves farther afield. Due to the number of jobs being offered to me in London, I was anxious to secure a place on the books of a very powerful manager, who at the time, was also managing the major West End star Stephanie Lawrence. Stephanie possessed an amazing talent but, Christ Almighty, she was one emotionally unsteady girl. Needless to say, it didn't sit well with her that people were starting to talk about the new name in town. Admittedly, it worked in my favour that Irish entertainers, such as Eamonn Andrews, Terry Wogan and Gloria Hunniford, were all achieving great heights of popularity in England at that point. They were adored by television audiences and as a result, people were eager to see more of the Irish on their screens. I knew I had all the skills necessary to make it into their league, all that was left was finding the right representation. Unfortunately, the agent I wanted had found herself in a predicament with Stephanie.

'There's no easy way of saying this,' she began. 'I really think you are going to be huge here,

definitely the next big Irish name in Britain. You have everything they like – you can sing, dance, act, "comeed", it's all ahead of you. There's just one problem – Stephanie barged into my office the other day and told me if "the Irish bitch is in, then I'm out". I'm afraid you have become just a bit too talked about for Stephanie's liking. Unfortunately, she is my biggest client; I made her a star. I have to stick by her because I owe it to her. I am actually disgusted with how this has turned out because I really wanted to sign you.'

I was crushed but I could completely understand how my presence in the agency would cause tension with Stephanie. Moreover, I would never have expected the agent to drop someone she took on as a protégée and subsequently transformed into a big star. Looking back, I probably should have known from the beginning that Stephanie would have felt threatened by me. After all, we were both blonde and shared the same set of skills required to work in British television and theatre. As such, she probably sensed we would be sent forward for the same jobs and naturally this didn't sit well with her.

As she apologised profusely for the turn of events, the poor agent admitted that she thought I would have reacted in the style of a thundering bitch. Like anyone else, I have my 'thundering bitch' moments, but fortunately that's not my style when it comes to the professional world. When I arrived back at my friend the Hubbards' house following the meeting, John took one look at me and remarked, 'Well that's not the happiest face I've ever seen!'

When I told him the story, his immediate reaction was one of, 'Well, fuck her! Fuck the pair of them! We'll get you a bigger and better agent than her!'

John and Ros kept their word and the following day, I was sent out to meet six different agents.

❖

Looking back on all those meetings and auditions, I don't know how the poor kids do it today. I could never go through that process again. It's so disheartening, not to mention degrading. On one particular occasion, for instance, I arrived at the offices of a potential agent and gave my name to the male receptionist who then phoned upstairs to let the agent know I had arrived. Clearly, the agent asked him what I looked like, because he then leaned out slightly over the desk, very obviously looked me up and down before replying, 'Not bad, not bad, quite pretty, actually!'

I felt like I was in a bloody cattle market. The agent himself was a big name in the business but a absolute toe-rag. God, was he a slime ball! I wasn't interested in working with him, and that incident finished it.

Another big agent I was scheduled to meet with was Natt Berlin from London Management. He was an absolute gentleman and we hit it off immediately. No sooner had I arrived in the front door of Ros Hubbard's house when she told me that London Management had phoned

Almost exhausted ... and that was just the warm-up!

confirming that they would be delighted to represent me. 'Ecstatic' doesn't even come close to my reaction that evening. Granted, I was less than a year married but, in my line of work, I had to go where the jobs were. I genuinely wasn't worried about leaving my new husband because I planned to make regular trips home.

All in all, life was going terrifically well. Even though I was still a relatively new face in Britain, I was beginning to make a name for myself and people of influence were starting to notice. Des O'Connor had seen me on *3, 2, 1* and wanted me for his show, as did many others. I was very fortunate that I wasn't entering the London scene on my own. My good friends Ros and John Hubbard had offered me a room in their beautiful home in Mill Hill, north London, while I was finding my feet and their support helped enormously.

❖

The British theatre scene gives new interpretation to the word 'vicious'.

It's a place where you have to really crave the stage to be able to stick it out. Anyone who goes over and has the tenacity to see through the whole gruelling experience automatically has my respect. One of these people is my dear friend John Sullivan. In the late sixties, John announced he was going over to London to try his luck in the West End, a place where even the best dancers in the world are made queue for jobs. Before we knew it though, John was winning one job after another. One of my proudest moments was when he was chosen to be the dance captain for the production of *Singing in the Rain* starring Tommy Steele in the London Palladium. On the opening night, I sat proudly in the front row of the dress circle, looking on in awe as my lifelong friend danced his heart and soul out on this magnificent stage.

Siobhan McCarthy is another good friend of mine who made it big in the golden circle of the West End. A former Young Dublin Singer, whom I nicknamed 'Mchyarthy', she was the first to create and play Donna Sheridan, the mama in *Mamma Mia!*. I think one of the biggest thrills of my life was seeing her on huge posters around London as Eva Perón in *Evita*, Fontaine in *Les Mis*, Mrs Turnblad in *Hairspray*, the list goes on! Remarkably, despite all of Siobhan's incredible successes in London, she still has to audition for *every* part. That's the bit about the London scene that wrecks my head. For two people such as John and 'Mchyarthy' to leave Ireland and crack the toughest business in the world, well I can't but take my hat off to them.

Even though Vegas would knock the naivety out of a newborn, I think there was still probably an element of 'rose-tinted glasses' in my approach to the London scene. On one occasion in 1984, an agent of mine brought me to an up-market restaurant in Chelsea to meet the producer of a very well-known television show. When we arrived, he showered me with compliments and, as we were chatting, my agent suddenly pinched

me underneath the table and said, 'Right, well, I'll leave you both to it'. She then bid us goodnight, picked up her coat and left.

I was suspicious, but I honestly didn't cop exactly what was going on, so I continued chatting away until suddenly I began to feel 'the love' ... in the form of his hand moving up my thigh. In the space of a minute, his side of the conversation managed to centre around nightcaps at his place. In all my years in the business, this had genuinely never happened to me before, not once.

I had heard talk of the 'casting couch' in Britain where you don't get *on the air* until your legs are *in the air*, but never in a million years did I want to find myself in that position, if you excuse the pun! Dashing to the ladies room, I stood in the toilet cubicle for what seemed like ages just shaking with fright. Once I returned to my seat, the hand immediately went to resume its place on my leg. With all the self-assurance I could muster, I faced him and explained that we clearly didn't share the same intentions. In a split second, his attitude changed.

'Aw you know what goes on here!' he argued. 'This is showbiz, sweetheart! Remember the golden rules … he who has the gold makes the rules!'

He didn't show any signs of stopping, so I simply stood up and walked out. When I got outside however, it was pitch dark and the place was absolutely deserted. I didn't even know which direction to walk in; I just wanted to get away from that restaurant. To make matters worse, I then became petrified that he would find me walking along the roadside on my own. At least in the restaurant there had been safety in the fact that I was surrounded by people. I don't think I was ever so relieved when I saw a London cab light in the distance. Even though it was around two o'clock in the morning when I arrived at the Hubbards' house, all I wanted to do was phone

David and hear his voice. I felt he would be the only person in the world who could give me the comfort and consolation I so desperately needed at that moment.

At the time, David and I were living with my parents until we sorted out our own house, so I dialled the number hoping my parents wouldn't panic at such a late-night phone call. Don't forget, these were the days when a mobile phone was merely a glint in a scientist's eye.

My mother answered and immediately she sensed I was upset. After a comforting chat with her, I asked for David. That's when she half-reluctantly told me that David wasn't in the house, and hadn't been so for the past number of nights. Straight away, I phoned a mutual friend of ours. As soon as I asked him where David was, I knew by the way he answered that he was covering for him. I would later discover that David had often stayed at his place in the company of his latest bit-on-the-side.

In later years, I found some old notes of David's from when he used to stay over at his friends house. One of them read: *'For God's sake wake me in the morning, I don't want to be caught here with Yvonne.'* While another note revealed: *'Am here with Yvonne, need to be out at 9.15. Please please wake us.'*

That phone call certainly compounded what was already a memorably awful night. When I met with my agent who had abandoned me in the restaurant that night, I recalled in disgust what had happened only to be met with a response all too similar to that of the producer geezer, 'Aw come on, Adèle, you know how the business works! If you don't put out, you don't get on!'

I never in my life had to 'put out' to get a part and, to be brutally honest, I would have swept the streets of Chelsea before even considering doing so.

Around that time, David bumped into Pat Kenny who asked how I was getting on in England. Unfortunately, David told him about my upsetting episode and Pat, being a journalist, decided it would make an interesting subject for his radio show. The theme was a topical one and unfortunately my story gave it a new angle. Pat was going to run with the piece on his show regardless of whether or not he had my participation, so, on the advice of my agent, I took the call. After outlining the incident and explaining what I had gone through, Pat suddenly announced that another actress was joining us on the line. Sure enough, some two-bit actress came on air and basically lambasted me from the word go, proclaiming that my story was rubbish and that I knew exactly what I was getting myself into. In fact, I think her words were, 'You know what, Pat, if you go looking for it, it'll always be there. There's a casting couch but you have to be putting it out there before they take the bait.'

I'm listening to this mouthy little git and thinking: (a) Who is she? and (b) How dare she! I had been in the business all my life and any job I landed had been secured on the strength of my talent and merit. When I told her this, she hit back with the low response, 'Like sleeping with John McColgan, the head of light entertainment in RTÉ?'

I shouldn't have to justify it to someone like her, but I pointed out that I was already a household name long before I ever began a relationship with John. I had worked in television all my life, it was hardly unusual that I would develop a relationship with someone else in the same business! The inference of her remark was both distressing and defamatory not to mention suggestively nasty, but then you live and learn. Mind you, I should add that I have never heard of her in anything or on anything since ... not even a casting couch!

❖

Even though my career in England was only in its infancy, the number of job offers being directed my way indicated that great success still beckoned. Unfortunately, however, not everyone was happy for me.

Dear Adele,
I miss you so much when you're gone. Come back soon
I love you
David
XXX
4/V/81

Out of nowhere, I began receiving phone calls late into the night. Naturally, Ros was growing increasingly annoyed by these calls as her two young children, Amy and Daniel, were constantly being woken up by the sound of the phone ringing at three in the morning. The calls, which came from women in the orchestra, usually involved them leering down the phone and saying things like, 'Do you know who David's with now? You stupid cow! You haven't a clue, have you?'

They would usually sound quite drunk and if the incessant laughter in the background was anything to go by, the calls clearly tickled their churlish sense of humour. I was already aware of a number of women in the orchestra who were annoyed that I had married David. A lot of them had fancied him at the time and, as a result, they didn't take too kindly to me. They were also infuriated by the fact that someone outside the orchestra had married him. (Musicians tend to be a little clique of their own.) The nature of the calls turned particularly malicious, but sadly, there proved to be some truth in the content.

I would later discover that even during our first year of marriage, David had been playing away. I began hearing reports back from all quarters, truthful rumours if you will, and in the end, I had to decide between carving out a successful career in England or returning home to save my marriage. When I explained my situation to Ros, she responded by sending me a bill for a few thousand pounds for all the time she had 'wasted' on me. I felt it was a particularly nasty backlash considering my circumstances, although I was later told by a mutual friend that she really regretted doing that.

From a career point of view, I should have remained in London. In fact, I would even go so far as to say that returning home to save my marriage was the most stupid thing I have ever done in my life. My only consolation was that I ended up having two incredible children, Chloë and Naomi.

Here's a LOL joke!

(For those of you older than sixteen, LOL is text talk for 'laugh out loud'.)

Two priests decided to go to Hawaii on holiday.

They were determined to make this a real holiday by not wearing anything that would identify them as clergy, so, as soon as the plane landed, they headed for a shop and bought the most outrageous shorts, shirts, sandals, sunglasses, etc. The next morning they went to the beach dressed in their tourist garb. As they were sitting on beach chairs and enjoying their drinks, they suddenly noticed a drop-dead gorgeous blonde walking towards them, topless. As the blonde walked past, she smiled and said, 'Good morning, Fathers!'

They were both stunned.

'How in the world did she know we were priests?' one remarked to the other. The next day, they returned to the store and bought even more outrageous outfits. Once again, in their new attire, they settled down in their chairs to enjoy the sun. After a while, the same gorgeous topless blonde came walking toward them. Just like the day before, she waved and said, 'Good morning, Fathers', as she walked past.

One of the priests couldn't stand it any longer so he stood up and said, 'Just a minute, young lady! How on earth did you know we're priests, dressed as we are?'

Looking a little taken aback, she replied, 'Ah, for God's sake, Father! It's me! Sister Kathleen!'

My Dear Vinny

It was early 1987 when I first noticed Vincent Hanley had become quite thin. He just seemed so small and cold inside his big parka jacket, but then New York is known for its biting winter breeze, so I gave it no more than a passing thought. A few weeks later however, David called me into the room where he was watching Vincent on *MT USA*.

'What's the first thing that comes into your mind when you look at him?' he asked.

I took one look at the screen and I think my heart skipped a beat with the shock. 'Rock Hudson! Oh my God, he's starting to look like *that* picture of Rock Hudson.'

Two years earlier, while David and I were on holiday in Marbella, we had bought a newspaper that carried the headline: 'Rock Hudson Dies'. The Rock Hudson everyone knew was outstandingly handsome, but that wasn't the picture that accompanied the headline. In this particular photograph, his cheeks were concave, his eye sockets sunken, and his emaciated frame left him looking like a completely different person. As I looked at Vincent on the television screen that evening, I could see there was now a frighteningly distinctive similarity between him and that final picture of Rock Hudson.

I looked at David, 'He couldn't have the dreaded … could he?'

'Looks like it to me,' came the reply that confirmed my fear.

When Vincent arrived home from New York, he phoned me from St James's Hospital. I visited him the first chance I got and, even today, I vividly remember the shock I tried to disguise when I saw him. He was a shadow of the vibrant man I knew and loved. To be honest, he looked wretched.

When he left hospital a few days later, he went to stay with his mother in the countryside. The word 'AIDS' was never mentioned once. It was seen as a very closeted, tawdry word and so instead, the condition was always quietly referred to as a 'blood disorder' or 'secondary problems associated with pneumonia'.

Within a matter of weeks, Vincent was back in hospital again. He was suffering from chronic eczema at the time and when I visited him, he wouldn't even let me hug him. 'Don't want you catching this,' he smiled.

We both knew this was the last time we were going to see each other and I can still remember sitting in that hospital room trying to fight back the tears while we chatted. His attitude was fatalistic.

He was talking about how he'd had so much to live for, how life was so short and precious and how it should be lived to the full.

Vinny and I as DJs in an RTÉ's Christmas Spectacular called **Castle Backtax**.

'We've had some great laughs together. Do you remember us doing the DJ skit on *Castle Backtax*?' he reminisced.

'How about that lunch in London with yourself and Charles? You two had me crying with laughter!' I replied.

'I love to hear you tell that story. I hope you think of all our great memories and that they make you smile when I'm … whenever you think of me.'

We looked at each other and we both wanted to cry, but, for each other's sake, we held back from doing so. We were such good friends and had created so many great memories over the years that it was hard to believe there would be no more on the horizon for us to share.

A few days later, 18 April 1987 to be exact, I received a phone call from Bill Hughes.

'Adèle … Fab Vinny's gone.'

Cherchez la femme (look for the other woman)

We always joked that if you were to post David a card, you would need two envelopes just to fit the number of letters he has after his name, H-dip, Bachelor of Music, Bachelor of Science, Doctor of Science, Doctor of Botany … you get the drift. To add to his array of talents, David was also a gifted photographer and ornithologist in his spare time.

Theoretically, the man was a walking prodigy.

Unfortunately, everything David did had a sneaky nature to it. He was the kind of person who would tell a lie even when the truth would do.

For instance, any time he wanted a cigarette, he would sneak out around the back of the house like a teenager. I would later find little stashes of cigarette butts in the strangest of places. I had absolutely no objection to him smoking and even after I pointed this out to him on several occasions, he would deny ever having smoked in the first place. For some reason, David always seemed to get a kick of out doing things he knew he shouldn't.

There were so many nights where I would walk the house wondering and worrying where he was. Phoning him wasn't an option because his mobile was always conveniently 'out of battery' or 'on silent'. When he did arrive home, he always looked and smelled as though he had just stepped out of a shower, which in hindsight of course he had … some *other* woman's shower! Whenever I asked him where he had been all night, his response was always to the tune of, 'Ah, just out with the lads'.

I don't know how he expected me to believe that line. What man goes out for pints with the lads and arrives home at three in the morning freshly coiffured and perfumed?

Some pub that!

❖

On any occasion – such as birthdays, St Patrick's Day or Easter – David would start a blazing row that would always result in him storming out of the house and driving away. It would also happen most Sunday mornings, always unprovoked and completely out of the blue. There was, in fact, a pattern developing which I didn't realise until much later. Whenever he stormed out, I always felt like I had to get away from the place, and so would bring my parents, my two girls and their nanny Anna, out to the Glen of the Downs Hotel for Sunday lunch. I would wait and wait for him to ring, and usually by the afternoon, the call would come and his grovelling would begin. Each time, I fell for it.

I later discovered that all the rows had been staged. They were his escape route when his 'bit on the side' wanted him at her house for whatever occasion was taking place in her life at the time. Whenever I asked him where he had been all day, I would be given nothing more than a gruff reply about how he had gone to his mother's house.

It also wasn't unusual for him to storm out right before his daughters' birthdays, leaving me to organise the entire party myself. I would stay up for hours arranging party bags and birthday treats, always determined that I would give my girls birthdays that were as memorable as those my dear father had given me.

I never considered this to be 'spoiling' them. In 'Toyland', Perry Como sings the saddest line: 'Childhood toyland, each little girl and boyland, once you pass through its portals, you can never return again.'

When you think about it, there are so many children out there who will grow up despising the childhood they were given. Some kids are constantly exposed to the sight of a parent with a syringe stuck in their arm; some see their parents spending more time in the pub than with them; others are sleeping on the streets and turning to petty crime.

My main wish was to give the girls a childhood filled with the happiest memories, always balanced, and never overindulgent. They were never spoiled brats, but rather well-mannered kids who were always appreciative for what they were given. If ever there was an overabundance of gifts, they *always* donated them to children's hospitals.

Even though I miss those birthdays now, the one thing that tinges those treasured memories are

the rows David would create. He would literally throw a few items in a gear bag and leave for three or four days. Sometimes, he would phone on the morning of the birthday and then swan in as though nothing had happened. He would kiss me on the cheek and mumble some excuse as to why he had lost his temper before brushing it off with his usual line, 'We'll talk about it tomorrow'.

None of those tomorrows ever came.

As you can see from the detail of this 1989 portrait, David is a seriously gifted artist. In fact, I have jokingly nicknamed this painting my 'Titanic moment' as a nod to that iconic scene when Jack paint's a beautiful portrait of Rose as she lies naked on the couch!

The amazing thing was that when he did arrive back from his tantrum, he would be Mr Personality himself, handing out sweets to the kids, greeting the parents and taking their coats. At night, he would enjoy the craic and banter while dishing out food to our guests. I lost count of the number of people who would say to me, 'Isn't he fantastic? You are so lucky. You've got a great guy, Adèle! He's the perfect husband'.

Even though I would be sitting there biting my tongue, I was always more than complimentary in my reply and never let him down. My girlfriends all believed he was a saint until the rumours began to surface in later years.

❖

I didn't want a masquerade, I wanted a marriage. David, unfortunately, preferred the masquerade.

My initial reaction towards any rumours of him having an affair consisted of a period of reflection followed by a determined enquiry to see if they proved true. I didn't want to confront him unless I had cause to, but even then there was little point as he was a brilliantly convincing, grade-A liar. Any time I asked him straight out if he was having an affair, he would somehow manage to turn it around and make *me* seem like the bitch for even suspecting. He would then tell me I needed help because I was so insecure. In the end, I was always left feeling like the guilty party even though *he* was the one in the midst of an affair, which I would later discover lasted seven years.

The laugh about this is that he was also cheating on his mistress with other women!

I never told my mother about David's infidelities, but then I didn't have to. Mothers always know. She and my aunt Meta would often catch me crying, and for a while, I remember being constantly on the verge of tears. Any little thing would set me off.

Funnily enough, my mother never really approved of David, nor did she trust him. It wasn't until the latter years of her life that she admitted this to me, and even then it had to be coaxed out of her. When I finally got her to open up, she simply pointed out that I had been working very hard since I was a child and that she would have preferred to have seen me with someone who took better care of me.

My wonderful friend Brian Merriman, never trusted David either. David likewise was never particularly fond of Brian. They were always very civil to each other for my sake, although I imagine if one of them was on fire, the other would have probably reached for the petrol canister before the fire extinguisher. Nowadays, however, I hear they have been spotted having coffee on Camden Street together. I'm just as glad … sure petrol's a ferocious price these days!

A true friend, Brian has always looked out for me and been a wonderful mentor to my girls. He's the kind of person you feel blessed to know. In another life, one where he's not gay, I'm pretty sure we'll marry … although he may have competition if Fr Brian D'Arcy has lost the feckin' collar by that point.

❖

Most people harbour the preconceived notion that people who play in an orchestra are wealthy. After all, the picture of the orchestra is so grandiose with the members all dressed in their dinner suits, looking every inch the upper echelon of society. The reality, however, is that the pay is dreadful and most of the members have to take on second jobs just to make ends meet. At the time, I was doing really well in my career, so I helped David set up a video shop in

Donnybrook, a business venture which I knew he would enjoy. After a short time, he employed an assistant called Yvonne Clifford. I didn't know her but if first impressions are anything to go by, I didn't take to her, and funnily enough, neither did my friends.

Our instincts certainly didn't fail us on that one.

One day, as I pulled to a halt at the traffic lights on the Templeogue Road, Arthur McIvor, a fiddle player with the orchestra, arrived up beside my car on his bicycle. As I rolled down the window to say hello, I glanced at my watch. It was one o'clock.

'Arthur, did you guys finish early today?'

'No, why?'

'Are you not working until six?'

'No, we were always scheduled to finish at one o'clock today.'

David had told me the orchestra was due to work until six. In fact, he would sometimes complain that the workload had kept them there until eight or nine o'clock. I phoned the radio centre. The woman I spoke with checked the list and confirmed that the orchestra had only ever been scheduled to work until one o'clock that day. I requested that she put me through to the RTÉ gym where I then asked if David was around. No sign of him. Out of curiosity, I phoned his mother to see if he was at her house. Bernadette, however, hadn't seen him in weeks.

At around six o'clock that evening I phoned the RTÉ gym again where I was told that David still hadn't been in. In fact, it was ten past eight when I heard Chlo and Nay shriek, 'Daddy, Daddy', as his car finally pulled into the driveway. I remained in the kitchen making dinner but I could clearly hear him outside chatting excitedly with the girls as they raced out to see him. He

arrived into the kitchen, put his arms around me as he embraced me in a long hug and asked, 'How's my gorgeous, sexy wife?'

I smiled, played it very low key and asked him about his day at work. While he recited his pretend grievances of the day, I just listened with a stony silence.

'Aw, it was the same crap as usual,' he began. 'Work went on until around half six, then I went to the gym and worked out for an hour.'

Complete lies. I later found out that he had spent the afternoon on a romp with his employee-turned-mistress Yvonne Clifford.

While he casually fed me more and more lies, I stood at the oven shaking with a mixture of anxiety and rage. I didn't tell him I knew. I felt I would fare better in the long run if I kept it to myself – more ammunition if you will.

One night, I decided to follow him. A glutton for punishment perhaps, but I had to see where he was going. My curiosity would not abate until I knew. He had told me he was going for drinks with the lads so I arranged for a friend of mine to pick me up and follow him out the motorway. We ended up in Finglas. Yvonne Clifford's bungalow to be exact. She and David greeted each other at the front door with a passionate kiss and they certainly didn't seem to care who saw them. Later, at around 3 a.m., he hopped into bed beside me talking about the wonderful night he'd had in the pub with the lads. I didn't let on I knew. As far as he was concerned, I knew nothing.

❖

David went through a lot of mistresses. I won't repeat the *exact* term he used to describe them, but he would always follow it up with, 'the lot of them are only good for one thing – sex'.

Personally, I think he intentionally went for women who were of a lower stature because it made *him* feel like the big name in the relationship. Newspapers sometimes referred to him as 'the less successful one of the duo', which was understandably very hard on his self-esteem. On another occasion, just as we were making our way into a big event, the then-Táiniste Mary Harney jokingly greeted him with the words, 'And you must be Mr Twink!'

As you can imagine, comments like these put an enormous strain on the relationship. Behind closed doors, we were not Twink and David Agnew, we were just Adèle and David. I did everything I could to encourage his career because I genuinely loved his music and felt his unique tone as an oboist could have led to international recognition. When he completed a master class in Trinity College with Maurice Bourgue, one of the world's leading oboists, he probably could have enjoyed his pick of opera houses had he put his mind to it. Unfortunately, David had a self-destruct button. There were always far too many skeletons in his closet holding him back from progressing.

He was always terrified of the media, never allowing them to get too close. So many beautiful photoshoots for publications such as *VIP* magazine portrayed us as a happy family with the perfect life, yet it was the complete opposite at the time. The reality was that before each shoot, David and I would have the most horrendous rows which almost always resulted in him storming out. Looking back, it probably all stemmed from a fear that the media might unearth details of his 'extracurricular activities'. I can only presume he was afraid of a journalist revealing the truth to me. So the next time you see a photograph of a smiling family, just remember, folks, while a picture can tell a thousand words, sadly they're not always a thousand truthful ones.

Pierce, can I buy you?

It's impossible to listen to Pierce Brosnan, and trust me, it's pointless even trying. He's so stunningly beautiful that you will inevitably find yourself drifting out of the conversation and thinking, 'My God, Pierce, if I got my hands on you …!'

When I worked with Pierce on the set of the film *Taffin*, I, like every other woman, was taken aback by his charismatic good looks. Dear God, the man had a face like a chiselled work of art. His personality was equally beautiful. Two dancers I was working with at the time presented me with a good luck present in the form of a clapper board which read: '*Taffin* starring TWINK … *with* Pierce Brosnan.' Self-effacing as ever, Pierce loved it and immediately saw the funny side.

People, mostly women, would actually gawp at him (I should know, considering I was one of his biggest gawpers!).

The thing about Pierce is that while he's so warm and approachable, the moment you find yourself in his presence, you end up standing there, mute in admiration. At the time, he was married to the beautiful Cassandra who would often join him on set with their sons. He always had his arm around her and together they made such a stunning family.

On one occasion, we were shooting outside Phil Healy's pub in Wicklow Town on a perishingly cold night. Both he and I were wrapped up in duvets and given a cup of hot soup, except the soup kept spilling on the duvet because we were shaking with the cold so much. Pierce turned around at one point and said to me, 'Adèle King, is this not the most perfectly ridiculous way for two grown human beings to make a living?'

As the night progressed to dawn, I remember seeing him sitting there in the morning sunlight, totally unaware of how beautifully flawless he was. In fact, I couldn't help but ask, 'Pierce can I buy you? Just name your price, dear and I'll get the chequebook!'

Another insanely handsome actor on the set of *Taffin* was my lifelong friend (and former teenage love) Jim Bartley, who was once famous for his role as the divine heart-throb in *Tolka Row*, not to mention his musical career with the showband Seán and the Raindrops, and to this day the indisputable star (Bella Doyle) of *Fair City*, or, as the cast jokingly call it, *Fairly Shitty*!

❖

One of the most memorable productions Jim and I performed in was a very controversial play entitled *Extremities*, a production that literally transformed the career of Farrah Fawcett-Majors. She herself admitted that prior to taking on that role, she had been typecast as the blonde bimbo from *Charlie's Angels*, however the moment she opened with that play on Broadway, the acting community immediately began to recognise the strength of her incredible talents.

It is, without doubt, a very harrowing part to perform. The play essentially centres around a woman called Marjorie who is victim of attempted rape. Her attacker, Joe, subjects her to a torrent of mental and physical abuse before she manages to overpower him. The story focuses on his obsession with Marjorie and her room-mate, as well as the grief she experiences following the ordeal. In the end, Joe is remanded

to a psychiatric hospital while Marjorie is left rocking and crying uncontrollably. As the curtain comes down, the audience are left wondering which of the two is really the victim. While the story is unquestionably traumatic, it's still a thoroughly captivating production, albeit not for the faint-hearted. Every night, we would hear a few people leave because they found the violent nature of the play so uncomfortable to watch. Even following rehearsals, Jim and I would continue to work on the script for hours, both of us desperately wanting every scene to be as perfectly realistic as possible.

Of the entire play, I think one of the most difficult scenes for the two of us was when Jim had to try to suffocate me. Ever the gentleman, he was always checking to make sure he wasn't hurting me. To be honest, though, there's no avoiding injuries in a production like *Extremities*. It's just part of the territory when you take on the main character of such a physically demanding story. Cuts, bruises and even broken bones I can deal with, unfortunately, this particular role led to a more unusual side-effect – a swollen tongue.

I had to smoke for the part which, as an asthma sufferer, I absolutely detested. Knowing how much I loathed cigarettes, the producer gave me herbal cigarettes to smoke instead. Unfortunately, they smelled like marijuana, which then led to complaints from people in the theatre that I was smoking dope! I couldn't bear to smoke an ordinary cigarette, so the next best thing were those menthol cigarettes. I had to smoke so many of the bloody things on stage that when I woke up one morning, my tongue was seriously swollen and inflamed. I was in absolute agony. Immediately, I went to the doctor who, in turn, sent me to an orthodontist. As I was sitting in his waiting-room, I began to read a magazine, anything to distract from the pain,

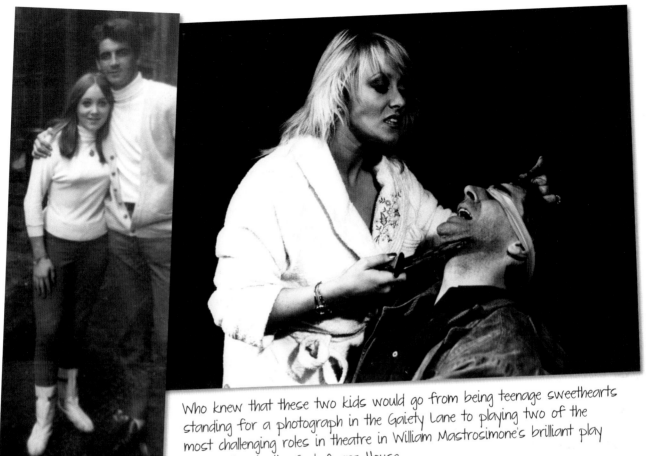

Who knew that these two kids would go from being teenage sweethearts standing for a photograph in the Gaiety Lane to playing two of the most challenging roles in theatre in William Mastrosimone's brilliant play *Extremities* in the Cork Opera House.

and in doing so, came across an interview with Farrah Fawcett-Majors. In the article, she was asked about the downsides to her acting roles. Much to my astonishment, one of the incidents she recalled, involved an allergic reaction to the menthol cigarettes she'd had to smoke when she played the part of Marjorie in *Extremities*. She went on to explain how as a result of her tongue becoming massively inflamed, she ended up in an orthodontist's surgery having injections to bring the swelling down.

There I was sitting in the waiting-room with my tongue inflamed and reading that Farrah Fawcett-Majors had gone through the exact same ordeal when playing the exact same role. I guess you could say we both suffered the same penance for our art!

❖

My idol, the opera singer Maria Callas, once explained to an interviewer, 'An opera begins long before the curtain goes up and ends long after it has come down. It starts in my imagination, it becomes my life, and it stays part of my life long after I've left the opera house'.

I think any actress who has had to perform a sinister storyline will completely understand those words. I know I certainly do. Everything in our *Extremities* performance was as realistic as we could make it and I think this led to my difficulty in 'switching off' when the play was over.

I became so absorbed in playing Marjorie, that I would have to try to leave the character behind when the play had finished each night. I know that sounds so 'actressy', a trait I despise in a lot of artists, but I genuinely had difficulty relaxing and easing myself out of the role. I could never just snap out of it and go for dinner as though nothing had happened. It was such a gruelling part to play that it couldn't but have a huge emotional impact on the person playing it. You find yourself thinking about all the women who have actually experienced such an ordeal in real life and the trauma they endured in their struggle to overcome it.

❖

While I was rehearsing for *Extremities*, I received a phone call from a Mayo showband manager.

'Twink, howya! It's Louis Walsh.'

(Yes, *that* Louis Walsh.)

'Ah, howya, Squishy!'

(Yes, I really do call him that!)

'Tell me, have you ever been to Turkey?'

'No!'

'Aw it's beautiful, Twink. You would love the country and you would love the people there. Anyway, there's a big television festival taking place in Çeşme (pronounced Cheshmay) and I want you to represent the Republic of Ireland.'

Turkey was unheard of back then. No one went there, primarily because no one knew it was there to begin with. Louis was certainly right when he said I would fall in love with the place. I think everyone has somewhere they love as much as their home and for me, that place is Turkey.

During the flight out to the festival, I was sitting with a contingent of Irish journalists who had been assigned to cover the competition. They drank the plane dry and by the time the coach picked us up in Izmir, there was no disguising the fact that they were well and truly sloshed. I don't know which was funnier – the carry-on of the drunken reporters or the expression of horror on the face of every onlooker who passed them.

I think everyone's lasting memory of that trip is of an incident that occurred just after the coach pulled up outside the hotel. The driver had parked on a slight incline downwards and unfortunately for the film critic Michael O'Dwyer, his door opened onto an area that was full of loose gravel. The poor man was so schmozzled that the he found himself shuffling downhill through the gravel, picking up speed as he went. Sure enough, he ended up falling flat on his face and sliding down the remainder of the incline clearing a six-inch path towards the wall with his chin. Of course the rest of his colleagues were so polluted drunk, they were almost wetting themselves laughing at the sight of Michael enveloped in sand. I can still remember the hotel management looking out the front door both horrified and bemused by what was going on. As the rest of the contingent spilled out of the coach and into the lobby, one of them piped up, 'Lads, where's Michael?'

Michael, it turns out, was still lying face down in the bed of gravel outside.

I'm not joking when I say that three of us went to help him up but were laughing so bloody hard, it was pointless even trying. He was too drunk to realise where he was and so kept insisting, 'I'll … I'll be fine here!'

The following morning at breakfast, the lot of them were all diseased with hangovers. Head complaints soon turned to hysterics however, when Michael walked out with plasters covering his face. Unfortunately, the heat was so ferocious that it caused the plasters to lose their grip and slowly they had begun to peel. For the entire time we were in Turkey, the poor man had to endure a litany of jokes at his expense. To add to his troubles, his face was lobster-red from the sunburn, except for the little white rectangles outlining where the plasters had once been!

❖

On the day of the press call, pandemonium ensued when a singer became rather buckled drunk at lunch. In the poor guy's defence, the weather in Turkey is shockingly hot and resisting the temptation to knock back a few cold beers is next to impossible. While everyone in the hotel had turned either red or brown from the sun, Louis Walsh on the other hand had turned a shade of pale he was so panic-stricken. He and I spent ages trying to coax the singer out of his drunken stupor, all to no avail however.

Noticing a rather tall, good-looking Turkish maître d' nearby, I summoned him over to ask for his help. Unfortunately, he had only a smattering of English so I tried to explain that the man comatose on the chair in front of us *had* to be sobered up in time for his performance at the festival later that night. He seemed to acknowledge our problem before running back into the kitchen where he remained for what seemed like an hour. At one point, I even said to Louis, 'That son of a bitch must have gone home!'

Just as we were about to give up, out he arrived carrying a tray of sandwiches along with a huge pot of black coffee and a jug of iced water. Without hesitation, he grasped the jug of water and poured it over our guy's head, ice cubes and all. It was one of those moments where in the midst of the panic, you just have to laugh. Sure

enough, the Turkish shock treatment had the singer wide awake within seconds. Lifting up his chin, we opened his mouth and literally poured a cup of black coffee into him before feeding him sandwiches. The guy was absolutely soaked to the skin but within an hour we had managed to get him coherent enough to talk.

When I later approached the maître d' to thank him for his help, we ended up enjoying quite a nice long chat. Introducing himself as Ibrahim, he told me about his life and how he had once been a chef in Ankara. He then went on to tell me about his love of languages, although I could have easily guessed that, as I had often witnessed him chatting with the Italians, Germans, Spaniards and Russians with the same ease of fluency as one of their own. When it was time for me to leave, he asked if I would like to join him and his friend Peter, whom I had met once before, on a boat the following day to go swimming in the beautiful clear blue seas of Çeşme. Peter was known for having a dog that was also called Peter, however in order to distinguish between the two, everyone always referred to the dog as 'Entel Peter' which translates as 'Intelligent Peter!'

Although somewhat hesitant to go at first, I ended up enjoying the most fantastic day with Ibrahim and Peter. Later, Ibrahim taught me how to play backgammon, or tavla as it is known in Turkey, before bringing me into the village to see old men play it with such incredible skill, all the while blinding their unwitting opponents with nifty and ingenious side-steps. We enjoyed so much fun together and I adored being in the company of a man who treated me so lovingly. Now, ladies I won't lie, I welcomed the flirtation as a much-needed break from the misery I was having to put up with from David. I had sacrificed my career in London to try to save my marriage and yet the same crap still continued.

Every time I was off on tour, I would hear reports of him bedding some dancer. I always found out because, frankly, there was always someone only dying to break the news to me. I think I had reached a point where I just thought, two can play your game darling.

I even told him straight out that I had begun to look at other men myself. I made it quite clear that I harboured no intentions of wasting my time on someone who was out screwing the nation. David hurt me with lies, whereas Ibrahim lavished me with love … is it really any wonder I treasured the feeling of being in his arms whenever I travelled to Turkey?

❖

In the run-up to the competition, my interpreter, Rana Orhuntak, translated into Turkish a verse of the brilliant song 'Bolt of Lightning' that my musical director Andy O'Callaghan had written for me. Needless to say, the moment I began singing in Turkish, the crowd went ballistic with excitement. In the end, I came second place to a wonderful Turkish singer. Of the two of us, though, I think I fared better in the long run as my career went from strength to strength following the competition.

Unfortunately, there was a slight downside to the new-found popularity my performance had garnered there, namely that of fan mobs. On one occasion, I was nearly crushed to death by a crowd outside a venue. I couldn't breathe with the weight of the crowd against me and there was a moment when I genuinely thought I was going to be killed. I was trapped up against the limo unable to move until my bodyguard Michael managed to push a few of them out of the way so that we could open the door and get me inside the car. As we went to drive off, there were fans climbing up on the bonnet and the roof.

The following day, a man who managed a number of big acts in Turkey, asked me if I would be interested in flying back out the following week to appear on a television show. Suddenly, I was being flown out regularly to do more shows and festivals. At some stage, government personnel had also seen me perform and booked me to sing at a big official dinner. Out there, I was known as Tvink because the letter 'w' doesn't exist in Turkish.

Due to the number of jobs I was being offered, I felt I should learn how to converse in the language – nice idea in theory, however, considering that Turkey was practically unheard of back then, any assistance in learning the language was rare to say the least. This fact was certainly cemented when, having phoned the Linguaphone Centre on Abbey Street, I was informed that Turkish wasn't one of the forty-three languages they specialised in. They did however, put me in touch with a company in Knightsbridge who made Turkish language tapes for the overseas forces. A few weeks later, the postman arrived at the door with a kit of cassettes along with a massive tome of a book. Honest to God, I would have learned five European languages in the length of time it took me to learn the basics of Turkish. In most languages, the majority of the words bear some resemblance to their English version. In Turkish however, even the simplest of words are the most difficult to remember. For instance, orange juice is 'portakal suyu', a simple bit of 'bread and butter' is 'ekmek ve tereyaği' so you don't want to try to order two fried eggs which is 'iki yumurta kizaurtma' and that's before you get a cuppa tea!

Needless to say, I was seriously struggling and eventually, I decided that professional assistance was necessary if I was ever going to master the very basics alone. In a bid to source information on Turkish tutors, I went to the Turkish Embassy in Dublin where I was introduced to the diplomat, Mine (pronounced Mena) Gürekan. The moment I enquired about learning the language, she quite literally looked back at me in shock before asking why in God's name I would want to study such a challenging subject. I explained about the work I was doing in Turkey and how I had already tried to learn some vocabulary from an old book. Immediately, she warned me to be very careful where I learned my Turkish from, otherwise I might inadvertently find myself saying the Turkish equivalent of 'howya love' to diplomats.

Instead, Mine arranged to teach me herself and it was at that point that a wonderful friendship was formed. In fact, I wanted her to be Chloë's godmother, but unfortunately, the Catholic Church will not allow a Muslim to be a godparent, so instead she became Chloë's fairy godmother.

While she was tutoring me, Mine was always encouraging me to speak the language any time I was visiting Turkey, and so, one night, while I was having dinner with friends in Çeşme, I decided to act on her advice. I summoned the waiter and in Turkish I asked, 'Where is toilet, please?'

Or at least that's what I thought I was saying.

My friends around the table nearly choked on their pizzas when they heard me. It turns out I had used the word 'aptesame' for bathroom. What I didn't know was that an aptesame is the kind of bathroom you would find in a sultan's palace. It's the size of a small ballroom and features servants holding massive ostrich feathers ready to fan you down if the heat gets too much while you are sitting on a velvet-padded seat powdering your nose. Also on hand is a team of ladies who do everything from wiping your bum to flushing your toilet. It is the height of opulence reserved for sultans' wives, mistresses and ladies of the court.

It seems the book I had originally been learning from was so bloody old that the word 'aptesame' hadn't actually been used in Turkey for over fifty years. At this point, the table are all but roaring laughing at my mortifying blunder. The waiter, who was now also trying not to laugh, gestured me in the direction of the bathroom. I could only see one door.

'But where's the ladies toilet?'

'Doesn't matter, it's all the same!'

That alone should have been an indication as to what awaited me.

Behind the bockety old door was a small stinking kip of a room with a hole in the ground and two planks on which to place your feet and squat. A tin kettle filled with water sat nearby, there for you to wash 'your bits', so to speak, and unless you brought your own toilet roll, you would have to do without. It was about as far removed from an aptesame as a nunnery was from a brothel. I honestly don't think I spoke Turkish for the following six months, not even to order an ice-cream. Needless to say, I dumped the book and from that point on, learned everything from Mine before progressing to a point where I could continue my studies in the language unit in Trinity College, Dublin.

❖

I was flying to Turkey so often that I became good friends with the airline staff. In fact whenever I was flying with Club Air, I would often sit in the cockpit and enjoy some banter with the pilots. As we were flying into Turkey, they would even let me speak to the officials in the control tower, who also knew me very well at that stage. Whenever we were landing, the pilots would always hand me the microphone and have me greet the passengers in Turkish.

My God it's so hard to believe that there was once this level of freedom in the airline system, particularly when you compare it to today's regulations that prevent you from even carrying a bottle of water on board.

❖

On one of the rare occasions that David collected me from the airport, it was a miserable dark day and the atmosphere inside the car was no brighter. In fact, we barely said two words to each other. As we parked outside Nutgrove Shopping Centre where I had to pick up a gift for a friend's birthday, I casually remarked, 'God it's so miserable and grey here, why do I bother coming back!'

'That's what I was wondering,' came the cross reply.

Those five words stung more than a tirade of abuse.

'David is this marriage going to work?'

'You tell me, you're the one that goes away.'

'No, I'm the one who has to go away *to work*. To earn money, I have to go where the work is.'

'I'm sure there are plenty of other attractions for you in Turkey.'

'Oh, David …' I smiled, 'be *very* assured there are!'

The way I looked at it, there was nothing sneaky about what I was doing. At least when I was having my indiscretions, I didn't hide it – in fact I bloody well told him straight out. I made a point of letting him know that I wasn't prepared to waste my youth on a man who couldn't hold fidelity in place for a week.

The sad thing about our situation was that when we were on holiday together or even if we just shared a bottle of wine together at night, it was like we went back to being hopelessly in love. When there were no other distractions, we returned to the early days when he only had eyes for me. Each time, I would be convinced that the love we shared would make him want to change his ways, but unfortunately, my anticipation for a faithful husband always ebbed to a sinking disappointment in the days that would follow.

❖

Flying back and forth to Turkey was exhausting, and, combined with all the other travel miles I was clocking up, I don't know how I didn't collapse. I was also at a point in my life where I was beginning to get broody. When you find yourself nipping into Mothercare to get their catalogue, you know your biological clock is screaming at you.

I remember one day when I nipped into a shopping centre to buy a jacket I'd heard David say he liked. I don't know how, but I ended up in the baby department of Roche's Stores, browsing through the tiny clothes. I just had the weirdest feeling that I would be shopping for them in the very near future. Of course, none of this would have happened had it not been for two friends of mine, Andy and Clodagh O'Callaghan. To this day, I blame them for my kids. You know those T-shirts that read: 'I blame the parents!'? Well, I have always considered having one printed that reads: 'I blame the O'Callaghans!'.

It all started when I was booked to do a gig for the Irish ambassador's St Patrick's night ball in Zambia, Africa. Andy, my musical director, accompanied me on the trip but he couldn't stay on for the sightseeing excursion that had been arranged for us as his wife, Clodagh, was pregnant and very close to her due date. Not having any children of my own at the time, I couldn't understand why anyone would want to leave a place as amazing as Africa to go see someone giving birth in a hospital in Dublin.

The fuss was entirely lost on me until a year or so later when I was the one in labour.

When I arrived back home in Ireland, I went straight to the Coombe Hospital to visit Andy, Clodagh and their new arrival, Sheena. While I was there, a phone call came through to reception for Clodagh and as she stood up to go out and take it, she very casually handed me her newborn. Up until that point, I had never held a baby. Not once! Honest to God, I thought they were going to have to call the paramedics for me with the shock I got of suddenly being handed this tiny sleeping bundle. Gradually however, I began to fall in love with her and as I paced the room with this tiny person in my arms, I caught sight of myself in the mirror. I remember stopping in my tracks and thinking, 'I could get to really like this!'

Something about it looked and felt so right and from that day on I was hooked on the idea of starting a family. Now do you see why I blame the O'Callaghans?

When I left the Coombe, I remember telling myself that my priorities needed to change. My life was revolving around the airports of the world. In fact, some mornings I would wake up and need five minutes to remember what country I was in. It's that old traveller joke of: 'Well if it's Tuesday, it must be Japan!'

I remember with much mortification the morning I woke up convinced I was in Israel. I phoned reception and because I didn't have a good grasp of Arabic at the time, I instead began sounding out the words as best as I could. A voice that was anything but Middle Eastern replied, 'Ma'am, is there a problem?'

The embarrassment didn't stop there either as I then had to ask, 'I know this is going to sound ridiculous but can you tell me what country I'm in?'

'Ma'am, are you alright?'

'I will be when you tell me where I am!'

'You're in Toronto, Canada.'

'Oh, Jesus, I thought I was in Israel!'

'Ma'am … are you sure you're alright?'

I know some people reading this will think I'm an ungrateful wretch for not appreciating the opportunity of travelling the world, but let me tell you, the veneer wears off everything after a while. I was extremely grateful for the travelling prospects my career had afforded me, but there came a point when I'd just had enough. I had been travelling since I was a kid with Maxi Dick and Twink and to be honest, I wanted nothing more than to have my feet in one country for more than a week at a time, preferably Ireland. In the end, an unforgettable plane journey proved to be the very final straw.

One night just as we were feet away from touching down in Izmir, the plane suddenly shot up into the air again. Believe me, rockets from NASA haven't taken to the air as vertically as that plane did. People were screaming with terror and I would safely say there wasn't one person on the plane even remotely convinced we were going to survive. Clearly, the pilot had overshot the runway and in doing so, decided to abort the landing. Despite the terrifying ordeal endured by the passengers, we were never given so much as an explanation or an apology. In fact, at the end of the flight, an air hostess took to the intercom to say, 'I hope you enjoyed your flight. Please do fly with us again!'

That night really sealed the lid on my plane days. In fact, I have flown so much throughout my life that I'm convinced my luck is running out. On one occasion in Africa, when I had to take a flight to Botswana, the plane I was boarding was in such a dilapidated condition that it might as well have been held together with chewing gum and twine. I remember taking one look at it and saying to myself, 'There's no way that heap of crap can fly!'

Between the broken toilet window that was stuffed with loo-roll, to the toilet flush that looked more like an eject lever, as we finally came to land, it brought to mind that great old Al Banim gag, 'We flew so close to the Zambezi, you could wash your underwear … in fact you had to!'

Like I said, planes are not for me.

Ibrahim and I.

Lying on the beach in Turkey one night, despite the fact that the sex was hotter than the Turkish weather, I found myself saying goodbye to Ibrahim.

I don't think I will ever forget him saying to me, 'Will we see each other next week?'

I nodded and replied, 'Maybe, Ibo' – but I knew I was saying goodbye for good. I had made the decision to try to rescue my marriage for a second time. Little did I know then, that thanks to the magic of Facebook, we would become friends again after all these years.

If only I'd had the luxury of hindsight at the time I needed it most, it would have saved so much regret in later years. When I arrived home, I sat down with David and excitedly told him I was planning on remaining in Ireland. I laid my heart on the line and pointed out that we were both living totally individual lives and that there was nothing left in the relationship to indicate that we were married. Deep down, I wanted clarity in a situation that was very fast becoming intolerable. I know people will question why we didn't just split up considering the nature of the problems that had surfaced so early in our marriage, but you have to realise that it was too difficult to just discard the many, many incredible times we had shared. When we were together, we were so in love with each other, and, looking back, perhaps I was more in love with him than he was with me – I'll never know. But nonetheless, I always hoped he would change his philandering ways and give us a chance to truly enjoy a happy marriage.

Another LOL

There was an old lady standing at a corner with both hands clasped frantically on her hat while the wind blew her dress up around her waist.

A gentleman approached her and said, 'You should be ashamed of yourself, letting your skirt blow up like that'.

The woman replied, 'Look mister, everything down there is seventy years old; this hat is brand new!'

People always ask me about this photograph.

And no – I wasn't posing – I was dozing!

Although I didn't know it at the time – this was my first pregnancy photograph!

This was for a show called **She's Got It.** After it emerged that I was pregnant, the joke that went around RTÉ was, 'Well SHE certainly got it!'

It was taken in the RTÉ Stills Department where we were doing a photoshoot for a show called *She's Got It.* I felt exhausted that morning and at one stage during the shoot, I even remember hearing John Cooney the photographer saying, 'Oi, sleeping beauty!'

As you can see from the photograph, I had actually started to fall asleep.

Following the shoot, David collected me and dashed me across the RTÉ lot to the television building where we were due to join a number of other broadcasting personalities for drinks and canapés to launch the new autumn television schedule. For the short length of time he was driving, I kept nodding off, waking only when my head would smack against the window. I genuinely couldn't figure out what was wrong with me. As soon as I reached my dressing room in RTÉ, I crashed out on the couch. All I can remember after that is jumping up in a panic after waking to the sound of muffled chatter accompanied by champagne corks popping and the clinking of glasses (unlike the cheap plonk

in plastic glasses of today!). I still don't know how I managed to keep my eyes open during the photo shoot. That night, I arrived home and immediately took refuge on the floor in front of the fire, lapsing into a sleep that was almost comatose. Throughout that night and the day that followed, I was violently sick, I assumed a virus was the cause of my sudden ill health. On Sunday morning I visited my then GP, Dr Richard Harris, who carried out the necessary few tests. As we were chatting away, he casually began asking me about my future plans. I remember him saying at one point, 'You must be very busy with all that travelling between Turkey and Ireland. How do you feel about starting a family?'

I explained that I would love to have children but that there never seemed to be a right time. His reply? 'Well you better *make* time, Mrs Agnew! Congratulations, you're pregnant!'

I swear to God, the impact of the shock literally resulted in me screaming with excitement. I don't even know how my jeep made it to Anne Devlin

Road because let me tell you, those wheels never touched the ground once. The second I got home, I ran into the kitchen and screamed, 'Oh, my God! Oh, my God! Oh, my God! You're not going to believe it!'

Cool as a breeze, my mother replied, 'You're pregnant!' She had figured it out the night before! I guess mums just know these things.

When I told David the news, it very nearly prompted the verbal equivalent of a heart attack in him. I didn't know it then but at that stage, his employee Yvonne Clifford was already pregnant with his child. Oh, and did I mention Yvonne is a niece of Bill Cullen?

While Bill and I can enjoy some jovial banter these days, unfortunately at the time, Mr Hire-em-and-fire-em didn't have the liathróidí to speak to me about what was going on. Yvonne landed a job in the Europa Academy in France where she lives to this day.

❖

The first few months brought with it terrible nausea. At the time, I still had a number of work commitments to complete in Turkey and while I was out there, I would be dying for my friend Pier Flynn of Club Travel to arrive out with good oul' Marietta biscuits, Barry's Tea and Avonmore milk. The nausea was so bad that they were pretty much all I could hold down during those nine months. Fortunately, someone gave me a Kwells wristband which apparently works on the pressure points. If any expectant mothers are reading this, I can assure you they are amazing for easing the nausea. Unfortunately, they don't ease the cravings. During my pregnancy I had a massive hankering for Jaffa oranges. I was capable of eating six to ten of them in one go and, on one occasion, sent David to Terenure at three in the morning for a dozen Jaffas and three ginormous Cadbury's caramel bars.

I wasn't working as much when I was pregnant with Chloë so I became a lady of leisure and as a result, grew to such an extent that I constantly referred to myself as being the size of a small apartment block. I was pretty much pregnant in the front, back and sides. Even my obstetrician, gynaecologist and wonderful friend, Professor Colm O'Herlihy, who delivered Chloë, gave me a hard time over it. One day, as we were making our way into the ante-natal room in Holles Street, I noticed that popular poster of the large Buddha-like baby. When I started laughing at it, Dr O'Herlihy remarked, 'If you keep going the way you are, that baby will be only *marginally* bigger than the one you're going to have!'

In contrast, when I was pregnant with Naomi, I was as thin as a whippet because I was working in panto. I remember being five months'

So proud!

pregnant and doing things like abseiling from the roof of the Gaiety Theatre, not to mention performing strenuous tap-dancing routines in a small dress with a wide patent belt around a tiny waist. You wouldn't even have thought I'd had a big dinner inside me, let alone a child. It was such a small neat pregnancy. Funnily enough, Chloë reflects how I behaved during

Pregnant with Naomi.

year – a jumper his mother had knitted – while each Christmas he would receive just the one gift, a book. Consequently, he always thought I overindulged the girls. I always argued that a person only gets to experience being a child once in their lifetime, so why shouldn't it be a memorable one? I had no other reason for going out to work other than to pay for their schooling, clothes, and to give them the best life possible. Not once could they have been accused of being spoiled brats.

David, however, lived very much according to the values of his childhood, a fact that was made glaringly obvious one day when his father Arthur, who is an absolute gentleman, made a comment that will never leave my memory. We had a beautiful nursery in Beaufort House and when he visited on one occasion, I excitedly showed him the room. Around that time I had received hundreds upon hundreds of gifts and toys from wonderful well-wishers all over the country. I donated a large number of these to children's hospitals and women's shelters and the rest I used to decorate the nursery. When it was complete, the room looked sensational. Arthur however, took one look at it and just assumed I had gone out and bought all the toys. Suddenly I heard him mumble the word 'disgrace' under his breath so I confronted him about what was bothering him.

'It's ridiculous. That nursery is a mortal sin,' he argued.

I went to explain where the toys had come from, but before I could finish my sentence, he snapped back, 'You a have a sin to answer for. That's overindulgent. That child will never be sane or normal.'

The words 'pot', 'kettle' and 'black' sprang to mind but, how and ever, I held my tongue and silently accepted that some people can't be changed.

her pregnancy, in that she has a really cool, easy-going manner. Naomi on the other hand is very energetic and active, exactly the way I was when I was pregnant with her.

Even though David's parents were financially comfortable, he was brought up very frugally. He would receive the same birthday present every

'And what about the elastic stockings ...?'

Chloë's birth may not have been planned *per se*, but it was certainly predicted. I was informed about my future pregnancy in April 1988 to be precise. That was the year the Eurovision Song Contest was being staged in Ireland, an era when the competition was really at its earthy best. As part of the Eurovision week, organisers had arranged a wonderful boat trip around Dublin harbour for all the contestants, one of whom included a very young and little-known Celine Dion.

I was on the trip for two reasons: RTÉ had asked me to be the host, and I was also employed by the Turkish Embassy as the interpreter for the Turkish contingent. It was a memorably fantastic day of fabulous food, great banter and plenty of singing, with one of the highlights being Mr Eurovision himself, Johnny Logan, taking to the deck to belt out a few numbers. When the boat returned to the quayside, a number of coaches were waiting to transport us back to the Berkeley Court Hotel. On the coach, I was sitting next to my good friend Fergus Gibson, the gifted psychic and astrologer whom I had known since my Maxi Dick and Twink days.

For any sceptics reading this, let me start by clarifying that Fergie is the real deal. In fact, he was part of a famous showband incident in a hotel in Ennis, County Clare, where he invoked the spirit of a brother-in-law of one of the showband musicians playing there. The poor guy was plagued by his brother-in-law for months until, eventually, he had to call Fergie back to try to resolve the situation.

As we were chatting that day on the bus, Fergie suddenly turned to me and said, 'Now look, we have to talk about the pregnancy.'

'Eh ... pardon?'

'The pregnancy that you're going to have in ... I'd say ... about a couple of months. You're going to have to stay with me on this one! Don't worry, I can talk you through where it's going.'

'Sorry Fergie but ... where the hell *is this* going?'

'You're going to be pregnant! The baby will be due in about May or June next year. I'm going to have to talk to you about your legs because you're going to have problems with them. You'll definitely need elastic stockings and they're going to be a problem, because you won't look very glamorous in them, sweetheart!'

I don't know whether it was the idea of me being pregnant, or the image of me wearing elastic stockings but, either way, I was well and truly flummoxed.

'Fergie, can you really see a trained dancer in elastic stockings? Yeah, right!'

'Now Twink, you can laugh all you like, but you're going to be in elastic stockings. That's all I will say! Keep me number handy!'

Sure enough that September, there I was sitting in my GP's surgery being told I was pregnant.

Not long before I was due to give birth, Henry Mountcharles had invited me to his book launch in Slane Castle. Henry and I have enjoyed a wonderful friendship since our youth. We were, and still are, joined at the hip! In fact, his mother once said to me many, many years ago, 'I really wish Henry would marry you ... it would be very good for him'.

Her lovely remark was in rather stark contrast to that of my own mother-in-law who felt I was only 'almost good enough' for her son.

On the day of Henry's launch, I was scheduled to host the Texaco Children Art Awards in the Burlington Hotel as I myself had been a former Texaco winner. At that point, I was nine months and eleven days' pregnant and absolutely convinced I was going to give birth in the middle of the bloody show. For the job, I wore a beautiful Lainey Keogh knitted suit which I had paired with the most exquisite gold Italian shoes. Fianna Fáil's Mary O'Rourke was our special guest on the day and as I stepped out in front of the cameras to welcome her to the event, the right heel of my shoe snapped, presumably under the weight of my 'apartment-block' bump. Discreetly, I limped my way to the podium, and for hours and hours I stood there on one high heel and one broken heel. I could feel every drop of blood draining from my body and making its way to my legs. Never in my life have I been through such physical agony – believe me, the birth was a breeze by comparison. Following the ceremony, my legs were so swollen that I had to be transported to an ambulance in a wheelchair. Immediately, the paramedic recognised that I had oedema and opted to bring me home rather than to hospital. While he was tending to me, he took a massive pair of elastic stockings from his case and slipped them on my legs to help reduce the swelling. As I watched him put them on, all I could hear in my head was Fergie fucking Gibson saying, 'And what about the elastic stockings? You won't look very glamorous in them, sweetheart!'

Fergie was also right in his prediction that I would give birth 'around May or June 1989'. Chloë was due on 27 May, but arrived on 9 June!

Exhausted ... emotional ... ecstatic!

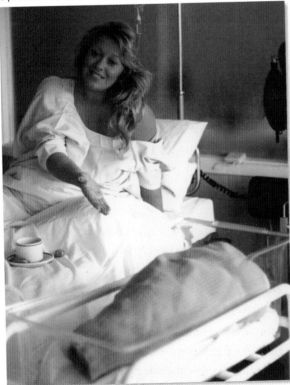

David, still in his orchestra dinner suit, kissing his baby daughter for the first time.

Twenty-three years on, I'm still none the wiser about how Fergie could have known such specific details about my pregnancy before I was even pregnant. Considering how his words proved to be 100 per cent accurate, I should have paid more heed when he subsequently made a prediction about David. When Fergie brought his kids to my panto in the Gaiety about a year later, I gave them a tour of the theatre, however, the real magical thrill for kids was to be brought backstage to see the various props and, of course, the coach and ponies.

As I was about to return to my room to pick up my belongings before heading home, Fergie stood and said, 'D'ya know wha', Twink? You're the best burd! Thanks a million for doing that for my kids. I can't begin to tell you how much that meant to them.' Turning slightly more serious, he then added, 'I'm going to tell you something now. I was looking at your chart the other day and, sweetheart, you need to ditch the baggage. Are you listening to me? If you don't ditch the baggage, and you know what I'm talking about, then it's going to bring you down and sink you further than the *Titanic*. You don't need the baggage. You're a strong woman, you can do this on your own. Ditch the fuckin' baggage … now!'

While he was speaking, he never referred to David by name.

Of course, I knew immediately he was right. Looking back, I had known for a long time, but when you're in love, it's very difficult to hear the truth, let alone act on it. Even though you know deep down that the person you love is not going to change, you become more defensive about them whenever anyone dares broach the topic. You silently convince yourself that your relationship is strong enough to survive the storm, but deep down, you know you're in denial.

Sunday March '89,

Dear Adèle, to the most wonderful woman and mother I love. I hope and pray I can be as good a father as you are a mother. Happy Mother's Day!

Love you always, David xxx

My girl, Jayne

My beloved dog, Jayne, was the most über-intelligent animal I had ever encountered and for fifteen years, she was my extremely loyal companion. Only for the four legs and coat of fur, she was practically human. When I became pregnant with Chloë, however, it was as though Jayne knew a change was imminent. She was already quite old, but at that point her health was beginning to visibly decline.

When I look back on Chloë's homecoming, it was tinged with equal measures of great happiness and sadness. There's a photograph of me taken the day after we brought Chloë home from hospital and in it, I look absolutely besotted by the tiny bundle in my arms. In the background, however, Jayne is seen looking on at us sadly, as though she knew that she could no longer be the centre of attention. To this day, I can barely look at that picture without welling up. Even though we still doted on Jayne and were completely in love with her, she sensed that things were different.

About a month after Chloë's arrival, Jayne's health had faded to a point where even the vet was concerned enough to keep her in for observation.

At one point, he phoned and advised that I come down to his surgery. He gently explained that Jayne didn't have long left and if I wanted to say goodbye, now was the time. Immediately I rushed to the surgery. Just as I stepped inside the door of the treatment room, my girl opened her eyes, and as I knelt down beside her, she slowly leaned out to kiss me on the side of my face one last time. With that, she lay down her head and quietly passed away. I was utterly grief-stricken.

To some people, pets are just animals, but to a genuine animal lover, they are so much more. Not long afterwards, I decided to have Jayne sent to a taxidermist. She is now preserved and placed in her own individual coffin. When I got her back, it felt like she was home again; like she had come home to rest.

My dog, Jilly, who died in 2010, has also been taxidermied, and I now plan to have both Jayne and Jilly buried with me. I know some people will be unable to understand such depths of love for two animals, but I promised them we would be together forever and I have every intention of honouring that commitment.

My beloved Jayne

Everything but nervous laughter

Around late March 1991, I received a phone call from the *Sunday Independent* journalist Eoghan Harris who explained that he was organising the Fine Gael Árd Fheis in the RDS and wanted to organise a comedy sketch that would lift it out of the doldrums once the main speeches were over.

When we met up to discuss ideas, we decided that I would begin my act by interrupting the Taoiseach, John Bruton, while he was on stage talking. At the time, a lot of people were hiring me for corporate events in which I would interrupt their speech at a certain point, often in the character of the cleaner Bernie, from the hugely popular 'rolls, TV and cinema ads' act Bernie and Rose Violet. Feargal Quinn, for instance, once hired me for a Superquinn 'highlighter' launch, where I arrived in on his cue, wearing my full cleaning uniform and wig, talking loudly about how I would never shop in Superquinn. I then clattered through the crowd, giving out shite about Feargal, whilst dusting the handbag of every woman I passed. Until they realised it was a skit, most people were genuinely looking on in shock.

After the event, I remember Feargal sending me a lovely hamper and thank you note which said, 'Brilliant comedy, witty, well scripted, great, great, performance – and you weren't bad either!'

It was a very funny routine and one that was in great demand at the time, so it seemed like the perfect format for the Árd Fheis. Eoghan wrote up the script and when we met for a coffee the week before the event, I suggested a number of changes. His script was too long so I recommended tightening it up. I also pointed out that he hadn't included a reference to the 'Úna agus a gúna' story, a well-publicised incident in which a female reporter from RTÉ was allegedly groped by a drunken Fianna Fáil TD. Eoghan was rather hesitant at first because he felt it was still a bit of a sensitive topic. My attitude, however, was that they were politicians and should be able to take it. After all, the whole point of the performance was to create a few red faces while at the same time giving everyone a good laugh.

Even though the general routine remained the same, I believe I made the script a little spikier. Whenever I have performed political satire, I have always been allowed to tweak the script to suit the way I would deliver it. When it comes to satire, you can't just repeat a script you have learned, you have to adjust it to suit your natural tone and delivery, otherwise it will sound too rehearsed and the jokes won't translate. This occasion was no different.

❖

Many a book has been written about the loneliness of the stand-up comic. Even when you're performing to a crowd of thousands, the stage really is the loneliest place in the world if your jokes are dying. The Fine Gael Árd Fheis, however, was one of the best audiences I have ever had. They were in pain laughing and a few guests were quite literally in tears. In fact, the only ones who were miffed at the end were the ones who hadn't been slagged off! It was absolute hysteria in the most positive sense of the word. Believe me, I've had enough stage experience to know when I'm on a roll and, that afternoon, I definitely had the crowd in my hands.

The cheers and applause were reverberating in my ears as I walked off into the wings and absolutely everyone left the venue in flying form. About twenty minutes later, as I walked into the make-up room, my dear friend the make-up artist, Evelyn Lunny said to me, 'Will it be safe for you to go outside? Adèle, it's all over the news, there's absolute uproar about your sketch. The media are going crazy. They're saying it's trivialised politics and that it will be the downfall of the government …'

I remember laughing it off thinking there was no way that what Evelyn was saying could be true. However, when I stepped outside the door of the RDS, a stampede of journalists and photographers were there to greet me. Microphones and flashing cameras appeared from over reporters' heads while questions were fired from all directions.

'Do you think you brought down a government?'

'Was that not a blasphemous thing to say about Úna?'

I was clearly being nailed to the cross; Eoghan Harris, on the other hand, was nowhere to be found.

The bloody sketch had nothing to do with government policy – it was entertainment for God's sake. I didn't go out on stage with any sinister, underhand intentions of causing the government to collapse; I went out to perform. If you don't like it then don't blame the act, blame the booker. Every radio programme that day was discussing it – RTÉ even changed the schedule that night so that an emergency *Prime Time* could be broadcast. I will never forget a well-known female politician voicing her disgust with the jokes on the show. The presenter, Brian Farrell, then introduced a clip from the Árd Fheis which showed her laughing hysterically at the sketch. He asked her to explain why she was suddenly so disgusted, considering she had obviously been so entertained by it. Her response was incredulous at best: 'Well, to be honest with you, Brian, in the case of most of us, it was nervous laughter.'

In fairness to Brian, he immediately shot back, 'Well it doesn't look very nervous to me!'

The party had known I was going to be there, and they were more than fully aware of the nature of the act. I still believe Fine Gael should have stood up and told people to get over themselves, that it was just entertainment. Had they done so, they would have more than likely remained in government. Instead, they were on the floor with their caps in their hands apologising to everyone from the pauper to the pope. The party was back in power not long after that, so I'm sure some people would argue that I didn't bring them down far enough!

When I look back on it, I am still bewildered that my performance brought a government to its knees. Nonetheless, I don't regret it; I was an entertainer doing the job I was paid to do. My gig description was to make them laugh and, by Jesus, did I make them laugh. It was a damning-yet-illustrious moment in my career and I traded on it for years. If there was a heckler in the audience, I would warn him to watch it otherwise I would 'do a Fine Gael on him'.

That said, heckling was never a common occurrence at my gigs.

You would really want a neck like a jockey's bollocks to try to heckle me on stage. I was always prepared for the idiots who tried though. I had a catalogue of one-liners to throw back at them – though if they were particularly nasty, I would hand them the microphone, tell them to stand up on stage and carry the rest of the show as I suddenly fancied the night off. I would then leave them standing there in the spotlight with 800 people looking back at them.

Men or women, I would tear them asunder. Funnily enough, it was always the upmarket people that would try it. Drink would fuel their sudden burst of comedic confidence and they would become arrogantly convinced that they, in their role as speechmaker of the local rugby club or golf 'clab', could show me how to do my job. They always think they have better jokes but once they are thrown to the centre stage, you will never see a mouth close faster.

Nay-nay

On 24 August 1993, Beaufort House became the epicentre of a cleaning frenzy. Unbeknownst to myself at the time, I was in nesting mode, preparing for the arrival of Agnew number two. With every nook and cranny sparkling, I still refused to go to bed until I had also cleaned every glass chandelier in the house. Just as I was polishing the one in our bedroom, however, I suddenly felt a grip of excruciating pain.

Baby Agnew, it seems, had decided the chandeliers could wait!

On this occasion, I was fortunate in that I made it to the delivery room in time to be given an epidural. This really reduced the pain and made the whole experience far more enjoyable, although I don't think I will ever forget the moment my poor doctor, Peter Boylan, the then Master of Holles Street, walked in, only to be greeted by the sight of my two legs up in stirrups! I was so embarrassed that all I could do was joke, 'Well, talk about looking up an old friend!'

That prompted a few hysterics and, as a result, our little girl was born to the sound of laughter and jovial banter. When she arrived, she was exquisitely beautiful; there literally wasn't a mark on her. David and I hadn't decided on one particular name as we felt we would have to *see* the baby first before we could be sure if the name fit. The list of potentials included Portia, Poppy, Daniella and Phoebe, however, the moment we saw her, we knew immediately she was a Naomi! I later heard that my mother-in-law, bless her, had apparently stormed heaven with prayers that I wouldn't have a boy for fear that I would call him Tarquin, a Scottish name I have always loved. Breffni Agnew was another potential name we had considered if our arrival had turned out to be a boy.

My two pregnancies couldn't have been more different. When I was carrying Chloë, I felt like I had butterflies in my stomach; Naomi kicked with enough vigour to rival a footballer. In fact, one night, I could actually see the outline of her tiny heel move right across my stomach. To this day, David still maintains that it was the most incredible sight he has ever witnessed.

I completely embraced motherhood and relished all the responsibilities that accompanied it, so much so, that my only big regret is that I left it so late. I genuinely would have loved a family of five or six girls. For so long, however, I had mistakenly assumed kids were not for me. Years before being pregnant with Chloë, I had suffered an ectopic pregnancy, one that nearly killed me. When I look back on that experience now, it makes me realise how lucky I am to be a mother. In fact, whenever I am asked about my proudest achievement in life, I don't think of the awards, the stage, or the television shows, I think of the two beautiful girls David and I created.

On holiday in Tunisia. Don't ask me how but, when this photograph was taken, I knew I had become pregnant just days earlier.

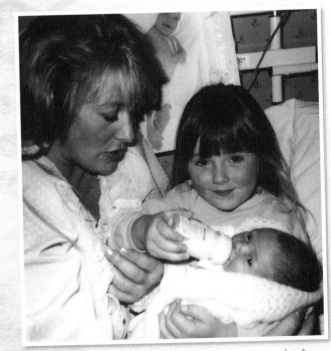

The new big sister doting over the new arrival!

Chloë

Hat queen to this day! Photographed while filming **Bon Voyage** for RTÉ in Naples.

Her first time in front of a microphone! With Dad in the Orchestral Booth for **Cats** at the Point Depot.

Lil' tomboy.

Practising her ballet in nappies.

Naomi

Some things never change (although the phone book has long since been replaced with Facebook)!

We always knew Naomi was going to be a class act when she would constantly hang her soother from her string of pearls.

My little ballet princess.

This shot is **SO** Naomi. She had a thorn in her little foot.

Romance and memories

On Butterfield Avenue in Rathfarnham, there sits a derelict house hidden behind cast-iron gates and surrounded by trees. Where once there were beautiful rose gardens and manicured green lawns, there are now overgrown weeds, strewn timber pallets and building blocks. Large boards cover the once-stunning old windows and doors, while discarded rubbish smears the entrance. On the wall beside the black gates sits a wind-beaten circular plaque that reads 'Beaufort House', probably the only remaining indication that the run-down building inside was actually once a much-loved home. Now very much a shadow of its former beauty, not to mention being further vandalised recently by fire, it's almost impossible for me to look at that house without breaking down in tears.

Shortly after I moved in, I received a welcome to your new home letter from Nuala Fennell, who informed me that her husband was raised in that house and they had very happy memories there. However, when I was a child, it was owned by John O'Donoghue and his wife, Meg Boucher Hayes, a champion rose grower. John also owned the surrounding orchard grounds on which he built a pub, aptly called the Old Orchard Inn. After John died in 1990, the house was placed on the market. At the time, David and I were living with my parents. While we had been looking at various properties, we didn't want to rush into buying anything as I had been securing quite a lot of work abroad. I had just given birth to Chloë and like any first-time mother, was walking around with her as though she were the best thing since the arrival of Jesus himself. I was always at my happiest when out walking the pram and showing off my newborn to anyone who asked!

One beautiful June morning, as I was walking up Butterfield Avenue, the heavens opened and rain began bucketing down. Naturally, I ran like the clappers, hoping to find some shelter along the way. John and Meg's daughter, Mairéad, who was maintaining the grounds while a buyer was being sought, was out pulling weeds when she spotted me mid-sprint with the buggy in tow. She and I had been great friends since childhood, having met through our mutual love of horses, so immediately she called me over and invited me inside until the shower had passed. As I stepped into the large square lobby of the house, I was dumbstruck. I had actually forgotten what a wonderful house it was. To me, it was the epitome of old world domestic grandeur.

While Mairéad doted on Chloë, I wandered the house, imagining how I could transform each room. When she told me the asking price was £200,000, I remember laughing in astonishment and saying, 'Sure you can get a nice semi-detached house for £45,000! Who on earth would have £200,000 to spend on a house?'

A month later, I read in the property section of a newspaper that an offer of £185,000 had been rejected. It played on my mind and that evening, as David and I were chatting about the house, I suddenly suggested that we put a bid in for it.

'And what bank in Monte Carlo are we robbing to pay for it?' came the enthusiastic reply.

David couldn't see it happening, but I remained undeterred, convinced we could negotiate a good deal. When I broached the idea to our solicitor, Elio Malocco, he assured me he would talk them down in price. After making a few enquiries, Elio then told me to collect whatever outstanding fees were owed to me because he knew a man in the building society who was a big fan of mine. He explained it was likely that the man would give us the loan primarily because it was an amazing property with colossal potential. Elio was young, but boy was he sharp. I *even* remember him telling me that something was about to happen with the property market and that if we could secure the house for the right price, we could be on the first step to having a really good home for the rest of our lives. We were within a hair's breadth of finalising the deal when a British man stepped into the equation and offered the O'Donoghue family £160,000. Elio immediately recognised the man's name and ran a search on him, discovering that he was a criminal who had been involved in umpteen squalid deals. When the O'Donoghues heard this, they realised they would never get their money from him and, consequently, the deal fell through. As soon as word of the botched deal filtered through, Elio was on the phone to me.

He explained that if we could get a £30,000 deposit, we would officially own the house of our dreams. In the end, we bought the house for £130,000. Our friends were close to calling in a psychiatrist to speak with us as they thought it was a mental amount to pay for a house. Today, you would be lucky to even buy a shed for that, but back then it was huge money. Our investment paid off and, within ten years, the house was worth over a million.

The man who owned Beaufort House before John O'Donoghue had built another house on the grounds for his Rolls Royce. Not a garage, but an actual little house! In order to help us fund the purchase of Beaufort, my parents had sold their home on Anne Devlin Road and moved into the 'Rolls Royce house', as it became affectionately known, which we had beautifully transformed into a fully furnished cottage for them. It was the perfect situation because they loved being so close to their grandchildren while at the same time maintaining their independence. The beauty about Beaufort was that it was structurally sound. All it required was an interior makeover, which was 100% my forte.

For me, the strength of the finished job could have been measured by the number of publications that requested photoshoots in the house. The place looked really incredible at that point, which is probably why it's so difficult for me to see it in such a dilapidated state today.

In the midst of the refurbishment work, two opportunistic gurriers broke through the fence one night and tried to smash down the back door with a crowbar. They were obviously aware that the house was empty and so figured they would make off with whatever they could find inside.

Following that incident, Gardaí advised us to maintain a presence on the property at night until the building work was complete and so David and I decided to place a mattress on the sitting room floor while Chloë slept beside us in her travel cot. We would often get a takeaway meal from the village and sit on the floor laughing and chatting. With only one working plug socket, there were candles everywhere and even though we had very little money at that point, those times were some of the happiest of my life. Back then our relationship appeared to have all the elements of a Nicholas Sparks' novel.

Sadly, however, the one acid drop that now mars the beauty of all those memories is knowing that David had another secret life at the time.

❖

Beaufort House has always had a bigger place in Naomi's heart than in Chloë's. When Chloë was a young child, she went through a phase where she would not go past the first landing because the 'big black wolf was there'.

Around the time this was taking place, David was going through a period when he wore nothing but black clothes. Some evenings, he would arrive home and be all smiles, but yet a few minutes later, he would emerge from the room looking like the devil incarnate. It was like looking at a completely different person. His face would be white, his eyes black, and his lips no more than a thin black line. He would also be in the most atrocious mood, screaming at the kids as well as myself. We came to know this 'look' and as soon as we saw it, I would instruct the girls to go up to their bedroom. I too would leave the room because he would be like an anti-Christ.

While Naomi was too young to understand what was going on, Chloë was terrified that David would come home with his 'evil face'. Some nights she would even try to peep out around the door to see if he was 'normal dad'.

If David was having a particularly bad episode, I would put the girls in the jeep and drive to the shops, anything to pass an hour. He would genuinely look like someone possessed. The episode itself could last anything from five minutes to two hours. Once it was over, everything about David would completely return to normal. The black would disappear from his eyes, and his face would resume its natural complexion. He would remember everything he had said and the way he had behaved, but he would always put it down to just being in a bad mood or a stressful day at work. Frankly, the physical differences in his face were far too frighteningly dramatic to just be a symptom of stress.

On other occasions, he would put it down to being a coeliac – my jury is still out on that one. It was as though something would build up inside him until he snapped. In fact, when I look back, I realise it all started around the time he began lying for a living. The more pressure he was under to maintain a façade, the more frequently it happened.

29th Sept. 1993
I have never thought too much about my marriage vows over the years. Mistakes have been made and I'm sure more pain and hurt to be inflicted. After 10 years however I would say "I do" again, without hesitation. Thank you for being there.

After presents like Chloë and Naomi who would want more?

... love you!
Happy Anniversary

Happy Anniversary.
Adèle
I love you always.
David xxx

The second coming of Jesus

When I was giving birth to Chloë and later Naomi, the arrival of flowers into my hospital room were almost as regular as my contractions. They came from all corners of the country – just the most beautiful gestures of goodwill. At one point, my room would have easily put the Chelsea Flower Show to shame. I received so many beautiful bouquets that I donated a substantial bulk of them to several churches and hospital wards. Even after having done that we were still left with hundreds.

Women from the Aran Islands sent me hand-made booties; an ICA guild, who specialised in lace, created bonnets; while many more women sent me the most exquisite crocheted clothes, including Mike Murphy's then-wife, the lovely Eileen, and a lovely Rathfarnham woman called Celcie Deveraux. Every single item I received, I still treasure to this day. These were extraordinarily warm gestures that left me deeply touched. As a result of the media coverage, there wasn't one person in Ireland who didn't know I was 'in the family way'. In fact, when the media first heard I was pregnant, a witty journalist once wrote that the child was 'more awaited than the second coming of Jesus'.

One magnificent bouquet of flowers that arrived into my room was accompanied by a card that read: 'Congratulations on your new baby. You'd want to hurry up though, we need two of them by Christmas as we're doing *Babes in the Wood*! Love, all your colleagues in the Gaiety Theatre.'

I laughed it off thinking it was a joke, however I wasn't a week out of hospital when I received a call from Aileen Connor asking to meet me to discuss the panto. Eleven days after giving birth, I was back on the set of *Play the Game*, so I arranged to meet her in the RTÉ canteen. She explained that she was putting in a proposition to do a whole new revamp of the panto and that she wanted my name for the top of the bill. I was only after having Chloë, so the idea of leaping around a rehearsal stage come September was not very realistic or appealing.

I also wasn't interested in participating unless drastic changes were made, simply because there was just so much wrong with it.

The previous January I had been flying back from London when one of the air hostesses began chatting to me about the panto. During the conversation, she mentioned, to my shock, that the show was finishing up that very night. Immediately, I knew it wasn't going well because, in those days pantos always ran until mid-February. When I left the airport, I took a cab straight to the Gaiety to catch the final show. Arriving a little early, I had my choice of seats and considering that frequent toilet trips are one of the delights that accompanies pregnancy, I chose a seat at the edge of the row near the bathrooms. I assumed the row would be full and so didn't want to disturb guests by constantly running in and out. The show was scheduled to start at eight o'clock, but by quarter to eight, there was no one to be seen. At five to eight, the director Mavis Ascot arrived in. During our chat, she asked if she could meet me afterwards to hear my opinion of the show. 'You don't have to be polite,' she added.

Now things are bad when on closing night of the panto, the crowd is minimal at best – however things are really, really bad when the panto director tells you that 'you don't have to be polite' in your analysis of it.

Sure enough, the actors arrived out on stage wearing utter tat for costumes. It was very obviously bought-in stock, the kind I wouldn't even put on my dogs for Hallowe'en. The show also lacked a decent script and the jokes were too adult. There were far too many 'toilet songs'… a term used to describe a boring element of the show that causes the kids to look for other distractions, usually a request for the toilet. I find kids only ever realise they have a bladder when they're bored. I kept my word and outlined for Mavis everything that I thought was wrong with it.

That was January, now here I was five months later facing the prospect of performing on that same stage. I think the Gaiety team were hoping that I would do for their panto what I had done for the one in the Olympia.

A few years earlier, Gerry Sinnott had phoned me and asked if I would rejuvenate their pantomime, which was really waning at the time.

I agreed, but only on the grounds that I could pick the people to be involved. I brought in talents such as Brian Merriman as director, Andy O'Callaghan as musical director, Des Keogh as the voiceover not to mention the brilliant Belinda Murphy as choreographer and the crème de la crème of dancers. As part of the show, we had to perform the full routine of Michael Jackson's 'Thriller'. I will never forget learning that routine in rehearsal. It was so unbelievably difficult, truly brain-damaging stuff. My personal choreographer for that show, Joyce Richardson, taught me how to moonwalk across the stage which really delighted the kids. In the end, I devised a whole new jaw-droppingly amazing production of *Cinderella* and, if I'm not mistaken, it was one of the biggest theatre hits in the venue's history. You could not get a seat for love nor money. Testament to this were the queues down the street at 9.45 in the morning looking for cancellation tickets. The following

year, we performed *Aladdin* which was another blockbuster.

The Gaiety and the Olympia had earned the nicknames 'fur coat' and 'rain mac'. The Gaiety, which is on King Street, was always known for its audience of 'fur coats', while the Olympia on Dame Street, was known as the 'rain mac' theatre. For the first time ever, all the fur coats were queuing up alongside the rain macs for tickets in the Olympia, thus prompting a newspaper to run with the clever headline 'Adèle King, the Queen of King Street now becomes the Dame of Dame Street'.

After two years, Gerry was still more than eager for me to continue, but I didn't want to become the resident panto queen and, anyhow, at that point, Turkey was beckoning once again.

Despite having just given birth, not to mention fulfilling other work commitments, I took on the Gaiety panto because I viewed it as a challenge, and if there is one thing I thrive on in life, it's a challenge.

Immediately, I set about enlisting the best in the business and work on the production began swiftly. When I arrived into the Gaiety Theatre following weeks of rehearsal, however, I remember feeling distinctly uncomfortable. The general modus operandi was still very much to the tune of Maureen Potter. Even though everyone had accepted that Maureen would no longer be gracing the stage boards of the Gaiety, staff were continuing to do things 'the Maureen way'. I remember thinking that if I'd heard the words 'Maureen did it this way' one more time, I was going to crack. It caused a great deal of pressure for me and I genuinely couldn't cope with the constant comparison. By that point, I had worked in theatres all over the world and was doing things my way but even though Maureen wasn't there any more, I still detected an air of 'the old way is the right way'.

My stress levels were not helped when people on the street would approach me and say, 'Oh you're the next Maureen Potter'.

Even though it was highly flattering, I never wanted to be the *next* anyone, I wanted to be the first Adèle King. Maureen was gifted, but she never had a 'let's do it this way' approach.

Instead, her husband Jack, who was also her scriptwriter, became her voice. That said, she was most definitely the greatest female entertainer of her time and like everyone else who met her, I adored her. The last time I saw her was when we both judged the Docklands talent competition in the National Concert Hall. Three days earlier, she had appeared on *The Late Late Show* for the very last time.

With Maureen Potter just days before she sadly passed away.

I received this beautiful letter from Maureen and her husband Jack in 1993.

Cuffe, Boardman, Claspy and Walsh

The Cuffe, Boardman, Claspy and Walsh women were a huge part of my life. They were genius women who worked behind the scenes in theatre and frankly, never got enough credit for their amazing work. Some nights they found themselves comforting and encouraging a broken-hearted woman (me), other nights they were holding a sick bucket for an expectant mum (also me!).

I had also grown up in the theatre with these women. In fact, when I was a kid, Annie Cuffe was the chief costumier while her daughter Sadie was her up-and-coming protégée. Annie and Sadie were the personification of brilliance; they just didn't know how to make something that was anything less than show-stopping. The grand finale costume was always the one that drew the biggest gasps of admiration from the audience. Of all the finale gowns I have worn, I think my favourite was the massive black and gold ball gown by Sadie & Co which was paired with an equally extravagant feather hat made by the gifted milliner, Marie Claspy.

Whenever I was doing a show, I would always lose my appetite. Always. In fact some of my lasting memories of theatre are of Sadie Cuffe and my dresser Frances Boardman fussing over me like two mother hens begging me to eat some toast before then checking the bins to make sure I hadn't dumped the last slice.

'Oh here's the start of it!' was Sadie's famous line when she would notice me getting thinner. She would always have to take in the costumes in order for them to fit me and by the final two weeks, she would usually have to re-cut them completely because I would always be half the width I had been when I'd started the show.

When I was pregnant and suffering from terrible morning sickness, Sadie and Frances always made sure a bucket was kept by the side of the stage. I remember when I was three months' pregnant with Naomi, I had to perform in morning matinées. Part of my role involved scaling a bockety little backstage staircase – a million years old – that ran right up into the roof of the building. Situated nearby was the Eastern Tandoori restaurant, an eatery I normally adored, but when its 9.30 in the morning and they're cleaning out their kitchen, you can probably understand its lack of appeal in the eyes of a nauseous pregnant woman, particularly one who has to abseil down over a theatre full of children firing out sweets. In fact, the next time you're in the Gaiety Theatre, look up at the beautiful chandelier that had to be removed to accommodate my flight!

Is it any wonder I lost my appetite?

On one occasion in recent years, I arrived into the theatre each morning with a peripheral cannula in my arm after having spent my nights in the Blackrock Clinic. As Frances helped me into my costume, the sleeve would inevitably rub against the cannula thus inciting the most agonising pain. To get through it, I would stand there shouting, 'Fuck, fuck, fuck, fuck!'

Even my dancers were warned not to grab me by the arm where the cannula was placed. I was so sick with my asthma at the time that I was practically living in the hospital. In fact after the show each night, I would go to bed in the Blackrock Clinic. Paul McGuinness (yes, he of U2-manager fame) was my wonderful chauffeur. As a gesture of gratitude for bringing his beautiful wife, Kathy, and their children, Max and Alexandra, on a backstage tour of the theatre, Paul insisted on chauffeuring me to the hospital. He was at the stage door every night for nearly two weeks ready

About to step on stage in one of Synan O'Mahony's beautiful designs.

One of Sadie Cuffe's many amazing creations.

and waiting to bring me to the Blackrock Clinic. He was such a sweet gentleman.

❖

In theatre, most actresses, particularly the leads, are very demanding when it comes to their costumes, however Sadie's great line about my attitude towards my wardrobe was, 'She would trust me'.

She was right. I always trusted her choices because I knew that when the time came for me to wear the costume, it would be absolute perfection.

Sadie also exhibited the most amazing craftsmanship when creating boned corsets. In all my years of theatre, I honestly never met anyone so skilled in the craft, until that is, a young man by the name of Synan O'Mahony came along.

Even though Synan was new to the theatre, he had the remarkable talent and creativity of someone with lifelong costuming experience. Rich opulent fabric, silk bodices and layered tulles, it really was the highest standard of costume-making in all its theatrical glory. Needless to say, I also loved taking to the stage in *his* exquisite pieces.

When people chat to me today about the pantos they saw me perform in, they will almost always comment on the costumes I wore. In fact, anyone who saw me play the fairy godmother in the Olympia production of *Cinderella* will definitely remember the show-stopping costume of the night.

For one particular scene, we had decided that I would talk to Cinderella as a little hunched-up old lady dressed in a small black cloak before suddenly transforming into a fairy godmother complete with the most exquisite gown. To carry this off however, we had to choose a dancer of similar height to me and dress her in the black cloak. She would then go on

I hate to squeal, but you're about to find out how one of the most memorable panto tricks was pulled off!

stage and mime the words to my pre-recorded voice. The audience would be led to believe it was me on stage when, in fact, I was actually backstage changing at break-neck speed into an unbelievable, corseted gown with a massive white tulle skirt.

Following the line, 'Oh you shall go to the ball Cinderella', a massive plume of white smoke would shoot up accompanied by an array of flashing lights, thus allowing me sufficient time to change places with the dancer. Once the smoke had faded after a few seconds, the audience would then see me standing there looking every inch the fairy godmother. It really was a devastatingly clever piece of theatre and nobody could ever figure out how we had pulled it off, particularly considering that my dress was so gargantuan. Incidentally, the dress became known in theatre land as 'the dress that ate Dublin'! I remember the audience gasping at the sight of it. I couldn't even guess how many yards of tulle went into its creation but it was indescribably beautiful. To this day, people beg me to know how that illusion was done.

Well now you know – but please don't tell your kids under ten this. Let's keep it magic for the little ones!

1. The magnificent finale in the Olympia Theatre.

2. Wearing my all-time favourite colour – white, another fabulous Sadie Cuffe design.

3. Oh that dress and that hat! Myself with Chloë, Niall O'Brien and Lisa Lambe.

4. One of the most popular costumes I have ever worn the famous, Liquorice Allsorts costume!

5. Love that hat!

6. & 7. Two more of Sadie and her team's super sweet panto costumes.

8.

10.

ROCKINSON CRUSOE '97 — GO ON YA GOOD THING!!

9.

8. Barney, Gerry Ryan, myself and a cast of millions in the **Sleeping Beauty (sort of)** at the Point Theatre.

9. With Dustin in 1997.

10. As Buttons in **Cinderella** at the Olympia Theatre.

11. All the puff sleeves and pantaloon dresses couldn't hide the skeletal frame underneath, and to think I was worried about being too thin ... ha!

That's entertainment

'Em ... I'm in doing the final edits of a show called *That's Entertainment* ... and we've been advised by our lawyers to clear something with you before the show goes on air. On the show, Gerry Ryan ... well ... he calls you Hitler ... and he says that you ran *Play the Game* like the Gestapo ...'

While Deborah Tudge the producer of *That's Entertainment* was telling me this, I was roaring laughing. In fact, I think she was shocked when I told her that Gerry was absolutely right in what he had said. I really did run a tight ship, but then that's why my team was so successful. As most people will remember, Ronan Collins presented the show, while I captained the ladies' team, and subsequent to the departure of my beloved lifelong friend Brendan Grace for greener grass in America, Derek Davis took over as captain of the men's team.

I would always crack the whip with the ladies' team because I genuinely didn't want them to embarrass themselves on television or end up looking like bimbos with sweet Fanny Adams between their ears. As a result, I invested a lot of time in training the girls and making sure they were familiar with the kind of topics that were likely to come up. Of course, there were always the few titles you could never prepare for. I will never forget the night I had to mime *Observe the Sons of Ulster Marching Towards the Somme*, a play by Frank McGuinness. Another equally memorable title I had to mime was that of the song, 'Miss Otis Regrets She's Unable to Lunch Today'.

Some days I was blessed with brainy participants; other days, I wasn't quite so lucky. But regardless of the level of intellect that was seated on the couch beside me, I was determined that no one would look bad or come across as being dumb.

To ensure that we were all more than well-prepared, I would look up the film titles that were on release, books that had won the Pulitzer Prize, people and events that were making the news, all the topics that I felt that the compiler was likely to put on the cards for the show. I would then put the ladies through their paces and make sure they had learned all the miming symbols to perfection.

During the afternoon, I would often hear, 'Aw, Twink, you're awful hard on us'. Following the show each week, however, these same women would come up to me and admit that while they had previously thought I was a slave-driving taskmaster, they were now incredibly grateful for all the techniques I had made them learn.

Contestants always found that when the cameras rolled, everything they had learned would suddenly click into place. I would also receive the most beautiful cards and letters from past participants thanking me for the effort I had invested in them prior to their appearance. This training meant we became quite successful. In fact, the ladies' team ended up winning so many times that the viewers began to write in, complaining that the show was quite obviously rigged in our favour. It didn't help matters that Derek would often shout 'fix' or 'partiality', or on other occasions, voice his belief that we were being given easier titles to mime. (Although I think it's safe to say *Observe the Sons of Ulster* … proved otherwise!)

There was not even a slight chance of the competition being fixed, simply because the production team were very strict with the cards on which the titles were printed. Each pack was sealed and only given to Ronan Collins when the opening credits were rolling. Not once in my ten years on the show did I *ever* see the cards before we went on air.

Another subject that inspired people to contact the show was my choice of fashion. I think at one point, I became synonymous with Lainey Keogh knitwear. The process of procuring clothes for the new season was relatively straightforward. I would be given a budget and if I spotted something while out shopping, the shop assistant would reserve the item until RTÉ collected it. On one particular quest for outfits, my mother and I were browsing in a shop in Dublin city

centre. Also in the shop at the time was another mother and daughter, who seemed to take more than a passing interest in the kind of clothes I was looking at. I swear I'm not exaggerating when I say they followed us around the shop, commenting loudly to each other on every little thing I picked up. One item I looked at was on the cheap-but-cheerful sale rail. Noticing this, the mother turned to her daughter and remarked, 'Jesus the money that one must be earning in RTÉ, and look at the rag she has in her hand?'

I had long learned the art of pretending not to hear such barbed comments, so I continued browsing nonchalantly, while the two continued following. On the designer rack, I noticed a most beautiful, albeit very expensive, Frank Usher dress paired with a little black sequin-detailed jacket. As I held it up against me, a familiar voice behind me observed, 'Now do you see what she's picking up? Well 'tis the fuckin' likes of them that would have the money to buy a Frank Usher dress!'

Within the space of ten minutes, they had gone from calling me a cheap bitch to a moneyed cow. They were the kind of begrudging individuals that were determined to find fault regardless.

On set with Brendan Grace and Ronan Collins.

To be honest, I don't think I could print the other comments they made! All I will say is that the two of them were like a double act with the bilious comments they were making – the bitch community's Morecambe and Wise, so to speak. My poor mother was shocked by the whole thing and, as we left the shop, she just shook her head and said, 'Well, love, you're damned if you do and you're damned if you don't!'

I never said anything to those two women that day, and while I'm sure the mother is long since pushing up the daisies (Jesus, I hope she is), I'm sure her equally bitchy daughter is alive and reading this.

I'm sure you remember who you are dear.

I certainly do!

❖

To this day, people still ask me why *Play the Game* was cancelled.

The honest truth is, I don't know. Would you believe that not one of RTÉ's higher powers even bothered to tell us that the show was being axed? About a month before we were due to begin filming the next series, Ronan Collins took me aside and asked if I had heard any rumours.

'Rumours of what?' I asked.

'Rumours that *Play the Game* isn't returning.'

'What? Are you serious? Did someone phone you?'

'No, but I think the big fella knows.'

Seconds later, as we are walking towards the television building, who drives up but the big fella himself, Derek Davis. I think he had been approached by Network 2 who wanted him to front a new late-night chat show. Seemingly, the bosses on *Play the Game* had told Derek that he would be able to press ahead with it because they

were axing the show. Ronan and I both knew by his behaviour that he was uncomfortable with the fact that he knew more about the situation than we did. From that day to this, RTÉ have still never officially told us why *Play the Game* was axed. Although, when they didn't have the manners to tell us it was ending in the first place, maybe a reason is asking for too much.

Ronan and I had to hear about it through the rumour mill and the newspapers; we didn't get so much as a phone call, not even a polite letter. I know everything has a shelf life, but *Play the Game* was not waning in popularity. It was the anchor show for *The Late Late Show* and for the ten years it was on air, it was always up there with the station's biggest rating winners. Ironically, I remember Moya Doherty predicting that RTÉ would turn into a facilities house.

What's more, she was absolutely right.

I had the pleasure of working with Ben Kingsley a number of years ago. We had both been hired to provide the voices for a religious cartoon The **Sign of the Fish** in which he voiced the role of Pontius Pilate and I was his wife. A very quiet and charming man, his acting was incredible, just so understated and natural.

I dunno, say a prayer or something!

One particular night, as David and I were chatting in the front room of Beaufort, I suddenly heard a very faint snore emanating from an area of the room behind David. I even noticed David flinching when it first started. The noise began to get slightly louder before travelling right down to the corner of the room. David's face was, as Paddy Cole would say, 'the colour of boiled shite'! By the time the noise had reached a different part of the room, it was a very loud snore.

It wasn't menacing, in fact I think I was more bemused by it than anything else. David on the other hand, not so much.

'Adèle, do something!'

'What the hell do you expect me to do?'

'I dunno, say a prayer or something!'

In my innocence, I stood up and said, 'In the name of the Father, the Son, and the Holy Ghost … if there's anyone there, you need to know that this is a house of the living, and if you're not of the living then we need you to pass on peacefully.'

As soon as I said it, the noise quietened down to a tiny whisper before disappearing completely. Immediately, David looked at me and said, 'If you tell me we bought a haunted house, I'm out of here. What the hell was that all about?'

I couldn't explain it either, until years later when I met Mairéad O'Donoghue out shopping. She had seen pictures of the house in the *Sunday Independent* and told me how much she loved what we had done with it. As we were chatting, I invited her up for a coffee to show her each room. As she stood at the door of the front room, she looked in at it with awe. Mairéad then explained that her father, towards the end of his life, wasn't able for the stairs and so had used the front room as his bedroom. In fact, it was in that very room that he had passed away. When she then pointed to the part of the room where her father's bed had been, I could have dropped with the shock. That was the exact area of the room where David and I had heard the snoring.

❖

While I never thought of Beaufort as haunted, there was certainly no shortage of ghostly incidents during our time there.

The snoring appeared to be a one-off, but there were other occurrences that were far more prominent.

One Sunday morning for instance, while Chloë and David were fast asleep, I brought the Sunday newspapers up to bed for a quiet read. As I was flicking through them, I began to hear the shuffling of teacups in the kitchen accompanied by the low mumbling of conversation. It was as though someone was serving tea to a number of people. Next, I heard the cries of a baby.

At first, I assumed the television had been left on, but then it occurred to me that it was probably a few friends of ours who had long been threatening to turn up some morning with a bottle of house-warming champagne. As I made my way downstairs, I could still very clearly hear ladies chatting and drinking tea, however the moment I reached the top of the landing, everything suddenly went silent. When I went into the kitchen, there was not a teacup nor a person in sight. I was beginning to question my sanity until David also heard it the following Sunday. It continued every Sunday morning at around

10.20 a.m. and it actually reached the point where David and I would be lying in bed just waiting for the chatter and tea serving to start. Whenever we went to go downstairs, all noise would abruptly stop the moment we reached the same spot on the landing. I often thought about waiting downstairs for it to start but when I broached the idea with David, he wasn't long informing me that I would be waiting on my own.

We often tried peering over the banister but we could never see anyone, all we could hear was the noise. The voices were always clearly audible as was the distinctive clinking of the teacups and the cries of the child. Even though there was nothing frightening about it, the whole episode was beginning to worry me slightly, so I turned to the family's resident priest, aka my cousin Hubert Condron, and asked him if he would carry out a blessing on the house. Whatever he did worked, because it was the last we heard of the phantom of the ten o'clock mass tea party.

Papa, can you hear me?

Sitting at home in Beaufort one night, the strangest feeling suddenly came over me. I don't know whether it was intuition or otherwise, but something was telling me I needed to be with my father.

He was in hospital at the time and when I arrived at his ward, he was slipping in and out of a consciousness. Sitting beside his bed, I poured my heart out to him, thanking him for all the chances he afforded me in life. I had been an expensive child to rear, particularly as my parents were not wealthy, but despite all

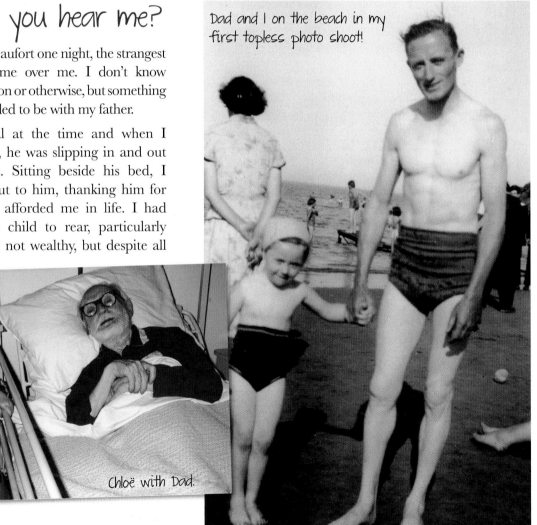

Dad and I on the beach in my first topless photo shoot!

Chloë with Dad.

my dance, music, elocution and sports lessons, neither he nor Mom ever once complained.

I sat with him for two hours and spoke to him about everything. I recalled my wedding day and how he was my prince charming escorting me up the aisle; I recalled the time he cried tears of pride when, in the national stadium, Donal Lunny asked me up on stage to perform two complicated guitar duets, Carolan's Concerto and Classical Gas. I also reminisced about the wonderful Christmases and birthdays we had shared. Dad was a fantastic carpenter and one Christmas, when I was quite small, he made me a beautiful desk with special compartments for my paints and pens. He had been up until five in the morning varnishing it and, of course, with varnish being anything but subtle, the house reeked. When I woke to see what presents Santa had left me, I found to my delight this beautiful desk. In a suspicious tone, I turned to Dad, who was trying his best not to laugh, and asked, 'How did Santa deliver this if the varnish is still wet?'

As I was recalling these stories for him, his eyelids flickered and his hands moved, as though he too was thinking back on all the memories. As I thanked him profusely for everything he had given me in life, I singled out the tennis racket which he bought for me by pawning his Christmas present. I had been participating in a major tennis tournament when my coach told me I needed a new racket. I didn't know it at the time but the firm that Dad worked for had just folded and the only way he could afford to buy me the new racket was to pawn the Christmas present of a snazzy electric razor my mother had given him. He never knew I had found out about it until I thanked him that night in the hospital. I kissed him a hundred times and told him a hundred more how much I loved him.

At around eight the next morning, the hospital phoned to tell me that dad was fading and that it would be good if I went in.

Panicking, I sped to the hospital, but when I arrived at his room, a cleaning woman greeted me.

'How'ya, Twink! Sorry to hear about your da, you must be very upset.'

'Why what's wrong?'

'Oh … eh sorry, did you not know he was dead?'

That's how the news of my father's death was broken to me, something the hospital later apologised profusely for. When I went into the room, he was laid out with a candle lit beside him. I can still remember the shock I felt when I saw him like that; nothing can prepare you for it.

The news of Dad's death devastated my mother. She never saw it coming because she truly hadn't realised how ill he was. Mom had been in such pain with her arthritis that she often joked to him that she would be the first to go. Mom actually went on to live for eight more years. They were both such fantastic parents, so much so, that I often questioned how on earth I got so lucky with the parents I was given.

My childhood memories were so good that when I became a mother myself, all I wanted was for my own children to experience the exact same sense of happiness, freedom, and yet discipline, my beloved parents had given me.

My beautiful Mama in her eighties.

Letters from the enemies

In the late 1990s, I fell extremely ill which resulted in me being hospitalised. As soon as I mentioned to the doctor that I had just been to Africa, he enlisted the assistance of consultants from the Department of Tropical Illnesses who, upon carrying out a battery of tests, informed me that I had E. coli.

Regardless of whether you are sick with a flu or a fever, the one thing you absolutely need is silence, as every little sound feels like a punch to head. Unfortunately, in the corridor outside my room each morning, there was one particular cleaning lady who would make so much noise that she probably could have woken the dead in the hospital morgue. She would shout everything out to her fellow cleaner who was further down the corridor. I heard all her troubles, what she'd bought when she'd been out shopping, her schedule for the week, the problems she'd had with her washing machine – Jesus, there was nothing the whole ward didn't know about her.

When she was hoovering, she would wallop the vacuum off every door and skirting board as she was making her way along. She would then barge into your room to empty your rubbish bin, all the while continuing her conversation very loudly with her friend outside in the corridor. This would all take place at around six o'clock every morning so, needless to say, it wasn't the most peaceful environment to wake up to particularly when you are violently ill.

I remember when I was eventually allowed out of my room, I went to the day room with a cup of coffee. While I was there, I got chatting to a lovely woman and, during the course of our conversation, she happened to mention that she had asked her husband to bring in her mail. One of the letters in the bundle was an ESB bill which, she laughed, almost gave her a bigger shock than the one she got from 'that wagon waking everyone up in the morning with banging the hoover and roaring'.

She too had found it so distressing when she was ill. The section we were in was for seriously ill patients, some of whom were facing the prospect of being there for quite some time. I just felt that considering how ill we all were, we could do without waking up to the sound of this inconsiderate 'wan' hollering at the top of her voice. Furthermore, a number of people in this particular area were genuinely in their final days and it just didn't seem right that they were being denied a peaceful passing. God, if I thought I was going to have to leave this world with the sound of that woman's voice in my ears, I think I would have probably taken the oul' bag with me.

When she still didn't quieten after a few days, I politely asked the matron if perhaps she could get her to tone it down a little. Sure enough, peace and quiet was soon restored. The day I was leaving the hospital, however, a badly written note was slipped in under my room door, rather charmingly addressed to 'Scab'.

It was a vitriolic letter about how I was a stuck-up bitch who got people into trouble. Any time I appeared on television after that, I would receive another vicious letter with the same distinctive handwriting. Fourteen years on and she is still writing to tell me how much she hopes I will die alone. It's nothing more than verbal vomit in an envelope. In fact, I know her dreadful penmanship so well at this stage that I don't even bothering opening the envelope; I just throw it straight in the bin.

My father used to say, 'My darling daughter, when they have *you* nailed up on the cross, they're giving someone else a break down off it.'

So maybe by writing to me, she is giving some other poor soul a break.

❖

There was another man who actually went one step further and followed me for years. I always got the impression that he had been a literary intellect back in his day, because you could clearly see strong traces of academic genius in his writings. Sadly, it seemed as though his mind had completely derailed at some point during his life. When he first started writing to me, I was in my twenties and he was in his fifties.

He would write to me religiously when I was doing my Saturday morning radio show, his deranged letters and postcards like those of an eccentric professor. His letters would often begin with something like 'as I was reading Shakespeare today, I saw you within the lines', before then progressing into reams of gobbledygook.

When he realised I wasn't going to write back, he began arriving at the stage door of the Gaiety, demanding to see me. One night, he even brought with him a pile of books and slept on them outside the stage door, waiting for me to leave. He then began waiting for me in the car park of RTÉ after my radio show. Whenever he was there, my wonderful producer and dear friend Kevin Hough would drive my car out to the front door for me so that I wouldn't have to walk through the car park on my own.

People encouraged me to report him, but I brushed it off as the infatuation of a harmless aul' soul. Unfortunately, however, there's no such thing as harmless when you start ignoring them. Sure enough, the cards suddenly began to take a

nasty turn and it got to a point where I became quite fearful. Everywhere I went, I would find myself automatically looking around to see if he was nearby. He would write to me demanding to know why I was not paying him any attention and not long after that, the stereotypical stalker lines began to surface.

'Why are you ignoring me? You know you need my advice', or 'Why are you doing this? You shouldn't be allowing these morons to interfere with our wavelengths!'

On another occasion, he wrote: 'You know you and I are intellectually joined. When you broadcast your radio show, there is a special wavelength between your brain and mine. I'm picking up on all those things you don't say to the listeners but I know you're saying them to me. I hear your hidden signals and messages. The air is carrying your wavelengths from RTÉ into my brain.'

Unfortunately, the air around RTÉ must have been strong enough to have carried him to Rathfarnham, because when I opened the door of Beaufort House one morning, I found him asleep on my front doorstep. As always, he had a stack of books as his pillow and was lying underneath a check blanket. Fortunately, I managed to close the door before he jumped up. At that point, I had no other choice but to call the Gardaí. It clearly didn't deter him though, because he turned up at the Gaiety two nights later. Up until around five years ago, he was continuing to send me cards.

I never knew his name, but I have often wondered if he was the strange man I encountered during the latter days of Maxi Dick and Twink. We were very popular interviewees in the Irish media back then and so I didn't take any notice when, one day, I received a phone call from a man who claimed to be a journalist from *The Irish Times*. The interview he wanted to conduct was not taking place in a coffee shop or in an office but rather in a house near the Grand Canal. Testament to my naivety was the fact that I didn't even so much as question it. I arrived at the address ready for the interview when this head case opened the door. The moment I stepped inside, he immediately put the chain on the door and clicked the lock. The first thing that hit me was the strong musty smell throughout the house. He smelled too, having clearly not washed in a long time. Escorting me into a small sitting room, he ordered me to sit down. The room itself was the weirdest sight I have ever seen. It was stacked high with what looked like thousands of books. When I asked about the intended nature of the article, he just replied, 'Oh, you'll find out'.

There was absolutely no fucking way I was hanging around to find out. Calmly, I asked if I could have a cup of tea. Once he was in the kitchen, I ran to the front door and tried to quietly open the lock without arousing suspicion, before then running for my life until I found a cab to take me home.

When I told my parents about it, my father quite rightly hauled me over the coals for being so stupid in the first place. I still can't believe the depths of my breezy naivety whenever I think back on that day, although, to be fair, Ireland was a very different place then to what it is now. I was sixteen years old at the time, and as most readers will remember, sixteen-year-old girls back then were not particularly wise to the ways of men with hidden agendas, primarily because we never needed to be. I have never forgotten the sight of those books piled high in his living room and have often wondered if he was the same man who stalked me all those years later.

Now that Chloë is in Celtic Woman, she too is going through a similar experience albeit on a much grander scale. The band have a stream of burly bodyguards, with each girl assigned her own one. Celtic Woman is currently the biggest touring concert show in America, Japan, Australia, China and Europe so personal security is not so much a luxury but rather a very real necessity. While the group has millions of beautiful loyal fans, there are always the few who take it a step too far.

It wouldn't be unusual for me to receive letters addressed to just: '*Twink, Ireland*', demanding to know why Chloë hadn't replied to all the letters they had sent her.

On one occasion some years back, Celtic Woman were performing in the Wang Theatre in Boston. During the interval, the lovely American couple sitting next to Naomi and me noticed our accents and asked if we were 'genuine Irish'. When I replied we were from Dublin, the woman exclaimed, 'Oh, my God! Don't you just love Celtic Woman? Aren't they just the greatest group in the world? We have never missed a show yet!'

Her husband intervened at this point and said, 'Chloë's our favourite! We just adore her. We would walk on hot coals just to hear her sing.'

When I said I would pass on their sweet comments to the girls, they both looked at me in shock.

'You know them? Like you actually know them to talk to?'

'Well I should! Chloë's my daughter.'

'Oh, my God, you're Twink! Every Christmas we watch the show you did with Perry Como. Oh, my God! I can't believe we're meeting Chloë's mom!'

Within seconds, they were kissing and hugging Naomi and me, almost trembling by the prospect of meeting someone with a connection to the group. They seemed so genuinely nice that when they asked if it would be possible to meet the girls afterwards, I agreed to bring them backstage with us. They nearly lost their minds with excitement.

When I brought them to the stage door, however, Maggie Seidel, the tour director, took one look at them and shot me a glare. If I thought Maggie's look was bad, then Mother Mary of God you should have seen the look Chloë gave me when I walked in with them. The term 'if looks could kill' springs rapidly to mind.

It turns out the couple were well-known obsessive stalkers of the group who would adopt any ruse to get backstage. They had also sent poison pen letters to the girls over things like not being invited to a 'meet and greet' following a show. They were actually so bad that they were on a blacklist. Talk about feeling like a right thick! You'd have thought I'd have learned from my own stalker experiences.

My other great gaff occurred not long after the Chloë Agnew fan forum had been set up. While reading their lovely messages in the kitchen one

night, I decided to thank them for their heart-warming comments about my beloved girl. The response went something like this:

'You're sitting in your kitchen in Ireland? How cute! Where is this kitchen, dear? Chicago?'

'Do you know how many people have come on here pretending to be Chloë's mom? Ugh, get lost!'

Then they began talking amongst each other:

'Did you read the asshole that's online pretending to be Chloë's mother? Hahaha! As if!'

Boy, they got it wrong that night!

An entrepreneur with an adventurous spirit

Elio Malocco.

Witty, undeniably.

Charming, undoubtedly.

Menacing, unfortunately.

For all his handsome looks and charm, Elio was not a metaphorical god on Mount Olympus, but rather an ordinary person whose imperfections had serious consequences. That said, I think I was probably a little bit in love with him. I certainly fancied him, every woman who met him did because, frankly, it was impossible not

to. Elio was dangerously good looking, a great *bon viveur*, not to mention a witty raconteur to boot. There wasn't a story he couldn't tell that wouldn't have you enthralled.

When telling a joke, he had the humour and timing of a professional comedian and could take off any accent brilliantly. All I knew of his background was that he hailed from Irish-Italian stock. Funnily enough, I always found him to be extremely cagey when addressing that part of his life, although I do remember one night at dinner when he regaled us with the memory of how he used to tell his friends in Trinity that his father was in the oil business. They were all wildly impressed but never enquired far enough to find out that the oil he was referring to was in a chip-pan. His father ran a chipper in Drogheda!

It reminded me of when David Agnew would tell his friends at school that his father was an astronaut, although why none of them questioned why an astronaut was living in Santry I'll never understand!

❖

I first met Elio through a young accountant I knew at the time called Pat Finn, Dermot Morgan's best friend. He told me that a very good friend of his was a real up-and-coming, hot-shot solicitor and would be well worth hiring. He wasn't wrong; Elio's career was undeniably on the rise. He was so sharp and incisive that to have him on your side in a dispute would practically guarantee you results in your favour. Absolutely everything about him was high-flying and suave. He lived in a stunning mansion in Foxrock with his wife Jane, granddaughter of Eamon de Valera, and their beautiful son, David (better known as Doco).

Elio wore only the most impeccable suits wherever he went, all designer right down to the polished shoes and the gold Rolex. Even his legal offices in Chatham Street looked like something out of *Dallas*.

One evening, however, a chance encounter with a friend led to me looking at Elio's success from a different perspective. After leaving his office, I nipped over to Sawyer's fish shop where I picked up some black sole for dinner. As I was paying for the fish, I heard the familiar voice of my then bank manager Brendan Kearney behind me. He was also a good friend of mine so we chatted away for a while. Just as I happened to mention that I had been at my solicitor's office, out walked Elio who gave us a quick wave before taking off in his Mercedes. The conversation that followed is one I will never forget.

'How old is he, Adèle?'

'Ah … I don't know, in his twenties or something.'

'Must be a very big practice!'

'Not big, but it's certainly busy.'

'Well, it must be very busy for suits and a car like that. Be careful, dear. When I see young fellas with a lifestyle like that, I always feel they have their hand in my back pocket and I'm paying for it. Just be careful.'

Elio, Jane and Doco enjoying Chloë's first birthday in the RTÉ crèche.

God Almighty, Brendan, when I think of those words now!

A few weeks later, David and I went to Elio's office to pick up a number of documents. We had tried to phone him several times, but he wasn't answering his phone or returning calls. When we arrived, we were met by his secretary Teresa who looked utterly distraught. She told us that a number of people from the Law Society had been to the office demanding to see the books. The poor woman couldn't contact Elio and didn't even know where he was.

The following day, I was in the kitchen when a slightly panicky David called me into the living room where the *Six One News* was on. Just as I entered the room, I caught sight of Elio being escorted away in handcuffs. He had been charged with forty-nine offences, including fraud and larceny. I couldn't take it in. It was just too hard to believe that Elio was capable of *any* crime. To try to make sense of the situation, we drove out to his house the following day in the hope of speaking with his wife, Jane.

When we arrived at the gates, however, there was no response so I decided to leave a note. With not a pen to be found in the jeep, I improvised by using an eyeliner pencil and lipstick. My note read: 'Elio, no matter what's wrong or what has happened, you have friends in us and we love you. Please don't be a stranger and just phone us. Everything can be sorted out, I'm sure it's all a misunderstanding. We're here if you need someone to talk to.'

Little did we know at the time that we ourselves had been one of his main targets.

In the months leading up to Elio's arrest in 1993, we had been experiencing problems with the building society and the financial dealings regarding the sale of my parents' house on Anne Devlin Road. Irish Permanent were threatening to sue us because they had never received the mortgage money from the sale. As far as we were concerned, however, the money had been paid, so we wracked our brains trying to figure out the source of the mix up. In the end, we concluded that it must have been an administrative error, there was just no other valid explanation we could think of.

It later emerged that the funds from the sale had never gone anywhere near the building society. The Fraud Squad produced for us a bank chit from the Bank of Ireland in Westmoreland Street where the money had basically come in one side and gone out the other to some apartment block in Spain. These weren't the only funds Elio had forwarded to that apartment.

By this stage, we were under terrible threat from the building society. One person I tried to discuss the matter with was Miriam Hedderman. I had come to know Miriam from the time she was vying for the position of Lord Mayor of Dublin. I always liked to help women get ahead, so I had invited her to participate in *Play the Game* on several occasions where I gave her great PR. Even in interviews, I spoke very highly of her and encouraged people to support her campaign. Years later, Miriam had gone on to become the CEO of the Building Society Board, so I wrote her a letter outlining the situation with Elio and the fact that there was a case pending involving him being suspected of fraud. I explained that we were embroiled in the matter and asked if she could call off the pressure until the issue was resolved in court. I'm presuming she got the letter and just didn't have the manners to reply – ever.

If anything, her heavyweights got heavier.

When Elio's trial came about, the newspapers plagued me for a comment. I refused on the basis that I was not entirely *au fait* with the exact details of his wrongdoing and I also had no intention of being his judge and jury. Furthermore, I still considered him a friend.

Yes, you read my words correctly! Despite what he had done, a part of me genuinely felt very sorry for him because he wasn't a deliberate gangster. He had made a series of investments using other people's money fully believing it would all come good in the end and that he would be able to return the cash before anyone noticed. A more charitable way to describe his crime is to deem him an entrepreneur with an adventurous spirit. People will think I'm crazy for saying this, particularly considering the financial damage he wreaked upon David and me, but I knew Elio well enough to know that there was no intentional malice underpinning his actions. I liked him and I really believe it's very hard to 'unlike' someone. As my mother once said, 'You can't un-ring a bell!'

I didn't particularly like the people who tried to sell my wedding details, so pulling them by their hind legs hadn't bothered me in the slightest, but I did like Elio. I couldn't believe it when I read he had been sentenced to jail for fraud. The Law Society returned to us the money for the house, but we had lost so much more besides that. The legal fees were colossal and as a newly married couple, it really scuppered us. In fact, I don't think we ever fully recovered financially from that experience.

We weren't the only ones who lost out. The *Irish Press*, which belonged to Elio's in-laws, was another client of his who failed to survive the financial pandemonium he created. Sadly, a lot of small businesses also collapsed following the sting, while many others were left picking up the charred remains of their lives. Meanwhile, Jane was nowhere to be seen, with rumours abounding that she had fled to Italy with Doco. I haven't had the opportunity to speak with Jane since, which is quite a pity given that she and Elio had been such good friends of ours.

One night, in the company of my darling Gay Byrne and Kathleen Watkins, I began reminiscing about those nights out with Elio and Jane. During the chat, I recalled how Elio had been such a gentleman in that he never once let me put my hand in my pocket to pay for dinner.

Ever the man with the quick line of wit, Gay quipped back, 'That's because he already had his hand in your pocket. You *were* paying for the dinner dear, you just didn't know it!'

Gay, of course, was speaking as the voice of experience having endured his own financial nightmare at the hands of Russell Murphy.

❖

The spell in prison definitely broke Elio, as was evident from a letter I received not long after he was sentenced. The letter, which arrived in an envelope stamped with 'Mountjoy Prison' turned out to be a vicious four-page rant that contained the ramblings of a person undoubtedly suffering from issues of anger. The author of the letter identified himself only as 'a dear friend' of Elio's. He then launched into a vitriolic diatribe in which he blamed me for Elio's imprisonment. The pen-man went on to point out that 'Elio has a lot of information on you', before stating his knowledge of a rather mundane situation about a house we had tried to buy a few years earlier which ended in the deal falling through. Just when I thought the letter had reached the highest possible degree of stupidity, he added:

'You must be the most foolish person on earth because Elio is in the process of writing film scripts and you could have been in his films.'

That night I decided to pen him a short, but sharp, letter.

Dear Elio

What dark Monday morning must you think I was born on to believe that that letter was from a friend of yours? I feel really sorry for you if this is what prison has done to you. In relation to your 'inside knowledge' on us buying a house some years ago that didn't work out, let me remind you that there's no

Despite the circumstance that inspired it, this mock-up of a film poster, featured in Phoenix Magazine, featuring Elio and me never fails to give me a laugh! It reads: 'Blackhall Place made him a lawyer, the Irish Press made him a mint, Twink made him a legend.'

law about gambling with your own money. I gambled with my own money and lost. You, however, gambled with other people's money and lost.

That's precisely why you're on the inside and I'm on the outside.

Sincerely,

Adèle

❖

For some reason, Elio was very bitter about me at first. A person who had dealt with him in prison subsequently confirmed this for me. Where this angry bitterness had sprung from is anyone's guess. I never once said a bad word about Elio and any time a question regarding him was put to me, my response was never anything less than gracious.

I always publicly gave him the benefit of the doubt in that I maintained he had taken the money with the intention of returning it once the property investments he had made with it paid off. I still attribute his behaviour to that brash stage of youth where you think you are infallible. Elio had been the sharpest suit in town in every sense of the word. He was winning cases left, right and centre, not to mention having also been the arbiter in a hostage situation where he talked a man out of shooting himself. When you have that level of power and praise at such a young age, of course you are going to be of the notion that you can do nothing wrong. It's an illusion of immortality exclusive to youth.

Unfortunately for Elio, his luck ran out, and with it, his charade.

❖

One day, as David was dropping me off near East Essex Street in Dublin city centre, a lone figure walking towards us suddenly caught his eye.

'Dear God above, is that Elio Malocco?' David remarked.

Given that we were the only people on the street, there was absolutely no avoiding each other. All I could do was prepare myself for the inevitably awkward small-talk.

When he saw me emerge from the car, his face said it all. He appeared completely lost for words. I walked over to him and immediately greeted him with a hug. To be honest, he was almost unrecognisable. His once beautiful sallow skin was now red raw from what appeared to be eczema or psoriasis, while his shock of black hair was now grey and thinning. That confident film-star panache he once exuded had been replaced with hunched shoulders and a broken spirit. He look bewildered, almost as though he had been confined within the prison walls for so long that he was unsure of to how to deal with being out in the real world again. Neither of us brought up the court case or the crimes that had sent him to jail, although he did mention that he had been disbarred from practising but had since taken to pursuing his dream of writing film scripts. He appeared to harbour great ambitions of making it in the film industry in Ireland and, at one point, asked if I was still interested in taking up a role in one of his scripts, should it come to fruition. I laughed it off and told him I was always interested in work if it brought in a few bob. I asked about Doco, but felt it best not to make any reference to Jane as I was unsure if they were still together.

Clearly I was right because when I saw him three years later on Christmas Eve, he introduced the woman next to him as his partner. He appeared to have recovered a bit by that point. He looked more together, more composed. It was a very brief encounter where we basically wished each other a Happy Christmas, but from the few words we shared, I got the impression he was happy with where his life was going.

Looking back on it now, it would have been nice if he had said sorry at some point, but even having said that, I will go to my grave not wishing any badness on Elio.

Weight

There's a great line in the *Absolutely Fabulous* series where Jennifer Saunder's character, Edina Monsoon, turns to her friend Patsy and says, 'You know, Pats, there must be a moment, about a week after death, when women finally achieve the size 8 figure they desire'.

I was a skinny child but once I entered my teens, the thin bitch left me and I became prone to weight gain. I now only have to look at food to put on weight, and if I looked at it long enough, I'd put on ten pounds. When I'm thin, it's because I barely eat or drink. Plain and simple. I might have a main meal two evenings a week and, even then, the meal might consist of just a piece of lean chicken or fish with lettuce. Even my own children wonder how I survive on such a diet!

Back when I was doing panto, I had phenomenal fitness levels and a killer figure to boot. I would have done three shows a day in the Gaiety beginning with two and a half hours in the gym that morning. My show diet would consist of a small Slim-Fast milkshake for breakfast, a small Slim-Fast biscuit for lunch and half a banana. In the break between the matinée and the night show, I would eat half a kiwi and a handful of mixed fruit and nuts. I would also have a pint of

Here's another LOL joke

A woman was sipping on a glass of wine, while sitting on the patio with her husband. Softly she said, 'You know I love you so much. I don't know how I could ever live without you.'

Surprised, her husband turned and asked, 'Is that you, or the wine talking?'

'It's me ...' she replied, 'talking to the wine.'

At my fighting weight.

fizzy water and two cups of black coffee, along with plenty of chewing gum. Following the night show, I would eat another handful of nuts, the second halves of the kiwi and the banana followed by another cup of coffee.

When I was on *The Late Late Show* some time back, I admitted that I ate virtually nothing in order to remain thin. No sooner had I said the words, than some nutritionist was lambasting me in a newspaper for encouraging anorexia. It was actually one of the first times I wrote to a newspaper editor to have my say.

Let me get one thing straight. This is what works for *me*. I'm not suggesting that everyone does it,

I'm just saying that I have tried everything and this is the only thing that I find works. I know it's crazy and I know it's not good for the bones, but to be perfectly honest, at sixty years of age, I'm a hell of a lot healthier than a lot of women I know who are half my age. Not eating suits me. I never feel weak, if anything I enjoy phenomenal energy. I know it's not normal, but that's precisely why I don't recommend it to others.

That said, I honestly love food too much to go through life without it. In fact, I'm so bloody bored by weight watching now that I'm tempted to let myself become twenty stone and just live my life, fat and happy.

My parents passed on a number of traits to me; unfortunately their metabolism wasn't one of them. Neither of them could gain weight if they tried. 'You can't fatten a thoroughbred', was my father's great line. He also used to say that the only way to lose weight was to take your nose out of the nosebag and exercise. Of course, that's easier said than done. I should know, as one of the unfortunate side-effects of my asthma medication is a ferocious appetite. My heart goes out to anyone struggling with their weight. Unless you have been through it, you have no idea how much it can affect a person's life.

When I was thin, I could have worn a bin liner with Sellotape for a belt and looked like I was head-to-toe in Gucci. Believe me, the man who invents the thin pill will be richer than Bill Gates. I'm all for disease research, but I do think the women of the world wouldn't object to a little funding for diet pill research, eh, ladies? I don't want the one that leaves you with diarrhoea, cramps and facial hair, just the one that makes you thin. There was a great diet pill which I took for years. It was a fantastic appetite suppressant and helped maintain my weight brilliantly. I, like a lot of people, thrived on it, but it seems many people suffered a number of adverse reactions and, before I knew it, the pill was taken off the market.

Before the PC brigade mount their bloody high horses and begin berating me for my thin-talk, I would just like to point out that 'thin' doesn't always necessarily equate to 'anorexic'. Everyone has what is termed their 'ideal weight' and once they exceed that weight, they begin to feel tired and sluggish. For some people, their fighting weight is eight stone, for others it's eighteen stone. There is no one set standard.

All I know is that when I am thin, I look and feel my best.

Another thing that really gets my goat is how the media crucified Kate Moss for once stating in an interview that, 'Nothing tastes as good as skinny feels'.

Do you not remember when that same line was the famous Weight Watchers' mantra we all proudly quoted to each other on a daily basis 'Nothing tastes as good as being thin feels'?

The bitch behind the Bic

Even though this memorably horrendous story occurred many moons ago, it still galls me even when I recall it now.

It began when I was involved in a show in the Olympia. During rehearsals each day, the cast would often go to a bar called the Granary for coffee. While I was there one evening, I noticed another actress nearby looking very disconsolate. It transpired she had auditioned for a production in the Olympia but hadn't got a recall. We got chatting and I bought her a few drinks to help cheer her up.

My favourite theatres

1. The Gaiety/Olympia Theatres, Dublin
2. Limerick University
3. London Palladium
4. Radio City New York
5. All the beautifully refurbished theatres now flourishing in Cork, Wexford, Waterford, Galway, Killarney, Kilkenny, etc.
6. The Courthouse, Mullingar is my new 'right up there' gig!

She didn't have the money for a taxi home, so I offered to drive her out to her flat, and as she was getting out of the car, I handed her £60 to help her get by. She was amazed by the gesture and said she couldn't accept it because she wouldn't be able to pay me back. I assured her she didn't owe me anything. Acting is one bloody rough business and if I was making a few bob then why shouldn't I help out someone who wasn't?

'You never know,' I jokingly added, 'the next time I meet you, it might be your turn to help me out!'

❖

A matter of weeks later, I was living in London when I received a phone call from Muriel Quinn who was over the very popular cabaret venue, Braemor Rooms, Churchtown, Dublin. At the time, they were holding an Irish cabaret in the venue where, unfortunately, it wasn't so much losing money but rather haemorrhaging it. During the phone call, Muriel explained her situation and told me that she had no other option but to give the cast their notices and pay them off. She explained that she needed to make some money from the show in order to afford to pay them and so asked me if I would perform for a week because she knew I would bring in the crowds. My agent at the time was a wonderful woman called Margo Tracey, so they liaised with each other and sorted out the various arrangements. My only stipulation in the contract was that no one would be out of work as a result of this new turn of events. Muriel, however, explained that regardless of whether or not I did the show, the artists were still going to be given their notices but at least with me bringing in the crowds, she would have the money to pay them off.

On the opening night of the show, my dressing room was packed with beautiful bouquets from well-wishers. One in particular immediately caught my eye. A bunch of nettles, thorns and weeds styled in the form of a bouquet wrapped in newspaper was placed on my table beside a small shoebox. Inside the box lay a decaying rat. The accompanying note read: 'You scumbag, you have done your colleagues and friends out of work. You stinking showbiz rat.'

Everything about it was positively putrid.

I don't know what it was about the handwriting but it was distinctive enough to be familiar to me. I knew I had seen it somewhere but couldn't figure out where. Then it occurred to me. The actress I had met a few weeks earlier had written down her name and phone number for me and that very same handwriting was now on this note.

Following that night, she began composing the most vicious hate mail; the epitome of the poison-pen letter. She then began sending me nasty postcards but would address them to RTÉ so that everyone could read her insults. The open postcards were of the same nature as the letters. Anonymous and filled with whatever new litany of insults she had added to her 'vulgarcabulary' that week.

❖

Around this time I had begun working on *Can't Stop the Music* in the Gaiety Theatre alongside Red Hurley. As I was chatting with Red's brother, Fran, I began telling him about the letters I had been receiving. I told him who I suspected was behind it but said that I couldn't confirm it. Fran, however, had a friend who was a detective and so he arranged for me to meet him.

I knew the actress was due to be at the Gaiety for another set of auditions, so I conspired with Fran's detective friend to try to find out if she was, shall we say, the bitch behind the Bic biro. To do this, we arranged a set-up that would have made

CSI's Horatio Caine proud. We had the barmaid primed to give our actress a drink, and when she had finished it and left, the barmaid would then use a tea towel to pick up the glass and give it to the detective. Everything went according to plan and, sure enough, after the detective ran a fingerprint test on the glass, the prints were an exact match to those found on the letters.

The following Friday night as I was chatting to my friends and family after the show, the bitch actually had the audacity to walk up to me and in faux-excitement exclaim, 'Ah, hiya, Twink! I haven't seen you in ages!'

Considering how fond she had been of sticking the proverbial knife in, I figured this was my one chance to return the favour.

'So you've been a busy little beaver with the pen,' I smiled. 'Written any good letters lately?'

Her face visibly fell.

'You know, I was going to send you a bunch of ballpoint pens because surely you've run out of ink by now with all those poison letters you've been writing. I'm just wondering though if I'm the only one you've written to?'

Without saying a word, she turned around and legged it out of the room. I was given the option of pressing charges but I declined. I'd had my satisfaction of seeing the look of shock on her face and that, for me, was better than any courtroom result.

Even recounting the story now, I can vividly remember recoiling in horror at the idea that there was someone out there sick enough to go to the trouble of finding a dead rat not to mention picking nettles and thorns to arrange in a bouquet.

Believe it or not, I feel sympathy rather than animosity towards her. After all, what God awful miserable place must her mind have been in to enable her to do that to another human being? Our paths have never crossed since and, frankly, I hope it stays that way.

Remarkably enough, she's still very much in the business, which is why I can't name her! A number of people in the industry will know exactly who I am talking about when they read this.

I know where the bodies are buried!

When Chloë was a child, she had a fascination with *Snow White and the Seven Dwarfs*. It was one of the stories that had to be read to her repeatedly. As her third birthday approached, I told her that Snow White might be bringing her a very special gift. Gus Bowman who owned Bowman's in Stillorgan had just brought into Ireland a beautiful new range of children's Wendy houses, some of which even had staircases in them! I decided it would be the perfect gift for Chloë's birthday as it was so similar to the one in the *Snow White* story.

The night before her party, we hauled her out to her grandmother's house for the night while Gus installed the foundations of the Wendy house. Operation Snow White had been planned to perfection. We had arranged for the nanny Anna to pick up Chloë from pre-school and when she arrived home, I pretended to find a note in the kitchen from Snow White and the Seven Dwarves in which they wished her a happy birthday. The whole surprise was pulled off beautifully. The moment she laid eyes on the house, she literally screamed and screamed with excitement. She was just besotted with it and everything inside it.

David's mother had bought her a McDonald's cookery centre while my mother had bought her a bed set and a tiny pink girlie dressing table for upstairs. It was a little girl's dream come true and even though she was only three, I knew she would remember it for the rest of her life.

Earlier that day, however, I'd had words with a member of David's family who told me in no uncertain terms how much she disagreed with giving a child such a gift. She pointed out that she didn't do Santa 'because kids need to know where money comes from' and that if she buys them something, they should know it's from her.

I couldn't understand why anyone would want to make life so practical and factual for a child. What will they have to look back on when they're older? Chloë fondly looks back and laughs at how convinced she had been that Snow White had left the birthday note and the Wendy house for her. As far as I was concerned, she would have enough time to learn where money came from when she was older. It wasn't a subject of necessity for her childhood.

Every day after school, the coat and school bag were flung in the hall and the Wendy house was given Chloë's full attention. She would have moved into the flippin' thing if we had let her. One day, she arrived into the kitchen and asked if she could have milk and biscuits for 'Mrs Burgoine'.

She explained that Mrs Burgoine was a very nice old lady who was quite tall and wore a black dress with her grey hair tied in a bun. She then began telling me how Mrs Burgoine was also 'a very good lady because she was looking after all the poor girls'.

'They're very poor, Mommy, they don't have nice clothes or anything, just awful clothes. They're very thin and they're always very hungry, so could I get some milk and biscuits?'

Naturally, I assumed her imaginary friends were the result of a fertile childhood mind, so I arranged some biscuits on a plate and gave her a glass of milk thinking she would be scoffing them herself as soon as she was inside the door of her Wendy house. The whole thing began to really escalate though, and, on one particular evening, a perplexed David turned to me and said, 'Who on earth is Mrs Burgoine? And *who* are the poor girls?'

Whenever David and I would ask Chloë if she had seen Mrs Burgoine that day, her answers were always so specific and knowledgeable. One evening, I remember her saying, 'No, she wasn't there today. She must have been busy because the girls have to work, you know. They don't go to school, Mommy, they just have to work. They're always very dirty. I asked them why they don't have a bath like me, but they don't know what a bath is, they just wash in a bucket.'

Chloë's stories soon began to get more and more factual to a point where there were almost too many facts coming out. There were times when I literally had goose bumps listening to her. One day, she arrived into the house absolutely distraught because one of the poor girls, Emily, had died from an illness. We comforted her, but we still had no reason to assume that Mrs Burgoine and Emily were anything more than imaginary childhood friends, a fairly normal occurrence in the social life of a three year old.

At the time, there was an area behind Beaufort House that contained a line of hedgerows and Chloë would often tell me how Mrs Burgoine and the poor girls would enter our garden through the hedge. Some time later, the owners of the Old Orchard Inn decided to transform the whole area

at the back of the pub which involved the grounds being dug up. While the work was being carried out, Chloë ran into the house roaring crying that Mrs Burgoine was gone.

'She came to say goodbye to me and that she wouldn't see me any more because they have no where to stay. There's bad men where they live,' she sobbed.

At that particular point, the car park of the Orchard Inn was like Mount Vesuvius with the amount of clay that was being excavated so I could only conclude that the 'bad men' she was

referring to were the builders carrying out the digging work. The following weekend, a lovely young local lad called Barry arrived at the house to cut the lawn for me. He did his usual trek of the lawn in which he looked for discarded dog bones hidden among the grass to avoid completely wrecking the lawnmower blades. After about fifteen minutes, he rang the doorbell. The poor lad was ashen-faced and absolute shaking.

'Eh, Mrs Agnew … I think you should … I think you should look at the … eh … bones.'

As he was talking, one of our dogs, McNalty, strolled past carrying in her mouth what appeared to be a large skeletal lower jaw of a man, with the teeth still intact! I let out a roar, 'Jesus Christ, Mackie, drop that now!'

It was at this point that Barry showed me the large black refuse bag of bones he had collected. Naturally he had assumed they were dog bones until he realised they were beginning to look … well, rather human. As we tried to figure out where they had come from, I remembered that the dogs had been digging a hole near Chloë's Wendy house. It was actually so deep that David and I had previously wondered what they had been searching for. After digging up another shovel full of clay, we could clearly see a human skull looking back up at us. Immediately, we phoned the Guards.

Don't ask me why, but we christened the skeleton Eugene.

The next day, I had been scheduled to do voiceover work in Tommy Eillis's studios, and, as I was on my way home, I was listening to the six o'clock news when suddenly a story caught my attention.

The newsreader stated that Professor John Harbison had been called out to a site in Butterfield Avenue where hundreds of human remains had been found. She added that a team of forensic scientists were trying to determine whether the remains were ancient or recent, and that the bodies in question 'had been discovered in the grounds of the house belonging to well-known Irish entertainer Twink'.

I don't know how I didn't crash the car with the shock. Hundreds of bodies? Seriously folks, *hundreds*? Last time I had checked, there was just the one, Eugene.

I arrived home only to be greeted by swarms of Gardaí and forensic units not to mention reams of yellow tape cordoning off the entire area around my house. The grounds of Beaufort had suddenly gone from being green with grass to white with forensic uniforms. A woman from the Natural History Museum accompanied by a forensic anthropologist also arrived out to investigate the scene. The team brought a number of bodies back to the museum for further investigation, but the remainder of the bodies were covered back in and given a blessing. I think the car park is sitting over the poor things now.

The evidence indicated that an early Christian monastery had used the grounds as a burial site for many generations. In fact, the bodies were buried three deep, the bulk of which the team believed, were directly underneath the house itself! Three strata of bodies? It was almost too much to take in. When I asked about the discovery of the children's bodies, the woman from the museum turned to me and said something that very nearly landed me in the ground beside Eugene.

'Well, Mrs Agnew, we're also investigating the presence out here in the mountains of a workhouse for impoverished little girls run by a Bretton couple called Mr and Mrs Burgoney,' she explained.

I must have turned pale, because I can distinctly remember her asking me if I was feeling alright. I told her all about Chloë's descriptions of a woman she referred to as 'Mrs Burgoine' and how she had said that the poor girls were wearing sacking cloth with twine. The woman from the museum agreed that sack cloth and twine was exactly what they would have been wearing 300 years ago. I have to admit, the entire experience gave me a whole new insight into the deep intuition possessed by children before the world gradually beats it out of them.

We were digging up bodies for ages. In fact, when we went to create a pond in the garden, we found another three bodies and had to call the forensics back in again. Even today, Chloë still remembers Mrs Burgoine and the poor girls. As for poor aul' Eugene, he's still there looking up at the sky. We hadn't the heart to fill him in so instead we ended up placing a mesh grid over him. In a rather bizarre way, he became a bit of a garden feature.

I wonder am I related to Stephen King after all!

❖

Whatever about hauntings, I do believe that all places retain energy, be it good or bad. When we were living in Beaufort, there was one particular neighbouring house that was the scene of substantial tragedy. It started when a woman had been found dead in a bath in the fifties after an electric fire fell off the wall and into the water.

In the eighties/nineties several previous owners had moved out shortly after they moved in! Then a couple called Frank and Esther McCann moved in. Apart from sharing a few brief words with Esther whenever she passed the gate with her baby girl Jessica, I didn't know the McCanns that well. Esther was very polite and quiet but there was always something about her that struck me as traumatised. She just seemed like a woman with a lot on her mind. When I think back now, I kick myself for not asking her if she was alright; for not asking the kind of questions that perhaps needed to be asked.

On 3 September 1992, I was a judge on a television show for BBC Northern Ireland and as I was driving home the following day, I nipped into a shop in Rathfarnham where I bumped into a lovely woman called Maeve Burkett.

'Isn't it awful about the McCanns?' she said.

'Why? What happened?'

'The McCanns house burned down and Esther and the baby are dead. The neighbours couldn't break the windows to get inside because they were double glazed. Esther and the baby were trapped upstairs.'

I couldn't believe what I was hearing, but sure enough, when I arrived into Butterfield Avenue, the local Gardaí had cordoned off the entire area. Frank had apparently arrived home the previous night to find his house in full blaze. Neighbours had to forcefully hold him back from scaling a ladder up to the second floor where Esther and Jessica were trapped. He was distraught, even fainting at one point when he realised there was nothing that could be done to save his family.

I don't think anyone who attended Esther and Jessica's funeral could possibly forget the scene of utter devastation. Frank, the most grief-stricken man you could imagine, had to be physically held up at one point. For the entire ceremony, he clutched a pair of tiny shoes belonging to Jessica. He was so broken and inconsolable over the loss of his two girls, that people were actually worried he might take his own life. Turns out, he was just a bloody good actor.

My heart broke for him when I saw him in the church that day so I decided to send him a letter in which I told him that his neighbours were always there for him if ever he needed to talk. Over the course of the month that followed, strange rumours began to circulate around the area about Frank. Sure enough, the rumours were not without substance and eventually he was arrested for the murder of Esther and baby Jessica. It transpired that Esther and Frank were in the process of adopting their foster child Jessica, but the Adoption Board had notified the McCanns' solicitor that they were rejecting their application.

Unbeknownst to Esther, Frank, a swimming coach, was facing child molestation charges. Apparently, the board received a phone call alerting them to the fact that Frank had fathered a child with a teenage girl. Three months following his wedding to Esther, the teenage girl gave birth to a boy whose adoption, it's alleged, was arranged by Fr Michael Cleary. Esther never knew.

Frank was informed of the Adoption Board's decision but decided against telling Esther, presumably fearing that she would leave him, thus sabotaging the family man image he so desperately wanted to portray. Every day without fail, Esther phoned the board's office in a bid to find out the cause of the delay regarding Jessica's adoption. Eventually, she was invited to a meeting with the board's representatives which was scheduled to take place on Monday, 7 September.

Esther was murdered on 4 September.

12.

13.

14.

15.

16.

17.

1. Flying with high with Foster & Allen.

2. Like myself, Mary Black is a former member of Young Dublin Singers, but she went on to conquer the world with that magnificent voice.

3. Chloë sitting on a flight with Terry Waite, the famous hostage hero.

4. While Gay and Kathleen are professional friends to me, they are lovingly known as uncle Gay and nanny Kay to the girls.

5. One of the great Irish minds, Eamon Dunphy.

6. Chloë with Aidan Quinn performed together in Frank McNamara's **Messiah** at the Point.

7. The one and only Van Morrison.

8. Joe Dolan & friends.

9. Amanda Byram.

10. Mary Coughlan — one of the nicest people you could meet.

11. Roger Moore 007 and me as host 006½ with Carol Hanna as 008!

12. Frank Kelly — better known as Father Jack, and the brilliant Des Keogh.

13. All the Agnews meet all the Reynolds family in New York at the time Albert was Taoiseach.

14. With the legendary Bono.

15. Myself and Stephen Gately always enjoyed a laugh together.

16. Engrossed in conversation with Milo O'Shea — come to think of it how did Michael Ball and Denis O'Brien end up in this picture?

17. With the wonderful John Bowman.

Shit in the shed day

The third of May 1993, celebrated by the Christians as the feast day of St Phillip, known to the Japanese as Constitution Day, detested by the Agnews as Shit in the Shed Day.

Every detail about that horrendously awful day will forever remain vividly sharp in my memory.

In the garden behind Beaufort House, there was an old shed which I had long promised the girls they could use to play in once the evenings became cool. The weather was so beautiful that day, however, that I spontaneously decided to clean out all the crap that was lying idle inside it. I began with the old filing cabinet David had used in his video shop in Donnybrook. Starting with the top drawer, I removed what looked like ancient tax documents and stored them in an old suitcase for his perusal. I then did the same with the second and third drawers. However, the fourth drawer seemed to pose a problem – unlike the others, this one was locked. I remembered noticing a key when I was emptying out the first drawer so I rifled through the suitcase until I eventually managed to locate it. Almost immediately, I could see why he had kept that drawer shut tight. It was full of crude birthday cards, really tacky vulgar items from joke shops stacked in amongst years of Christmas cards. Then I found a bundle of hand-made cards.

'Happy St Patrick's Day, Daddy, love from your Hayley.'

It had been given to him over a month-and-a-half earlier, around the same time he had sworn blind to me that he was not having an affair.

It was then that I suddenly remembered that the child of his employee, Yvonne, a child I had seen many times in his shop, was called Hayley.

It was the closest to a fucking heart attack I have ever come. This was the very first time I had ever known of the full extent of his affair with Yvonne. I thought David's encounter with her had been nothing more than a fling, like all the others he'd had before her.

The fact that he'd had a secret child was just mind-numbing. Even now, it's genuinely hard to put into words the searing pain that went through every fibre of my being. Everything was spinning in my head; then, of course, the numbness kicked in. All the trivial things that once seemed so major, suddenly disappeared into insignificance. In a way, it was like an out-of-body sensation, in that I couldn't quite fully believe it was happening.

While ripping apart a photograph of the man who wronged you is usually the domain of heartbroken teenage girls, I instead opted for the heartbroken woman approach and decided to rip *him* apart instead. I went inside and phoned the National Concert Hall. It was around 7.40 p.m. and David was due to begin his concert.

I explained to the person I was speaking with that I needed David to phone me urgently as there was a problem with the baby. Minutes later, he rang back. I didn't answer; instead I listened to his panic-stricken voice on the answering machine.

'Adèle, what's wrong? Please pick up. Is everything all right? What's wrong with the baby? Jesus Christ is Naomi all right?'

Half an hour later, still dressed in his orchestral evening suit, he burst through the door, frantic. He rushed into the dining room looking around manically to see where Naomi was.

'What's wrong with the baby? Where is Naomi?'

'No, not that baby … *this* baby!' I shouted, while throwing at him the stack of cards that I had found hidden within the filing cabinet. The life nearly drained from his face when he realised exactly what I had uncovered. Where one man might grovel or beg for forgiveness, David typically managed to turn it around and make *me* look like the one in the wrong.

'Well, is this what you have been doing with your day? Snooping?' he shot back.

Grabbing two cushions from the couch, he threw them on the ground with force. We had a major argument. I was so outraged, I seriously considered phoning the police and having him removed from the house and filing for a barring order.

David stormed out of the room. Suddenly, I got a whiff of burning charcoal drifting through the corridor. Immediately, I followed the smell as it became stronger and stronger, until I found him in the back garden burning the stack of cards on the barbecue. He just stood there stoking the fire, pouring paraffin over it. The flames were at least three feet high. I don't know why he was getting rid of the evidence. After all, the cards may have been burned to a cinder, but the child was still very much around.

That night he left the house and, as soon as he was gone, I ran upstairs and emptied every piece of clothing he owned into black bin bags. I discovered through a friend that he had spent the night in the shop, so, the following morning, I drove to Donnybrook. In full view of everyone, I threw the entire contents of his life on the path outside, accompanied by the words, 'I believe these are yours, dear!'

Afterwards, I phoned a good friend of mine, a well-respected psychiatrist, and asked her up to the house for a chat. I poured my heart out to her and together we dissected the situation while I conveyed my dilemma and obvious state of indecision. Walking out the driveway of Beaufort House towards her car, I asked her the most important question of all: should I take him back? She reminded me it was my decision but added, 'You're going to take him back, aren't you? I know by you!'

I admitted it was likely.

'Let me tell you something, Adèle. In my office, I have shelves and shelves of case histories of men like David, and, unfortunately, I have evidence by the lorry load to prove that leopards never change their spots. I wish you luck.'

With that, she drove off. The whole scene was timely poignant and sadly her *précis* would later be proven right. Sure enough, David soon arrived at the house pretty much on bended knees, begging me to take him back into the family fold. He kept insisting that it had all been a big mistake and that he didn't know what he had been doing. I can still hear him crying to me, 'I don't care about anyone, I only love you. The others were all only cheap oul' rides, it was only ever sex. I actually love *you*. I do have a problem. I'm addicted and I can't seem to stop, but, Adèle, I want you to know that I never loved any one of them. I want to live with you and the girls.'

While it was easy for him to say sorry for what he had done, it wasn't as easy for me to forget. After I had found out about Hayley's existence and his despicable seven-year relationship with another woman, I sank into an impenetrable depression.

❖

People have always been of the impression that my emotions are secured firmly underneath a steel helmet. They will say things like, 'Oh, but sure you're strong, Twink'. Look, I'm the same as the next person, and there were days when all I did was lie in bed, crying in devastation.

I was in such a dark place that on one particular occasion, the most horrifying thoughts went through my head. One day, as I was driving out to the Billy Barry Theatre School to pick up Chloë and Naomi from their dancing lesson, Frances Black's song 'All the Lies That You Told Me' was a big hit at the time and so, was on almost every radio station. In fact, I think I heard it about three times while I was in the car. Any time I hear that song now, my mind immediately reverts back to that truly awful day. In my head, I had everything planned out. I was going to take the lives of myself and my two daughters and finally end our misery.

As I was driving, I contemplated the various details of the different ways in which I could carry this out. First, I thought about driving the car off a pier, however, I'm quite a strong swimmer and I knew if I went ahead with it, my survival instinct would be to grab the girls and swim back up. I also didn't want to put the children through that psychological torture, so I figured I would have to drug them first. This then led to me considering the prospect of administering an overdose. I thought about lying down on the bed with them, taking a large number of tablets and giving them a drug-laced drink before reading them a fairytale and peacefully leaving the world together. It seems so frighteningly horrendous when I look back now on how I genuinely considered suicide as a valid option, but, at the time, David had dragged us through such depths of pain that I felt as though death would be our only relief.

Today, I honestly can't even comprehend how I entertained such a dreadful idea but, you know what? When you're in the blackest of places, your mind can travel to the darkest of corners.

I know most of you will ask why on earth I considered killing my two daughters when I could have just ended my own life and not touched theirs. The best days of my life were 9 June 1989 and 21 August 1993, the days my two beautiful girls were born. Every day with them since has been an absolute bonus and a joy. This is precisely why, when I was in that dark place, I just couldn't handle the idea of being without them. They were my life and I wanted them with me. Naturally I look back now, horrified by how I actually thought I had the right to end their lives, but I still maintain that unless you have been in a similar situation, you cannot understand what goes through the mind of someone suffering from that level of depression. Of course taking the lives of your children is an irrational decision but then who really knows what triggers a moment of insanity like that? All I can say is that I hope you never experience it.

One thing that really infuriates me is when people use the word 'selfish' when referring to someone who has committed suicide. Let me assure you, people who contemplate or commit suicide don't for one moment believe they are being selfish. If anything, they think they are doing everyone a favour. Their self-evaluation has reached its lowest possible ebb and they simply cannot see a way up.

When you are working off a full shiny deck of cards, you cannot comment on someone who might be missing a card or two. You *cannot* call them selfish and you *cannot* berate them for their actions. Instead, you should just thank whoever it is you believe in that you are not the one whose mind is steeped in darkness.

❖

When the girls were older, I told them of what I had planned that day. Their reaction was one of shock, but also a fine element of understanding. They knew how distraught I had been, and remembered how I would take to my bed and cry for hours, refusing to emerge. They too had been so broken-hearted when David left that they could see exactly why such thoughts went through my head. It took me months, even years, to remove myself from that horrendous darkness; in fact, there are days when I wonder if a small part of me will always be in that place. If you are currently in the midst of a depression where even getting out of bed seems like a chore, try with all your might to steal yourself back from the edge because I promise you that one day, you will be grateful you didn't give up. The light won't come back on like a 100-watt bulb, but it *will* come back. You will eventually see that glimmer of hope. It's just a matter of remaining strong and working on brightening that light a tiny bit more every day. A bit like a dimmer switch turning up the light little by little.

All her fault

Chloë and Naomi had no idea they had a half-sister and, frankly, I was torn about whether or not I should tell them or even introduce them to her. As it turned out, they were already familiar with each other. Long before I found out about Hayley, David had already introduced the girls to her, albeit not as their sister. I only discovered this in later years when Chloë began to remember occasions when she was playing with Hayley 'while that woman from the shop was with Dad'. He had also brought Hayley to Funderland with them when I was ill in hospital with my asthma.

It riles me when I think of how blatant he was about his infidelities. To be perfectly honest, I wasn't particularly keen on the idea of entertaining the child of some woman he'd screwed in his shop. I'm sorry if that doesn't sound very Christian but, you know what? It's easy to be an armchair critic. Put yourself in my shoes and ask yourself how you would have reacted. It's difficult to like a child that is basically the product of someone who got the leg over your husband, a woman you couldn't stomach being near in the first place. I wouldn't by any means begrudge the child her life, but I didn't want her life entwined with that of my children's any more than it already had been.

That said, there was no removing the fact that she was still their half-sister. That Christmas, David and I were in Smyth's Toys buying presents for the girls. As we were leaving the shop, he pointed to a particularly beautiful doll I had bought and asked if it was for Chloë or Naomi.

'Neither,' I replied. 'It's for Hayley.'

As soon as I said it, he broke down in tears.

I told him we would have to come to some arrangement with her mother and that I wanted him to give me a full apology in front of her. I'd had enough of being humiliated. He kept his word and drove me out to where Yvonne was living. Her face froze when she saw me standing beside him.

When we sat down with her in the sitting room, David didn't hold back in telling her that they were finished. He made it clear he was in love with me and that she had been nothing more than a bit on the side. Some part of me, as a woman, felt great sympathy for her. She just sat there motionless and in disbelief, looking at him as though her spirit and heart had been crushed to pieces. In true David style, he turned the blame on her, 'You knew I was a married man and you shouldn't have had an affair with me, Yvonne'.

I didn't say much because she already looked so broken by his words that she didn't need to hear mine. However, as we were leaving, she asked him what she should do with his computer and all the other stuff that belonged to him. He told her to 'stick it where she put everything else she shouldn't'. My heart hit the floor when I realised just how much of a secret second life he had been living with her. He had even given her a ring. It was as though he thought of her as his northside wife. Following that day, David was adamant there would never be a repeat.

For the first time ever, it really felt like we were starting over.

Fur coat and no knickers

Not long afterwards, we arranged a family holiday to Switzerland, sort of like the honeymoon we never had. The press had obviously heard of some marital disharmony in the Agnew camp because the day before we were due to fly out, a friend of mine tipped me off that some journalists had booked flights to follow us. A number of other journalists and photographers had been assigned to remain at the airport to photograph us as we were walking through.

I was panicked by the idea of some journalist approaching my girls and asking them about Hayley, so I phoned PR genius and good friend Gerry Lundberg and asked him for advice on what my approach should be. He, along with people from Top Flight Travel, arrived up to my house that evening and together we devised a plan. While Naomi was too young to fully comprehend the situation, Chloë was seven years old and at an age where she could take it in. I sat them both down and explained as gently as possible, that the girl they had been to Funderland with was actually their half-sister. An audible sigh of relief swelled from within Chloë and the words that followed completely surmised the innocence of a child.

'Is that it? Is that the bad news you wanted to tell us? Thank God! I thought you were going to tell us that you and Dad were splitting up.'

The idea of her parents separating would have torn her seven-year-old world apart, rather than the idea of her dad having an affair or fathering another child. In fact, the poor thing was so worried her father was going to leave, that she burst into tears with relief when I assured her he wasn't. That night, the Top Flight staff switched our flights from Switzerland to Austria and even though the flight wasn't until 10 a.m., Gerry arranged for a car to collect us at five in the morning so as to thwart any journalists intent on following us from the house. We were brought into the Gold Circle lounge where we were allowed sleep for a short while on couches. We then travelled on a seven o'clock flight to Austria while half the media were on a ten o'clock flight to Switzerland. By the time the press found out where we really were, we were on our way home, smiling at the thought of having pulled a master stroke.

Even though we had a wonderful time in Austria, I was still bitterly angry with David. I wanted him to experience the same mind-numbing shock that had gone though me when I discovered the contents of his filing cabinet. I wanted to use a place where we were so idyllically happy, that I could turn around and say, 'That's it, David! I want a separation'.

At the same time, however, part of me genuinely didn't want to call time on our marriage. First and foremost, I didn't want the children to have to endure such upset. Secondly, my heart kept reminding me of all the great times we had enjoyed together. You see, when things were good, they were amazing to a point where I would always feel convinced that we had reached a tipping point where David would change his ways and commit to married life. I knew deep down he really loved me. Unfortunately, his 'affair addiction' was the crevice into which all marriage-resuscitation attempts consistently fell.

In the end, I decided against my separation idea in favour of a more punishing form of revenge. The decision underpinning my sudden u-turn stemmed from a group skiing lesson we took under the guidance of a gorgeous instructor called Willie (pronounced 'Villie' in Austria). I was in very good shape at the time and, immediately, Willie took a shine to me. Even though I was an accomplished water-skier, thanks to my love of Lake Mead during the Vegas years, I was very much a novice when it came to skiing on snow. I was really struggling and even though I have always been a quick learner, a group setting

never suited me. Being an only child, I think I always had a tendency to learn better when I was on my own. Eventually, Willie gave me a private tutorial and, within the hour, I had picked up everything I needed to know. Within two days, we were skiing across the mountains together at tremendous speed, like Olympians.

Now, girls, I won't lie … there was some wonderful off-piste action as well! On one occasion when we stopped for a beer, our tryst started with a kiss (doesn't everything!). That day Willie and I skied off on our own and let's just say that while the snow might have been cold, the passion was sweltering hot. One night, he invited me to a bar where he and his fellow ski instructors were meeting for a drink. Some of the other instructors were female and as I had come to know them all quite well, I knew I wouldn't look out of place.

Earlier that evening, David and I had brought the girls out to dinner. I genuinely thought he would use the meal as an opportunity to apologise to the girls and me for all the pain he had caused and to maybe thank us for taking him back. Not a chance. He was in full-flight arrogance mode and his attitude was more, 'Ah, sure, she's taken me back again'.

When we returned to the hotel, I told him he was on babysitting duty because I was going for a drink with Willie and his friends. He was visibly taken aback by my rather blunt demand and, by God, I can tell you his jaw nearly hit the floor when I sternly reminded him that permission was not something I needed from him, particularly considering how he hadn't sought mine throughout our entire marriage. He asked me what time I would be home, to which I replied rather nonchalantly, 'No idea. When it suits me.'

Wearing a gorgeous tiny black dress, no underwear, a long fox fur coat and 'fuck me' shoes, I joined Willie for drinks and ended up having the most fantastic wild, guilt-free, full pleasured, passionate night … in Willie's bed.

At the end of the night, as I was gathering my things together before I returned to David and the girls, I had the most randomly marvellous idea.

Folding up my little slip of a black dress, I placed it in my bag along with my jewellery. I then put on my high heels, my fur coat and absolutely nothing else, before getting a taxi back to our alpine lodge. I was in brilliant shape at the time, so my confidence was soaring. When I opened the door of the suite, I tried not to recoil from the strong smell of cigarettes that greeted me. David was standing out on the balcony, looking as though he had been crying for three hours straight. He had been frantically worried and threw a litany of questions at me. 'Where were you? Why weren't you home earlier? Who were you with?'

One swift response answered them all.

'That's none of your business, darling, just like *you* felt it was none of *my* business to know where you were all those nights I stayed up pacing the house. Just be content to know I had a wonderful, wonderful night – phew, in fact, I'm hot just thinking about it!'

With that, I casually threw off my fur coat, stood stark naked in front of him before kicking off my high heels and heading off to bed with the words, 'Night night, dear!'

Fucking hell, his expression was priceless.

❖

Not too long before that, Lady Sarah, the wife of Sir Peter Graham-Moon, made headlines when she extracted revenge on her husband's philandering ways. Upon discovering he had been conducting an affair with a younger woman, she promptly cut one sleeve from each of his thirty-two Saville Row suits, later remarking that her husband 'only needed one arm for what he does best'.

She also poured white paint over his BMW and distributed the contents of his extensive wine-cellar to the village locals. Not surprisingly, she has often been described as the patron saint of scorned spouses. Well, I like to think of my fur-coat-and-no-knickers story as my own personal Lady Sarah moment!

David and I never spoke about that night, although you should have seen him the following day on the piste trying not to look Willie in the eye. Awkward doesn't even come close to describing it! A blonde in a fur coat, an angry husband, a handsome ski instructor and snowy mountainous surroundings … Lord God when I think about it now, it could almost have been a scene from a James Bond film, although, admittedly, the story is slightly more Jackie Collins than James Bond!

I felt so independent that night. Finally, I had done something for myself. Better still, I hadn't done it in the sneaky manner to which David had become all too accustomed. I proved the point that if he planned on continuing his role as Romeo, then I had no intention of staying home playing the Virgin Mary.

I wasn't hiding anything; I was honest and open … literally!

Meeting Mr Como

Around the time I was born, the number one song in the charts was Perry Como's 'If'. Given that I spent my childhood idolising Mr Como, I can only conclude that either my mother or the midwife was humming that song when I made my big debut into the world. I adored him. No, actually, 'adored' is far too light a word, the term 'hopelessly in love with' is probably more accurate.

Back when my age was still in single figures, I had those bubblegum cards that kids would collect and swap. I always exchanged the most coveted cards of stars such as Jane Wyman and Elizabeth Taylor for the different cards of Perry Como. With my guitar in hand, I would then climb up the tree by the river across the road, stick a picture of Perry in the bark of a branch and sing 'Catch a Falling Star' to him.

Ironically, he was one of the very few stars I didn't meet during my time in Vegas. He was reclusive by nature, and so wasn't seen about the place as much as his fellow stars. No matter how many times I went to hear him sing, it always astounded me that I had somehow gone from sitting in front of a television watching *The Perry Como Show* every day after school, to sitting in the front row of a Vegas show watching him perform live every Tuesday night.

❖

The series of events that would eventually culminate in possibly the most profound experience of my life, began when I flew over to London to record a voiceover. I had planned to stay with my dear friend Siobhan McCarthy, however I was barely in the door of her magnificent Camden Square mansion at midday when Moya Doherty phoned, insisting that I return home as she and John needed to speak with me urgently. She didn't divulge any details over the phone, other than I had to be at the Westbury Hotel for 4 p.m. that day. I still don't know how I did it, but I managed to get back to Ireland just in time.

It turned out that the meeting was with the representatives of a company called Black Cat Productions and PBS, a US TV channel. Moya and John had been to dinner with them the previous evening, during which the director, Bob Wynne, mentioned they were planning to do a television special in Ireland with Perry Como.

Perry had recorded his legendary Christmas show in many countries and there was a tradition that the top female name in the country of recording would be the special guest on the show. While they had looked at a number of Irish personalities, none of them fitted the criteria. During the conversation, Bob told them that everyone they asked had recommended an artist called Twink for the job, but that he couldn't track me down. Moya, however, knew I was in England and so promised him she would have me at the Westbury the following day.

When our meeting started, Bob and his team explained that they were holding a big show in the Point Depot and that they wanted me to be the leading lady. Granted, I was very flattered but I wasn't brimming with excitement by any means. Following a brief chat, they stood up to leave when one of them turned and asked me if I would be interested in flying out to London or LA to do a vocal test with the orchestra. I agreed at which point he replied, 'Fantastic! We think you will be perfect for the job!'

Bear in mind, I still had no idea what exactly their show was about whereas they had assumed

I already knew. After I enquired a little further, they explained that they had 'this major star in America who has been the number one hit since the fifties'.

It was then they dropped the five words that nearly knocked me in shock.

'His name is Perry Como.'

As soon as I regained my voice, I *insisted* that they couldn't give the job to anyone else. I had never before been so brazen in a meeting, but I was born to do that job and I was going to make bloody sure my name was on that contract. Immediately, they sat back down, clearly amused by my sudden surge of enthusiasm as I proceeded to tell them all about my lifelong love of Perry Como. Following the meeting, a man by the name of Shay Hennessy phoned me to say how they had loved the stories I regaled them with and were highly impressed by the footage they had acquired of my past performances. Shay advised me to start preparing because if I got the job, filming for the show would start in January. I should have been elated, but as soon as he mentioned the month, my first thought was 'Oh shit, please no, not January!'.

The panto I was performing in would be taking place at the same time.

That previous Christmas, I had been issued with a new set of contracts which outlined that the panto was now being run by a group of three people, two of whom I had opened many doors for within the industry. Mavis Ascott, Andy O'Callaghan and Aileen Connor had formed a company called Comet Productions (or as I later christened them, 'Vomit Productions').

Immediately, I arranged to meet Aileen in her apartment in Rathmines to give her advance notice of the audition I had done for the Perry Como special. I explained that if I got the job, we would have to form a plan around the night of the programme by compensating with an extra date at the end of the panto run. Considering that this was May and the panto was not taking place until the following November, I had literally given Aileen, Mavis and Andy six months to plan around the Como contract.

❖

Apart from a further meeting with the network people in June, I didn't hear a thing from them until the following November, by which point I concluded I hadn't got the job.

On the day in question we had been rehearsing for the panto in a cold, damp hall on Harrington Street. Outside, it was the kind of horrendous Irish weather that would drive even the strictest of dieters into buying a box of chocolates. Following rehearsals (and feeling cold, thin and almost as miserable as the weather itself), I arrived home to the sound of the phone ringing just I was coming in the hall door laden down with bags. Soaking wet, out of breath and in a foul mood, my voice was not at its most phone-friendly by the time I pounced on the receiver.

'Yes?'

'Uh … Adèle? Hi it's Bob Wynne here.'

Never was there a more theatrical change of tone. 'Oh, hi Bob!'

'Look, Adèle, I'm really sorry …'

With an opening line of that nature, I naturally assumed he was phoning to say I hadn't got the job, so motor-mouth that I am, I interrupted him politely at that point and said, 'Aw don't worry about it, Bob. When I hadn't heard from you over the past few months, I figured my name wasn't on the job. I won't pretend I'm not heartbroken, but …'

'Would you shut up for a minute?'

'Pardon?'

'Just shut it! I'm going to start again. I'm really sorry … that we haven't been in touch with you for so long. We thought we had lost Mr Como when he developed very serious pneumonia and then suffered a relapse. By that point, we reckoned there was no show, but Mr Como is made of stern stuff. He bounced right back and is now determined that the show in Ireland is going to go ahead. If you would do us the honour, we would be thrilled to have you as Mr Como's special guest. Mr Como can't wait to meet you!'

Once I put the phone down, I let out a scream that even Bob himself would have heard in LA. You know when you see a footballer celebrating a goal by clenching his fists and roaring up at the sky in elation? Well that was me in my front hall. Unfortunately, there wasn't one person in the house I could even hug. David was out collecting the kids from his mother's house and the dogs were already looking at me as if I had lost the plot, so hugging them wasn't an option either. I tried to get my head together and figure out who I should phone first. As I was mulling over it, the phone rang again. It was Gay Byrne.

'Well done, Dotey! Well done! We're here toasting a glass of champers to your name!'

Now Gay is a man of a million talents but, as far as I was aware, Tarot reading isn't one of them, and considering I myself had only just found out about the Perry Como job, I assumed he couldn't be talking about that, so I replied, 'Toasting me for what, Gay?'

I'm fairly sure the poor man turned fifty shades of pale at that point because he certainly sounded it. He honestly thought he had ruined the surprise. As it transpired, Gay and Kathleen had heard about my news when they were having lunch at the McColgans' house that day. Bob had phoned John that morning explaining that he couldn't find me, and so of course by that evening, Gay naturally assumed the news had been relayed to me and that it would be safe to make the congratulatory call. Had he phoned literally one minute earlier, he would have been the one surprising *me* with the news!

❖

The following day, I met Aileen Connor in the rehearsal room to discuss the date of the Perry Como show, where she told me quite bluntly, 'There's absolutely nothing we can do about it, you're under contract and that's final'.

Reminders of the six-month pre-warning proved fruitless and the meeting pretty much ended on Aileen's nonchalant words, 'Well, if you take the job, it's at your own peril'.

Gerry O'Reilly, the owner of the theatre at the time, couldn't have been nicer about the matter and genuinely did everything in his power to try to accommodate me. Aileen, however, opted to behave like an obstinate child and repeatedly refused all suggestions on the table, preferring instead to make me pay the cost of closing the theatre down for one night. She also demanded that I pay for security in the theatre on the night it was closed, as well as the cost of advertising the cancellation of the show (despite me asking her months in advance not to advertise bookings for that night).

To have one night off, I had to pay £11,500. The one infuriating element of the situation is that there were so many other options she could have chosen. I just felt it was all so unfair and, to be honest, it was years before I could even bring myself to speak with Andy, Mavis or Aileen.

No one took their side on the matter. Even the media expressed their disgust over the notion of me being charged almost £12,000 for one night off, particularly considering I had been filling the theatre and making pots of money for them every night I was on stage.

Looking back, I think Andy and Mavis felt bad about the way in which they treated the situation. Aileen, likewise, has since told me that she blames her rash decision on the fact that her 'head was in a bad place' as a result of a matter in her private life. I frankly couldn't have cared less if her whole body was in a bad place, there was no way in hell I would have turned down Perry Como.

Perry and I, the 'Star-crossed lovers'.

Before I begin to tell you about my subsequent friendship with Perry, I need to first explain a rather strange phenomena that has been occurring in my life from a young age.

Apart from my asthma, I have always been made of stern stuff. My father used to say, 'That child has the health and strength of a shire horse'. In fact, I only break bones because of the speed at which I go through life. While I don't usually get headaches, there was one particular day when I experienced the most searing pain in my head which graduated to a point where I honestly thought I was having a brain haemorrhage. This was accompanied by an immense feeling of wanting to crouch in under something, like a protection barrier. My girls had bunk beds at the time, so I immediately hunched in between them. I remember telling David that my head felt so heavy it was as though there was cement on it. I was clutching my head while screaming in pain, adamant I was under mountains of cement. It sounds bizarre but I genuinely could not control what I was saying. David was panicking at this point and went to call a doctor. To this day, he still remembers me saying to him, 'There's no point calling the doctor. I'm in another place, I'm in Turkey'.

It was like an out-of-body experience; I was having this vivid image of dying in a wreckage somewhere. After about half an hour, the ordeal abated. The following day, the news was dominated by headlines regarding the Turkish earthquake, which had claimed the lives of thousands of people. When I saw the news, I knew instantly that what I had experienced was a very real premonition. It was as though I had lived through the pain that someone else was going to go through. Immediately, I felt unbearably guilty because in a way I had known this was going to happen. Naturally, there was nothing I could have done to have stopped it, but that didn't prevent the guilt from overriding all logic.

Another premonition occurred the night before the Buttevant rail disaster. This time I dreamt I was on a train, however at one point during the dream I experienced a flash in which I heard a man say, 'We have got to stop this train, there's danger'.

Suddenly, all I could see were bodies being strewn about the carriage before the massive noise of impact occurred. I could hear metal crunching, glass falling, and people crying, before suddenly everything went completely black.

I can only presume that in my dream I had died from whatever injuries I had sustained. The following day, I heard about the Buttevant crash, which had also claimed the life of a young friend of mine. I was devastated by his death and I often wondered if what I had seen in my dream was what he had experienced.

I admit it sounds off-the-wall, but it has been happening to me since I was a child and I have never been quite able to draw a conclusion to it. The famous singer Dory Previn, with whom I performed in *Hunky Dory*, has also had eerily similar experiences. As she was walking up the steps of a plane one day, she was suddenly overcome by a deep sickening feeling. She told the crew she was not boarding and insisted that her luggage be removed. Twenty minutes after take-off, the plane crashed, killing everyone on board.

❖

I genuinely don't know how or why I am sometimes able to see an exact picture of what's going to happen in relation to certain disasters. In fact, a desire for a greater understanding of this subject has led to me reading countless books

on the subject. Unfortunately, I'm still searching for answers.

The last major premonition I experienced occurred the night before the St Stephen's Day tsunami in 2004. During this dream, I remember being on a fairground ride with my friend, Moya Doherty. As we reached the highest point, I turned and said to her, 'Grab the edges, we have to try and stay here'.

It was at that point that I distinctly remember looking down from a massive height on the sandbank where a ship was lying on its side. In my dream, I could feel the enormous pressure of the water gathering underneath us while we clung to the iron bars of the fairground ride. I even remember saying to Moya, 'Just hold on, it will be gone in a few minutes'.

Likewise, I can still feel the terror that burned through my nerves as I watched a massive seventy-foot wave crash through the area, swallowing everyone on the ground beneath us. While we were looking down on all this horror unfolding, we could see people and cars being swept away by the water. It all felt so shockingly real – the kind of dream that deprives you of a peaceful sleep and leaves you exhausted when you wake.

At breakfast the following morning, I described the frighteningly vivid scenes for David and the girls. When the six o'clock news came on the screen that evening, the three of them turned and looked at me in shock as headlines of the tsunami dominated the bulletin. It clearly hadn't been a dream, but a premonition. There was a clip on the news that had obviously been shot by a cameraman up on a height or a helicopter shot. He was shooting the scenes beneath him and everything he captured was exactly how I had seen it. The exact shot of the washed-up ship was also on the news. Even the scenes of the waves washing away people and cars were also 100 per cent identical to what I had dreamed. David was particularly shocked by the sight of the ship on the sandbank as he remembered me describing it to him and the girls at breakfast.

At one stage during my life, these dreams were occurring on a regular basis. They were utterly terrifying, often forcing me to wake up in a very real panic. In a way, they weren't dreams in the normal sense of the word. They were, in fact, so realistic that you felt as though you had actually been there in person. It was as though I was consciously awake and feeling the first-hand terror of being caught up in a disaster. I would wake up and know with every fibre of my being that I had been there. Even though the details of the actual disaster were always quite specific, I never knew exactly where it was going to happen. I think knowing that there was nothing I could do to warn people really added to the distress of the situation.

On some occasions, I would be absorbed by a terrible, overwhelming depression, crying for hours over what I had seen and felt. I was tortured by it and even as I recall it now, my eyes are welling up. There was also no way to prevent it from occurring either. After all, you cannot actively control your dreams. The only way I can describe the feeling I experience is to liken it to that strong sense of danger possessed by animals. They always know when an earthquake is coming or when danger is nearing. In fact, it was even reported that minutes before anyone knew there was a tsunami on the way, animals had begun to behave strangely with most of them hiding or seeking higher ground. Even though the tsunami dream was traumatic, I still maintain that the worst one I experienced was that of the Aberfan disaster in South Wales. When I was fifteen years

old, I woke up screaming in the early hours of the morning.

Immediately my mother phoned Dr Maguire and asked him to call to the house as she thought I was having a massive asthma attack. I distinctly remember being unable to breathe and feeling a very real sense of suffocation. Even though Dr Maguire injected me with a drug to relieve my distress, I remained in a terrible state for some time afterwards.

The following morning, when I was talking to my parents about what I had gone through, I blurted out that I had died in my dream. I'd had a vision in which I was sitting at my school desk when a black mountain of muck and tar broke though the classroom window causing me to suffocate. I could feel myself struggling to rise above it before being sucked back underneath again. I even told my parents how I could feel my life ebbing away as the mud rushed up my nose and down my throat. The following day, 21 October 1966, the six o'clock news reported that 144 people – 116 of them children – had been killed when a tip of coal waste had slid onto the village of Aberfan in South Wales. The moment I saw the pictures of the site, I knew that's precisely where I had been and what I had experienced in my dream.

When it comes to natural disasters, I always seem to live through them the day before they happen. The last major one I 'lived through' was the tsunami, however, there have been a few smaller incidents since then. I don't know if I willed it to stop or if it just stopped naturally, but I haven't experienced one in quite some time and I honestly hope it stays that way.

The first time my parents were aware of this, they informed me, was when, at around seven years of age, I told them I had died in a place called Pompeii in a past life. At the time, I would have been far too young to have known about the volcanic disaster that occurred there, thus leaving them baffled by the strength of detail I suddenly possessed on the topic. One night, I was able to recall for my mother so many specifics, such as the house where I had lived with my two uncles, that I think I left her freaked out by it. After all, such a statement from a very young child was certainly cause for concern, to say the least.

Many years later, when I was filming a segment for RTÉ's *Bon Voyage* programme, one of the places I had to cover was Pompeii. Our first night in Rome was memorably awful. Someone had smashed the windows of our rental car and stolen the entire filming rig, leaving us with no option but to approach the local Italian television station and hire some of their equipment, which had seen far better days.

By the time we arrived in Pompeii, we had missed our filming slot. To be fair, they have to deal with film crews from all over the world on a daily basis so a filming schedule is very necessary, however the red tape that accompanies it is ridiculous. Only the Italians know how red the red tape is! It was so late when we were allowed to begin filming that the crew were forced to set up arc lamps to light up the area.

While they were setting up the equipment, a curator called Edward was giving a tour of the area so I asked him if I could join him. As we were walking, I was able to point out the location of where the bakery used to be. I then pointed out where the perfumery had stood and recalled how the scent of the perfume emanating from there would change at certain times of the year. I had never been there before but, somehow, I was able to point out the different streets. I eventually brought Edward to the location of a house I had seen in my dream. I told him that two brothers called the Vetti brothers had lived there and that they had been my uncles. He was amazed by level of the detail I knew, all of which he confirmed was factually correct.

I always had a very clear image in my head of the precise location where I believe I was killed in Pompeii. I had never seen pictures of it in a book; it was just an image I have always been aware of. That evening in Pompeii I found the exact location and it was precisely how I had envisioned it. Standing there was overwhelming on a level I can't even explain. By that point, we had been filming for a few days and each time, my piece to camera was slick and professional. As we stood in this particular location, however, memories began rushing through my mind. Despite making several attempts, I could not recall my lines for the camera. To this day, I still can't even explain it to myself, let alone describe it for anyone else.

This is where the story regarding my darling Perry picks up.

As I was talking to Bob Wynne in a very plush suite in the Berkeley Court Hotel, I suddenly heard a familiar voice behind me say, 'Well, well, well! I finally get to meet her!'

It was Perry Como.

We looked at each other and for a moment, we both experienced the weirdest feeling. There was something so completely surreal about the whole encounter that it again seemed to transcend any kind of explanation. He said to me, 'If I didn't say that seeing you in reality makes me remember the beautiful kid who sat in the front row every Tuesday night for years at my show, I would say I know you from somewhere else in life!'

'I would say the same! Hello, Mr C!'

'I think we've been a long time waiting to meet!' he replied with a smile.

For several nights after filming, we would sit and talk for hours. During one conversation, he told me of how he had always felt a very strong connection with Pompeii. It was then he began telling me his own past-life story and suddenly everything seemed to fall into place. Upon sharing with him my stories, he was immediately convinced we had known each other in a former life. From that point on, the bond between us was unbreakable.

We became such close friends, speaking to each other on the phone twice if not three times a month right up until the week he died. We would pour our hearts out to each other. He knew all about David, and when his beloved wife Rosario died, he phoned me and said, 'Well there's one way of looking at it, at least we're free for each other at last!'

❖

I couldn't believe I had gone from being that child who had sung her heart out to photographs of him, to being the woman standing on a stage and holding his hand while we sang our hearts out together. Perry was such marvellous fun on the Christmas special and one night, much to the amusement of the audience, he even joked, 'My wife doesn't know this, but Twink is coming home with me!'

Following the television special, I performed alongside him in a number of shows in Florida as well as in the Marriott Marquis on Broadway. I think Bob Wynne suspected there was something deeper between us, as he often referred to us as the star-crossed lovers.

He was right.

We were.

Saying our final goodbyes. Perry is whispering the words, 'And I love you so'. That was our password!

1. Bernie, Rose Violet and my darling Paddy Cole.
2. My all time favourite dance partner, Colm Keogh.
3. My teenage bedroom.
4. A typical sixties shot of Maxi Dick and Twink.
5. Dressed for my role as the narrator of Joseph and his Amazing Technicolour Dreamcoat at the Gaiety Theatre.

6. In No. 1 dressing room in the Gaiety Theatre.
7. A Lucy Johnston (of folk group The Johnstons) Tashmia hat shoot.
8. Big 8 photo shot
9. As Lady Speranza Wilde – in a beautiful play called **A Chelsea Affair**.
10. Between shows in my dressing room in the Olympia Theatre.

Mrs Chamberlain

Apart from watching *The Perry Como Show*, my other priority after school was getting home in time to watch Richard Chamberlain in his role as Dr Kildare. He was my first major crush and I was convinced we would be married some day. I had great ambitions of being Adèle Chamberlain!

My mother was fascinated by my obsession and would often say, 'If you don't end up marrying Richard Chamberlain, there's no justice in the world because you have devoted your whole life to him'.

She was right! There wasn't a picture of him available that I didn't have. My room was a shrine to him and even featured a gargantuan poster on the ceiling so that every night I could look up at him and say, 'Night night, Richard! I love you!'

At the time I also fancied Oliver Reid. While Chamberlain was a quiet-spoken gentleman, Reid was a big hulk of a man with more than just a passing fondness for the bottle. In fact, he died from a heart attack during the filming of *Gladiator* after he consumed a bar tab worth $725. What's more, this drinking session took place during his bloody lunch break! There was always something brutish about Oliver that I liked.

Unfortunately, I didn't realise just how brutish he was until I met him one night in the company of my then-boyfriend John McColgan who had been given the job of bringing him to a nightclub following his appearance on *The Late Late Show*. True to form, Oliver became pie-eyed drunk and spent the night arm-wrestling with every man willing. Eventually, John and I managed to persuade him to leave the club, however once he was on the street, he immediately clung to the railings, pretending to be a baboon, much to the amusement of passers-by. Somehow we managed to extricate him from the iron bars long enough to pour him into the car where I then had to pin him down to stop him from opening the door and jumping out while John was driving.

At one point during the short journey, Oliver spotted two blondes leaving a pub and immediately lunged at the car door to try to make a break for them. When we reached his hotel, we managed to roll him out of the car where two burly hotel bouncers took over. By the way they were pacifying him, it was obvious they were well accustomed to his antics. In fact, as they were carrying him upstairs, I could hear a very ossified Oliver ordering his next round of drinks! As we sat into the car, exhausted, John burst out laughing and jokingly asked, 'Well, has that cured you of your love affair with Oliver Reid?'

❖

While I have always both liked and admired Gemma Craven, I kid you not when I say I could have stabbed her through the heart for the role she won next to Richard Chamberlain in the film *The Slipper and the Rose*. Even when I was filming my television series, my greatest wish was to have him on as a guest. He was contacted about it, but unfortunately there was no break in filming and so the plan never came to fruition. When I read in the papers that he had come out of the closet, I felt like my life was over! It turns out he had been with his partner for years! My kids still say to me, 'Oh Mom, for God's sake, what's happened to your gaydar? He's far too beautiful to be straight!'

So Richard, my darling, if you ever change your mind, do look up Rathfarnham on Google Maps. You'll find me there! At the very worst, dear, we can discuss knitting patterns together!

Tipsy table tennis

Every memory I have of the late Richard de Courcy (aka Dick Hill), my boss in RTÉ Two, is one of fun and banter. He was a great friend of mine, and whenever David and I played table tennis with his two sons, we always tried to get them slightly tipsy first in order to be in with a chance of winning a game!

One of Dick's favourite stories to recall was one we dubbed 'The Heist'. One day in his office I feigned offence that he hadn't remembered my birthday, however he assured me he had thought of it and left the room to get my present. To my surprise, he returned carrying a large gift, all wrapped up. At the time, the halls of RTÉ Two were lined with beautiful paintings created by various well-known Irish artists, including my all-time favourite artist, Pauline Bewick. Knowing how much I loved Pauline's work, Dick had left the room and grabbed the painting from the corridor wall before having his secretary wrap it up. Of course, I was ecstatic at the sight of an original Pauline Bewick and couldn't stop thanking him for having bought it for me. Unfortunately for Dick, an inventory was being carried out at the time and sure enough a report was quickly filed about a very valuable painting that was now missing from RTÉ Two. Poor Dick had the bicycle clips on with fright. Shortly afterwards, he phoned me and, in a very embarrassed tone, said, 'Dotey, I will make it up to you, I promise, but you know the Pauline Bewick painting? Please don't tell me how much you adore it because I need it back!'

The audit was being carried out the following Monday, so the painting had to be back on the wall as soon as possible. We agreed to meet somewhere we presumed would be so busy with cars and people that no one would notice. As he was travelling from RTÉ and I from Rathfarnham, we arranged to meet in the car park of the Goat Grill in Goatstown. Unfortunately it was a bank holiday and so the bloody pub was closed and its car park stone empty. There we were, transferring what was clearly a large painting from one car boot to the other, when a Garda squad car pulled in. To make matters worse, headlines were rife at the time with stories about the Beit paintings being stolen from Russborough House in Wicklow. Despite explaining to the two guards that it wasn't so much a Beit painting but rather a Bewick one that belonged to RTÉ Two, they still made us tear open the brown paper around it before they would let the matter lie.

Later that day, the painting resumed its position on the corridor wall and, as far as I'm aware, no heads rolled when the audit took place. Not long afterwards, I had Pauline Bewick on *Play the Game* where she mentioned that she had heard about an incident involving me and one of her paintings. I explained the full story much to her amusement and when she appeared again on *Play the Game* in 1989, she presented me with an artwork of my very own on which she wrote, 'To Twink, with love from Pauline, to make an honest woman of her at last!'

❖

Artwork heists aside, Dick was so wonderful to work for and an incredible person to have as a friend. He adored me like a daughter; I, likewise, adored him like I did my father. He was a myriad of things in my life – a friend, a mentor, a gentleman – but one thing he was not was a lover. On the night I was preparing for my performance on the television programme *Lifelines*, a member of the RTÉ audit staff remarked about how nice it was to see so many of my friends in the audience. She then singled out Dick Hill's presence, and, with an obviously suggestive tone in her voice, and a 'nudge, nudge – wink, wink', went on to say that I must be particularly thrilled to see him. She was clearly implying something untoward, so I asked her exactly what she was getting at.

'You and the Dick!' she replied with a smirk. 'The Dick Hill!'

Her face fell with shock when she realised from my reaction that this was the first I had heard of it. She went on to explain that rumours had abounded in RTÉ for years that Dick and I were an item.

I remember feeling so grossly offended by such a suggestion. It was the absolute farthest thing from the truth. Dick and I idolised and adored each other, but there was never anything more to it. Of course, all it takes is one caustic tongue to start a lie before it graduates to being accepted as an urban legend. Considering that this particular rumour had seemingly been around for many years without me knowing about it, I did wonder, and worry how many other myths were out there that I was not aware of.

Following the show I confided in Ted Dolan about the rumours, as he was second in control to Dick at the time. He admitted he had heard them but knew they were bullshit. Years later, after Dick had sadly passed away, I shared a long conversation with his beautiful wife, Sue.

Fortunately, she too was fully aware of the nature of certain people within RTÉ and therefore wasn't surprised by the in-house rumour mill.

Sometimes however, I wish 'certain people' would remember the proverb, 'What you don't see with your eyes, don't witness with your mouth'.

❖

When we were clearing out the old wine cellar, Naomi discovered an old music bag belonging to David. Much to her disgust, it contained love letters from some Swiss woman with a penchant for recalling their passionate love making, or as she put it, 'our skin melting together in the perspiration of our love'.

In amongst the letters, we discovered a note from her written on the back of ticket from Powerscourt Estate in Enniskerry, a place where they had obviously visited for a romantic time. That alone broke my heart in a million pieces as that was where *we* had fallen in love; it had always been 'our' special place. Once again, more wonderful memories were unforgivably tarnished forever.

Fortunately for me, she was stupid enough to include her address. Well if you thought the zip-up-your-mickey tirade was bad, you should have seen the letter I sent her! Let's just say I ended it with a very clear warning that if I ever heard she was performing in Dublin again, a few 'friends' of mine would send her knee-caps home to her mother in Switzerland – in a box!

And, yes, I meant it.

Bibi

Women who possess qualities such as strength, articulation, feistiness and intelligence immediately have my admiration. Bibi Baskin

was one such woman. I had always held her in high esteem, and Bibi, likewise, was a great admirer of mine. The last time we met, however,

was certainly memorable if nothing else. She had invited me to appear on what I think was the closing show of the *Bibi* series. Following the recording, champagne was plentiful and everyone was in high spirits. Even though there were taxis waiting outside the door of RTÉ to bring the cast and crew to a nightclub on Leeson Street, Bibi who had clearly enjoyed quite a bit too much champagne, was determined to drive herself there. I, however, was determined not to let her, and so offered to drive the car for her. When I parked on Leeson Street, Bibi suddenly began to move in quite close.

She was, shall we say, well-jarred, so I took no notice at first, however when she began running her hand up and down my leg, I immediately pushed her off and made my way into the club. Having been drinking coffee all night, I headed straight for the ladies' toilets. The latch on the door was slightly broken so I placed my handbag on the ground against it to keep it closed. Next, I heard someone enter the bathroom and drunkenly roar, 'Twink! Where the hell are you?'

It was Bibi.

From the cubicle, I told her to get a grip and sober up. Just as I was bending down to pick up my handbag, the cubicle door flew open, narrowly missing my head. She pushed me against the wall, hands all over me, and proceeded to kiss me. She was so drunk, she had developed this manic strength. Somehow, I managed to push her away, drag her out of the cubicle and into the bar where I asked the manager for some coffee or water, anything to try to sober her up. When we sat her on a bar stool, we literally had to keep her propped up. With Bibi being looked after, I joined the crew for a drink before leaving for home.

I was never a fan of the nightclub scene and this nightclub in particular held bad memories for me. It was in this venue that David got drunk one night before collapsing in the bathroom. A number of people had managed to carry him out to my car, however, when we arrived at our house, I couldn't carry him in on my own so my only option was to leave him in the car. The following morning, I heard him start the car and leave. I didn't see him for two days after that. When he returned home, he told me he had driven up the Dublin mountains to walk, think and just generally be depressed. With that memory still fresh in my mind, not to mention Bibi's amorous behaviour towards me, I would have preferred to have been anywhere but in that God-awful club.

As I was about to leave the enclave of people I had been socialising with, I stepped back and suddenly felt two hands reach up inside my dress.

Bibi was back.

'Ah, give me a hug, Twink. I've always fancied you!'

This was definitely my cue to leave. Grabbing my bag, I ran outside and hailed a taxi home. Our paths never crossed after that, although, in a way, they never had the chance to. From what I can remember, she upped and left Ireland in 2001, and next thing I knew, she was in India looking like Mother Teresa. Maybe she doesn't remember that night – but I certainly do! After all, to be fair, I doubt there's one person reading this who hasn't had a grope they regret when they've had a glass too many!

'Shifting the wagon's wheels'

The musician Fionnuala Sherry has always denied having an affair with David but yet, funnily enough, that never stopped David staying over at her place after many a late music session. To be honest, I don't know if they were having an affair but then David was sleeping with so many women at that point that it was hard to separate those he was bedding from those he was not.

One night, David arrived home and parked Fionnuala's car in the driveway, blocking in my jeep. It seems she had lent him her car while she was away in America.

The following morning, just as I was about to bring Chloë to school, I noticed the obstruction so I asked David if he would move the car out of my way. The response was gruff at best.

'I'm not moving it.'

'It's blocking the driveway!'

'I'm *not* moving it'

With my frustration rising, I went out and tried to manoeuvre the jeep around the car but there was literally no room so I went back inside, this time hoping for some compromise on his part.

'I can't get around the car and I need to bring Chloë to school. Will you please move it?'

'Move it yourself.'

The red mist descended and I decided I would do exactly that.

I hopped into my jeep and told Chloë to fasten her seat-belt. With the jeep in reverse, I revved it as much as possible before ramming Fionnuala's car four or five times until I had bounced it out of my way. David emerged from the house screaming. Chloë on the hand was laughing hysterically at the whole thing and, even to this day, she recalls that moment as one of the most fun things she did as a child.

As he stood there like an anti-Christ, presumably thinking of the mechanic's bill he was now facing, I reacted by waving nonchalantly out the window while I drove off. I'm sure Fionnuala subsequently found out about the incident because Terry Keane wrote the funniest article in the *Sunday Independent*, making reference to me 'shifting the wagon's wheels'.

Here's another LOL for you ladies

Walking up to a department store's fabric counter, a pretty girl asked, 'I want to buy this material for a new dress. How much does it cost?'

'Only one kiss per yard,' replied the smirking male clerk.

'That's fine,' replied the girl. 'I'll take ten yards.'

Fuelled by expectation and anticipation, the clerk quickly measured out and wrapped the cloth, then teasingly held it out. The girl snapped up the package and pointed to a little old man standing beside her. 'Grandad will pay the bill,' she smiled.

Idrone

We were heartbroken to sell Beaufort House, but it lacked space. Idrone House on the other hand, gave me the space I needed to rehearse my dance routines for shows; David, the music room he had always longed for; and the girls, their own bedrooms. We bought Idrone for around £750,000 and thanks to our renovation works, it was worth around €3.5 million within three years. Our friends concluded we were mad for buying it, particularly given how utterly wretched it looked, but I saw its potential from the very beginning.

Most people like to move into a showhouse, not me though. I'm one of the rare breed that adores the challenge of completely transforming a property. In fact, Idrone was so rundown that had David and I not taken ownership of it, a visit by the demolition squad would surely have been on the cards. We decided from the beginning that we would restore it to its former glory.

Heaven in theory, hell in practice.

I had known of Idrone House all my life. I even used to ride horses with the Gallagher children who were living in the house at the time. When Idrone was first constructed, it was the only building in the area. Back then, Knocklyon was considered 'up in the mountains' so there was quite literally no one else living there. From what I heard, Idrone House was bought by a barrister who returned from Egypt at the turn of the century. Apparently, the Law Society would come up and do their books in what is now my white room. It then became the house of the Archbishop of Dublin. During the era of the Black and Tans, they would hide the clergy in a part of the house that became known as 'the priests' hole' (I kid you not folks!). These days, we tend to stash the Christmas decorations there rather than members of the clergy!

Somewhere along the line, the house was let fall to rack and ruin. A dear neighbour of mine, Paddy Whelan, even once recalled himself and a group of men herding a bull through the front door of the house and out the back into the fields. He also told me about the time a number of squatters took up residence there with nothing but oil barrels in the front room for cooking sausages. While all this was taking place in a listed building, the county council did absolutely nothing to protect it. During the sixties however, John Gallagher and his beautiful wife Mairéad became the new owners.

As I was returning from a voiceover job in London one day, I got chatting with an air hostess from Rathfarnham. During our conversation, she happened to mention that Idrone House was listed as being up for sale in the property section of *The Irish Times*. When I arrived home, I went into the office only to find that David had left a note for me on the exact same property section that the air hostess had been talking about. On it, he had drawn a big red circle around the piece about Idrone House. He was out collecting the girls from school so I left a note telling him to follow me to Knocklyon as I was going to chance my arm at a viewing. As John Gallagher and I were chatting in the hall of Idrone, David and the girls arrived into the driveway. Well, if looks could kill, the faces on the two girls would have absolutely buried you. Chloë protested first. 'I hate this house! We're not leaving Beaufort, and if you sell it, we're staying there. This place is a

dump and it smells of cigarettes. We hate this place. Naomi and I don't want to live here.'

I took her aside and gave her a stern warning about her attitude. She didn't even want to look at the house and instead informed me that she was staying put. As she went to lean on the door of what is now my beloved white room, it fell open and she with it. The size of the room immediately left her in awe and suddenly she found herself warming to the idea of Idrone being the new Beaufort. All four of us were so utterly in love with the place that we decided to make an offer for it. The rooms were a disaster but everything just had so much potential. As I walked from one room to the next, I began envisioning how I would decorate them. I immediately knew the front living room was going to be an elegant white room, although considering the walls of the house were practically black with damp, a mountain of work awaited us before I would be anywhere near having the white room I dreamed of.

For the length of time we were working on the house, we got nothing but grief from the county council. They made our lives hell. They sent out a woman who literally sat in the house day in, day out, and commented on everything we did, right down to the shade of paint we chose. We were using the best of everything, from fine furnishings to Farrow & Ball paintwork, yet you'd swear we had intended on installing pink neon lights and a lap-dancing pole with the way she was going on. On one occasion, we pulled up the carpets in the guest room only to find that a whole section of the room had been re-floored at one point. Even the support joists were dangerously old. Immediately, the council warned us that we couldn't touch the floorboards because they were 'listed'. Their so called 'listed floor boards' were, in fact, MDF (medium-density fibreboard), so when the builder had

them removed, David left them outside in a stack along with the accompanying note: 'Dear County Council, here is your listed MDF.' When 'the wan' arrived at the house, I escorted her to her so-called listed floorboards and told them she could take the ugly things with her. Even if they had been genuine floorboards, they were far from safe; in fact they were so wet and rotten they reminded me of a biscuit dipped in tea.

The hall was nothing more than a clay trench and at one stage, there was even a mini JCB in the middle of it. The place was such a mess that even the poor dogs didn't know where they were allowed pee, because they couldn't tell the inside from the outside. All the ceilings and floors had to go and scaffolding was the only thing holding up the stairwell. We then had to have all the original Irish plasterwork re-created which was another time-and-money consuming project.

We were giving this old historic house a new lease of life, and rather than commending our hard work and dedication to renovating it, the council instead decided to become even more petty. They gave me nothing but grief, and very often went out of their way to make things difficult. On one occasion, I asked if I could remove the pebble dashing from the house because it was a 1960s feature, not a Georgian feature. It wasn't part of the original building and so I felt if we were restoring the house to its original glory then it shouldn't be there. The council said no. When I tried to compromise and ask them if I could instead pebble dash the front wall so that it would match the house, they again said no. Anything I asked for was met with a negative response.

I would strongly advise anyone to think twice before buying a listed building. If my experience is anything to go by, the authorities are uncertain and inconsistent. One council representative would arrive at the house and tell me one thing; the following day a different council representative would call out and tell me the complete opposite to what I had been told a day earlier. They were constantly contradicting themselves. I asked them what action they had taken when the squatters moved in or when a bull was being herded through the house? What did they do when someone blocked all the fireplaces before pouring bricks and cement down the chimney shafts 'for draft purposes'? Absolutely nothing! The council was nowhere to be seen. As a result of the chimneys being blocked up, a previous inhabitant installed a number of radiators in the house which left the Georgian woodwork underneath the windows very warped. Yet when we wanted to fit under-floor heating, we were told, 'It's not the Georgian thing'.

It really was a labour of love. The locals have always been more than complimentary about our work on the house, which really means a lot. While I'm very proud of the work we carried out, I am still incredibly angry over the manner in which the council fought so bitterly with us over the smallest of issues, particularly as they clearly hadn't given a fiddler's fart about the place before we moved in.

Mammy Jackson's curtains

I had looked everywhere for pretty lace curtains to put in my sugar craft room – the kind that had a *Little House on the Prairie* vibe to them. Simple as that may sound, they were impossible to find and, believe me, I trawled every shop in search of them. When I was performing *Dirty Dusting* in the Cork Opera House, a member of staff in the lovely Montenotte Hotel apartments where I was staying, told me about a shop in the old French quarter called Jackson's that made the most fabulous curtains.

The following day, I visited the shop and, sure enough, on display in the window were the exact curtains I had been looking for. Mrs Jackson ordered miniature versions of the curtains complete with pink gingham bows, to fit the small window in my sugar room. They were perfect, like something out of an old Shropshire country sweet shop. I gave her my address and told her to put the bill in with the box of curtains. The curtains arrived but there was no sign of the bill, so I phoned the shop and spoke with

Hard at work in my sugar craft room.

Mrs Jackson's son. I thanked him profusely for the beautiful curtains and pointed out that they had forgotten to include the bill. He explained that his mother wouldn't let him give me the bill.

She had been my biggest fan and because I had been through hell over the past few years, this was her token of good luck. When I spoke with Mrs Jackson, I literally begged her to take money for them, but she wouldn't hear of it. All I could do was send her some lovely flowers and invite her to the show as my guest.

It's women like Mrs Jackson that really restore your faith in the kindness of people.

❖

Naturally, I am sickened by the idea of losing Idrone House after all we went through to make it what it is. David's refusal to pay his half of the mortgage for six years has been a crippling battle considering that the repayments most definitely require two people working full-time. To try to keep our beloved home, Chloë and I have to pay him off with a very large sum. David is acutely aware of the strain he is placing on his family, but then his line has always been 'there's plenty more houses out there'.

However that's the difference isn't it? It's only a house to him. To Chloë, Naomi and me, it's our home. It's the place where Chloë phones when she is homesick; it's the place where Naomi curls up on the couch if she's had a bad day at school; it's the place where our seven dogs, two cats and twenty-three birds enjoy food, shelter and love. David might think of it as a house with bricks and mortar, but to the three of us (or thirty-five of us if you include the pets!) it's a home with beauty and memories.

In the midst of all my grief with the house, a friend forwarded me a comment made by someone on an internet forum which read: 'Have you seen the size of the bitch's place? She could sell the fucking house and buy five semi-ds and pay the bank.' Ha! As if! in this climate?

Barbed comments are easily made when you have the luxury of hiding behind the anonymity of a computer screen. If what I have read in the newspapers is anything to go by, Twitter in particular is quickly becoming the new platform for incitements of hatred. Makes me wonder if such spineless weeds would have the balls to comment on anything if they had to put their name to it?

My message to Mr & Mrs Online Critic is a rather straightforward one: since when was it *your* shaggin' job to tell me what to do with *my* house? Bugger off and mind your own business.

Another LOL

WITHDRAWN

I'm robbing this next joke from the great Al Banim:

'On my wedding night, the wife and I went up to the room.

She took off her hairpiece and put it in the drawer,

She took out her contact lenses and put them in the drawer,

She took out her teeth and put them in the drawer,

She took off her eyelashes and put them in the drawer,

She took off her bra and put the two chicken fillets in the drawer,

Jaysus, I didn't know whether to get into the bleedin' drawer or the bed.'

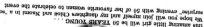

HOWEVER...
this Wednesday, the 4th, 2001.
this amazing little girl will be 50 YEARS YOUNG...
We hope you will join myself and my daughters Chloé and Naomi in a "sorta" surprise" evening with 50 of her favourite women to celebrate the event

And has still managed to live to see the 4th of April come around again and ... again and again.

From the day of her birth on Wednesday the 4th of April, 1951 ...

this little girl has ...

Danced ballet with Dame Margot Fonteyn,
Sung for Presidents, Prime Ministers, Princes, Kings & Queens.
Represented Ireland ten pin Bowling
Won the Texaco Art Contest,
Jumped horses over six bar gates,
White water rafted down the Zambezi
Para-glided over Tunisia.
Scuba dived in the Red Sea in Egypt
Won the Nestle Tennis tournament at 12.
Brought the Fine Gael Government to their knees.
Won TV awards from Jacob's to Monte Carlo,
Was marooned in Morocco
Won Ice skating championships at 19.
Lived through an earthquake.
Played everything from Samuel Beckett to Oscar Wilde.
"Rescued" Perry Como in the Point.
Looked after almost anything that has four legs and a tail.
Won every major Feis in Ireland... Singing and Dancing before she was 13.
Entertained the 007 cast at the Top of Piz Buin (mountain) in Switzerland.
Worked countless Tapestries and Needleworks.
"Did a ditty" with Kalinga - Linga Ceili band . . . in ZIMBABWE!
Water-skied for 4 years in Death Valley, Arizona . . .
Has been known to "work out" in a Gym 7 days a week!
Skied through the Austrian Tyrol.
Hosted a trip on the Orient Express.
Has more energy than a power station.
Won the Gas Cookery certificate for cooking age 9.
Has apparently graced more magazine covers than anyone in Irish History.
Played Polo with Eddie Macken & Harvey Smith in the RDS. (Charity)
Crossed a rope bridge over the Victoria Falls at midnight.
Can live for three months on chewing gum, apples & black coffee.
Has had every length, cut, and colour of hair in the history of the world.
Was dug out of a 16ft. snow drift in Alaska.
Won the Bord Iascaigh Mhara Award. (Cookery) aged 15.
Has "safaried" in Africa.
Bared all in St. Tropez!
Entertained 86,000 Turks . . . live . . . IN TURKISH!!!
Made dolls houses.
Knocked Dean Martin down in Las Vegas (on her bike)
Has Given birth to two daughters,

And you thought she only did Panto!!!!!!

Has survived,
Accidents . . . injuries . . . E-coli . . . money . . . marriage . . . AND ME!

'And you thought she was only a panto queen!'

If anything is capable of prompting a smile from me on my death bed, it's the memories of my fiftieth birthday.

In the run up to my big five-zero, I asked David what he thought I should do to mark it. He suggested that we go out for a family meal in a beautiful restaurant and although it sounded nice, I just felt as though I wanted to do something more memorable for such a landmark occasion in my life. What I didn't know was that David and the girls were already in the midst of planning a surprise party. Many months before I hit the milestone, Chloë and Naomi asked me, under the guise of a game, to name fifty women (as well as a few of my favourite fairies – sorry lads!) whom I would bring with me to a desert island. On another occasion, David asked me if I had ever written a list of all the things I had done in my life. We started compiling a list and when we had finished, he suggested I stick it on the fridge and add to it when I thought of something. I did exactly as he suggested and as the months passed, I kept adding to it. The three of them took note of the fifty women I mentioned and sent them the most phenomenal invitation which they created as a result of the information they had garnered from my list of achievements/endeavours pinned to the fridge.

❖

Unfortunately, Foot and Mouth disease had hit Ireland, resulting in every open public area, including their first choice, Rathfarnham Castle, being deemed out of bounds. Hearing of David's dilemma, my beloved Paul and Helen Goldin came to the rescue and offered their fabulous grounds for the party. Between the lot of them, they sent out the invitations and swore everyone to secrecy. David had

David and I with Frank McNamara and Teresa Lowe.

Myself and Linda Martin!

L-r: Alma Carroll, Ros Hubbard, Eileen Pearson, myself and Margo Tracey.

also organised coaches to bring people from the city centre to the Goldins' house in Rathmichael.

On the evening of my birthday, I got dressed up assuming we were going for dinner, but as David started driving, I noticed we were heading farther out the mountains rather than into town. As we made our way from Kilternan to Rathmichael, I then spotted a trail of luminous arrows with the words 'Adèle's party this way' hanging from trees. When we pulled into the gorgeous grounds of the Goldins' house, the whole driveway was lined with perfumed oil burners. David had also organised for the Vandenberg String Quartet

to play my favourite classical music as I arrived. As he escorted me into the marquee, everyone suddenly burst into a rendition of 'Happy Birthday'. I, on the other hand, nearly burst into tears with the excitement. Following a most amazing meal, the speeches began, as did the hysterics. David's speech was especially witty. I remember at one point he even said, 'Adèle has seen me through thick and thin … well there's the proof, I'm thick and she's thin!'

To help capture the magic of the night, he even arranged for a professional photographer to cover the event. I was literally left stunned by the amount of work both he and the Goldins invested in the surprise. It was just the most fabulous night and one which my friends and I still talk about with great delight.

❖

The late great Paul Goldin, the hypnotist, was one of my best friends. He was a brilliant showman but also an equally great intellectual with a list of letters after his name to challenge even David Agnew's! Coincidentally, he and David shared the same birthday of 15 April. There were many occasions where we all sat up until four in the morning in his beautiful house discussing subjects such as philosophy and medical science. I absolutely idolised and adored him.

A story he often loved to tell occurred back when I was going out with John McColgan. John and I had planned to meet Maxi and Dicko at Paul's show in the Pavilion in Dún Laoghaire. We were sitting five rows from the front and, as luck would have it, Dicko was sitting next to me. In the middle of his show, Paul informed the audience in his beautifully cultured voice that his next illusion wouldn't work unless he had the assistance of a very beautiful and intelligent woman. He then began looking around the audience before suddenly making a beeline for where I was sitting. Looking directly at me, he says, 'Now I *do* emphasise she has to be very beautiful and very intelligent …'

As he's honing in on me, I'm giving him the devil's look, the kind that says, 'Paul, I'm going to kill you if you bring me up on that stage!'

Walking towards me and smirking like a bold child, he adds, 'Now, would that beautiful woman please stand up?'

Without a moment's hesitation, Dick immediately shot up out of her seat. Flashing her Colgate smile, she promptly made her way to join Paul on stage while Maxi, John and I looked on, paralysed from laughing. Paul meanwhile had absolutely no idea who she was. In fact, he didn't even realise until afterwards that I knew her. He told that story at dinner parties for years. Poor Dicko on the other hand had no idea … until now that is!

We've met before, young man!

Some people arrive into our lives with such marvellous zeal that the impact of their friendship is strong enough that it's hard to remember what life was like without them. Jonathan Philbin Bowman was one such person. When he became part of *Play the Game* at nineteen years of age, I introduced myself to him with the words, 'We've met before, young man!'

I can still remember the exact moment I laid eyes on him. He was standing in the middle of a shop, a little boy of nine years with a shock of blondie-brown curly hair, not to mention an Usain Bolt level of speed when mastering the Rubik's cube. He was the epitome of the boy genius and even though the child of nine soon progressed into a man of nineteen, he never lost that same boyishly mischievous charisma that mesmerised everyone who met him. I'm proud to say that Jonathan and I became great friends, as did our kids.

❖

In early March 2000, David walked into the living room, sat me down, and told me the dreadful news that Jonathan had died. The shock was indescribable. I just kept thinking it couldn't be my Jonathan. Not the young man who could captivate people for life in the space of one conversation. Sadly it was. The moment he left us, Dublin became a darker place, devoid of his articulate writings and infectious wit.

Whenever I think of him, I don't envisage what he would be like today; instead my memories are of a man forever entrapped in a youthful persona. To me, he will always be the charming nine year old who wowed the crowd in the shop that day, or the incredibly handsome nineteen year old who enchanted all the female viewers of *Play the Game*. I always felt there should be a statue of Jonathan on Dawson Street complete with the dickey-bow tucked in by his shirt collar and the books tucked under his arm. After all, there wasn't one person in Dublin who didn't know or love him; it's only right he should be honoured. Following Jonathan's death, I wrote a letter to his parents John and Eimer Bowman, who later asked if it could be included in a tribute book to Jonathan. John Bowman wrote:

The broadcaster and comedienne Adèle King, better known under her stage name Twink, worked with Jonathan on RTÉ television's Play the Game. *She* was the regular captain of the women's team and so occasionally played against Jonathan who was on the men's team. He entered into the spirit of the game and hugely enjoyed it. I was unaware until I received this letter that Twink's first encounter with him had been many years earlier. Jonathan had been fascinated by the first wave of electronic gadgets and puzzles of all sorts, forerunners of the Rubik's cube and he quickly mastered them. He persuaded his parents that he should accept an offer from the proprietor of a shop in Dublin to spend two hours on a Saturday afternoon demonstrating them.

Adèle King wrote the following letter to me when Jonathan died:

'It is almost twenty-two years this week since I visited a shop in the Powerscourt Town Centre to buy a techno game of some sort for a friend of mine. As I walked into the small shop on the ground floor, I was drawn to a large crowd of customers standing watching someone or something with rapt attention. I approached them curiously and I was fascinated to see that it was a small tousled-haired little boy who was at the epicentre of the crowd. Within seconds of approaching the group, I was aware of the gasps of sheer astonishment and audible comments such as, 'My God, isn't he a little genius? Wouldn't it make you ashamed of your life?'

To my astonishment, the said little boy was giving all and sundry a breathtaking display of manual and mental dexterity with an entire array of digital games, pocket psions of the day. The manager, whom I knew from my college days, approached me and on seeing my astonished look promptly told me that the boy's name was Jonathan Philbin Bowman and that he was all of nine years old.

That was to be my first encounter with the boy wonder and I, just like the punters in the shop, was hooked. It was to be a further ten years before we actually met on a professional basis at a book launch we both had a part to play in. Shortly after that he appeared on the first of what was to be a regular stint in the ten-year life span of Play the Game on RTÉ. The energy and enthusiasm he generated to all around him on that show was breathtaking not to mention his inexhaustible knowledge of literature films and theatre. He put all his efforts into what was always a scintillating performance.

Off the screen, I became one of his ardent admirers. I was like most others, particularly women, drawn like a moth to the flame of this brilliant, effervescent young guy. He was like a battery cell, a force field and he had an extraordinary sense of the power of his own presence to all around him. It was to that most generous, witty, vivacious and energetic of people that we were all drawn willingly to what was sometimes hours and hours on end.

I bumped into him only a couple of weeks ago in Fitzer's in Dawson Street. I had my two young daughters with me and within seconds of meeting them, he had them laughing hysterically at some old school yard prank he re-enacted for them. I could clearly see that even though they were only aged ten and six they too were immediately sucked into the web and charm of good old-fashioned niceness that poured so effortlessly and unassumingly from him.

So it was with the greatest distress and utter grief that I tried to get my head around the events of the past few days. I have gone through all the stages, the shock, the disbelief, the endless tears and now the numbness and the eternal question when faced with the sudden loss of one so young and gifted – why? Concerning his passing, I can only say that few really ever make such an impression in their life and death as Jonathan did. He is now an immortal part of the Irish, and in particular Dublin, culture. I for one cannot imagine the *thought of driving into the city at some stage in the foreseeable future on a dull Dublin day without the prospects of possibly bumping into Jonathan somewhere to put the sun in the sky and a smile on my face …'*

Still miss you to this day – J.P.B.!

❖

Around this time, I had become embroiled in a conflict with the nuns of Notre Dame school, where my daughters were in attendance. All the parents had been summoned to a meeting in the school hall where the nuns announced their plans to close the junior school by phasing it out. There was uproar. A microphone was even passed around the room to allow parents have their say. One poor woman who had four young children in the school explained that her husband had been killed in a car crash and that she had deliberately moved to within walking distance of the school because she wasn't able to drive. Other parents, myself included, also voiced our outrage. Unbeknownst to us, reporters were listening to our comments. The following day, when I pulled into a petrol station in Rathfarnham, the shop assistant remarked that I was all over the newspapers. Sure enough the front pages consisted of headlines to the nature of 'Twink's fury with nuns'.

I couldn't see why the nuns should be allowed retire on the money of fee-paying parents so I carried out some investigation work and discovered that an old woman in the area had donated the land to the Notre Dame Sisters. It was to be used for, and I quote from the ancient papers I dug up, 'the further education of the young Catholic ladies in the area.' This basically meant the sisters did not have the right to sell off the land to developers. To help us with the legalities of our fight, I also hired a terrific solicitor.

In the midst of this drama, I received an invitation to the launch of the Bowmans' tribute book to Jonathan, which was taking place in his beloved Horseshoe Bar in the Shelbourne Hotel. John Bowman had also very kindly invited me to join himself, Eimer and around twelve other guests for dinner in the Unicorn Restaurant afterwards. When I arrived I was seated between Mary Harney and Liz O'Donnell. Why waste a golden opportunity? I sat down and immediately said, 'Now that I have you two ladies on the right and left of me, I need your attention!'

Once I told them about the story of the school, they did everything humanly possible to benefit our campaign. Along with the late Séamus Brennan, they added fuel to the fire and helped the parents in their fight. Around this time, I also went on Joe Duffy's radio show in a bid to highlight the campaign further. That, in itself, attracted strong criticism of the nuns' plans, and so they were left with no other option but to rewrite their proposal. Eventually, the issue was resolved and it was announced the school would stay open. In the meantime, I had to suffer a very vicious backlash from a priest in the west of Ireland. He wrote the most vitriolic letter to a newspaper in which he basically said, how dare Twink try to keep that school open for her spoiled, rich-bitch daughters and the other little spoiled, rich bitches in the area. Who does she think she is?

I remember reading it and being utterly appalled that these were the words of someone who wore the collar. First and foremost, it had absolutely nothing to do with 'fees' or 'spoiled, rich bitches'.

A woman had donated the land to the Notre Dame sisters for educational purposes. Why shouldn't her wishes be respected?

Joe Duffy has often asked me since if I ever received a thank you card from the school for my efforts. To be honest, I never even heard the words 'thank you', let alone receive a card. Most people don't believe me when I point out the stark contrast between the stereotypical image of a private school and the actual reality.

Long before the campaign against closing the school began, I approached the nuns and made a formal complaint about the school's conditions. The incident that prompted my action occurred when, after a sleep-over, I dropped a friend of Naomi's to the national school in Knocklyon. While I was there, a teacher asked me if I would come in and say hello to the kids. She brought me upstairs to the classroom where, to my shock, I was greeted by a bright and airy room that was also colourful and impeccably clean. Here was this beautiful school that was free of charge, and yet I was driving my child to a private school that still managed to be a kip, despite benefiting from humongous fees.

The nuns had always been more than happy to take the full fees without providing the adequate facilities in return, so I argued that all parents should pay a compromised fee, rather than the full fee, until the conditions were improved. The toilets were filthy and always blocked, and even though the nuns would insist on the girls being immaculately groomed, there wasn't even so much as soap or mirrors in the bathroom. Apparently, the lack of mirrors was the nuns' archaic way of teaching the girls not to be vain. The students underwent lessons in a nasty prefab on the lawn which, in the winter, was inches deep in muck. The nuns were so precious about their uniforms that they wouldn't allow the kids to wear their jackets in the winter even though it was freezing cold. During the summer, they sweated in rooms with non-open the windows, when they played sports in the summer, there was nowhere appropriate for them to shower or change, which meant they were stuck in sweaty tracksuits for the rest of the day. Naomi, like her fellow students, was permanently ill as a result. The only thing that concerned one particular nun was that the girls wore their Juliette cap; Jesus she was obsessed with that bloody cap.

The straw that broke the camel's back however, was when the head nun started telling us what we could and couldn't put in our kids' lunchboxes. They had actually banned a list of foods. When a meeting was held in the school, I duly attended and let fly. I reminded them that they were nuns not mums, and as a result, had no idea how much effort mothers invested in trying to vary the contents of the bloody lunchbox. As far as I was concerned, it wasn't the business of the Notre Dame sisters if a parent decided to put twenty sticks of chewing gum in the child's lunchbox. During the meeting, they were gormless enough to reveal that the reason they had banned certain foods was because there was no one to sweep the yard. It actually had nothing to do with the dietary benefits of the children. At that point, every parent in the room immediately asked, 'So what *is* the fee money being spent on?'

When I pointed out that under no circumstances would I be heeding their ridiculous list of banned foods, I was informed that Naomi would be sent home from school if she was found to have one of the listed items. They were shameless. When I put it to the room and asked if the other mothers supported me in my stance, there was a unanimous show of hands.

The nuns had their answer. These days the school is being run by a lay committee. I can only hope things have improved.

I can't believe how young David looks in this photograph. God he really was only a boy wasn't he? (I feel like a cradle snatcher now!) The bed he is sitting on is a waterbed which I had brought over from Las Vegas. I had decorated the attic of my parents house in a very zany style of den appropriate to the 1970s, which included covering the walls of the room in fake grass. I know that sounds bizarre but it actually looked spectacular. I had a drinks cabinet on one side and a little stash of marijuana with roach clips on the other. The waterbed, which was all the rage back then, was the main feature of the room. In fact before I could even bring the bed into the house, I had to first enlist the services of an engineer to determine whether or not the ceiling would be able to sustain the weight of the water. It was fine for years until a man fixing my stereo knelt on the bed, causing part of it to roll and catch against a sharp end. A puncture ensued, as did chaos. In the end, the fire brigade had to climb through the back window with a hose to drain the water from the bed before it flooded the top floor. It was a queen-sized bed and had it completely burst, the water would have wrecked the house. Mind you with some of the action that waterbed experienced between Ireland and Vegas, I'm surprised it hadn't burst years earlier!

Far-from-reality TV

Celebrity Farm, which was aired in 2003, was one of Ireland's first reality TV shows. It's one that most people still fondly remember – but one that I, quite frankly, would rather forget.

The idea of the show was to have eight Irish personalities work on a farm for seven days with one being 'turfed out' each evening. I was reluctant to participate at first but on the advice of my then-manager, I went against my better judgement and signed the dotted line. Following the show's launch on the *Late Late,* myself and my fellow farmhands – singer Mary Coughlan, artist Kevin Sharkey, socialite and columnist Gavin Lambe Murphy, *Fair City* actor George Murphy, presenter Mary Kingston, Rose of Tralee winner Tamara Gervasoni and presenter Paddy O'Gorman – were barrelled into a coach with blacked-out windows. Clearly the bus driver had been ordered to drive around for an hour so as to give the impression we were being driven out into the midlands. The reality however was that when we left RTÉ in Donnybrook, we only went up the road to Rathfarnham.

Once inside the house, our bags were thoroughly searched and items such as phones, magazines, music, radios and even wrist watches were all confiscated. Cosmetics, apart from basic toiletries, were also taken away. You couldn't seek solace in a book or escape a bad day by sticking on your headphones, instead you were forced to rely on your fellow contestants for entertainment. There were no clocks in the house, so in the evenings we would try to amuse ourselves by guessing what time it was. Every window and door also had a security man outside it, so you couldn't even step out into the fresh air until you were given permission.

On one occasion, a member of the production team arrived into the house and explained that because a contestant had smuggled in a phone and seemingly rung someone, we would all have to forgo dinner that evening as punishment. That immediately set in motion a sense of animosity within the group. Suspicions were being raised about different people and fingers were beginning to point. As it turned out, it was all psychological warfare. When the show was over, we discovered that no one had smuggled in a phone, it was just a ruse to set us against each other in the hope that we would start rowing.

Every day, we were brought into a room individually where we would have to talk to a camera. A man behind a screen would ask a variety of questions in an attempt to try and coax you into bitching about your fellow housemates. If you refused to insult your colleagues, he would then make out that they had all spoken badly of you. Again, it was set up to try and cause a rift within the group. With the exception of the bathroom, the cameras were on us twenty-four hours a day. Our microphones were on at all times, even when we were in bed.

In the world of reality television, a production team very deliberately brings together a group of people who will unquestionably wind each other up and get on each other's nerves. In this particular situation, I think the production team thought Mary Coughlan and I would lock horns. Much to their surprise (and ours) the opposite happened and we genuinely became great friends. She and I never had any reason to speak to each other before meeting on that show but when we did get chatting, we realised we were both the complete opposite to what we had initially assumed. As well as being one of the nicest people I had ever met, Mary was also one of the bravest. She has had a well-documented struggle with the bottle but, let me tell you, that woman has willpower made of steel. Most of the tasks throughout the week were based on a reward system of food and alcohol. When the wine bottles were brought in by the crew, Mary always treated the situation with amazing dignity and strength, brushing it off with a been-there-done-that attitude.

In the house, Kevin Sharkey and I would always call each other 'chef' because I had adopted the role of cook and, he, my assistant. He was always very complimentary about my cooking and really seemed like a sweet guy. At the time, I felt sorry for him. People had formed their opinions about him but I was convinced that if they gave him a chance, they would see he was just misunderstood. Even outside the *Late Late* studio as we were making our way to the bus, a very well-known international music mogul tapped me on the shoulder and warned me 'be careful of Sharkey, Twink!'.

During my short stay in the house, Kevin poured his heart out to me and I really began to consider him a friend, or at least a friend-in-the-making. Even though I got on well with everyone, I couldn't stick the confinement of the house and so became determined to be the first to leave. If I wasn't evicted, I planned to take the horse from the nearby field and jump the gate. I wouldn't have given it a second thought; sure I had been jumping six-bar gates on horseback since I was a kid. I knew exactly where I was, so I had it worked out in my head that I would ride out to Kilternan and phone the production team from

Palmer's Pub to tell them I had turfed *meself* out. I was so adamant on leaving that I had even showed the others how to cook different dishes so that they wouldn't be stuck when I left.

When my name was announced on eviction night, I was both euphoric and relieved all at once. The eviction routine however, soon knocked me out of my stride. I was escorted out to a pig trailer, which was embellished with the sign 'turfed out'. I was then driven out of the yard and over to the presenter, Mairéad McGuinness, at which point I was thrown into a live television interview. To be driven out on a pig trailer was humiliating for all the contestants, and not something we had been made aware of prior to joining the show.

At the time, I felt really guilty over leaving Mary Coughlan in the house. I could see that the alcohol was becoming more and more prominent within the house at night, primarily because there was no other form of entertainment. There was a temptation to get slaughtered drunk out of sheer boredom and, as such, I was afraid that the confines of the house would get to her. When I told the production company how unspeakably cruel it was to bring alcohol into the equation. The callous reply I received was to the nature of, 'Well we knew what we were letting ourselves in for.'

❖

While we had enjoyed a lot of great laughs in the house, we also suffered as much trauma. At one point, we all thought we were going to crack up. The noise of the security guards locking the doors at night was enough to put the fear of God through you because it reiterated the fact that you were not allowed out. As I left the house, I remember praying to whoever was in the heavens looking over me that I would never do anything foolish enough to find myself in prison.

I know in the grand scheme of things, it was just a show and we had the freedom to leave if we wished, but that doesn't make the experience any less horrendous when it's happening. Nobody, absolutely nobody other than those who have been through it, can describe what life is like in the trapped depths of a reality television hell hole. Even the biggest fan of reality television does not have the slightest concept of what it is like.

From my experience of being in that house, I can only conclude that anyone who has endured years of prison must be psychologically scarred after the experience. When I left the farm, John Gilligan's imprisonment was making the news. As a result, there were a few headlines to the nature of 'Twink comes out and Gilligan goes in'. As I looked at the papers, I couldn't understand how that jumped-up little shit was smiling for the cameras, considering he was about to be locked up for twenty-eight years. Even though I had only remained in the house for a very short space of time, my head was in a bad place when I left.

In fact, when I arrived home, David became extremely worried for me. I couldn't bear for the radio or television to be on and under no circumstances did I want anyone near me, not even my girls. Gerry Ryan had expected me to talk on his show each day about the other contestants and to predict the next evictee, but I was in no state to go on air. For some reason, a dreadful fit of crying came upon me. At the time, I felt like I was about to have a nervous breakdown, but now that I look back on it, I realise I was suffering from a form of post-traumatic stress.

I wasn't the only one who endured an adverse reaction to the situation. In fact, the reverberations for a few of the contestants were quite bad when they left the house. We met up for dinner several times after the show and we all agreed it was something we would never do again. The whole experience just seemed to have a debilitating effect on us. It's so easy to see how Jade Goody and Shilpa Shetty were set up as polar opposites in Celebrity *Big Brother*, and, to this day, I am convinced the psychological trauma from that show set in motion Jade's health problems.

Funnily enough, I still don't regret participating in the show. Let's just say, it motivated me to stay as far away as possible from ending up in prison.

Probably the biggest disappointment, for me anyway, was Kevin Sharkey. It was stipulated in our contracts that we were to be in the *Late Late* studio to meet the winner of the show, however on the night in question, a rumour began to circulate that Sharkey wasn't going to attend. The rumour proved to be true. It seems Kevin instead chose to appear on Eamon Dunphy's show which was broadcast at the same time as the *Late Late*. While in the hot seat, he bitched about all his former housemates, particularly me, thus ensuring it was he who secured the front-page headlines and not the winner, George McMahon. Immediately, journalists began phoning me for a response to his outrageous remarks. I didn't hide my disgust with him, and I admitted how up until that point, I was convinced everyone had him wrong, that he was just a misunderstood soul with a lot of issues.

Well I soon realised he was far from misunderstood, he was just a self-publicising hypocrite. He was so nice to our faces but yet he seemed to think nothing of lambasting us on television.

A month or two following *Celebrity Farm*, he sent me the biggest bunch of white flowers I had ever seen in my life; it looked like five huge bouquets in one. The accompanying message read: 'Happy wedding anniversary Chef, yours in admiration, love always, Kevin Sharkey.'

He had obviously remembered a conversation we had shared in the house during which I mentioned how much I loved plain white flowers.

Although he has never acknowledged the remarks he made on the *Eamon Dunphy Show*, I'm sure if I broached the topic, he would brush it off as just a bit of controversy and craic. Over the years since *Celebrity Farm*, he has kindly sent me invitations to his exhibitions, and I honestly began to think he was a changed man. Unfortunately, an incident in 2010 proved otherwise.

I had been paying David's share of the mortgage as well as my own for years until eventually I just couldn't do it any more. I approached the building society and told them that while I would continue paying my half, they could chase David for his. The house, after all, was in both our names. I paid my half and when the matter arose in court, David simply pleaded that he didn't have the money to pay his share. As a result, I was left having to pay the arrears in order to keep the house.

Following the case, I received a text from Brian Merriman who told me to 'buy if you dare' the daily and evening papers. It seems Kevin Sharkey had told the press that he would give me one of his paintings to auction off for money towards my mortgage. He then conveniently went on to mention an upcoming exhibition he was holding. Honestly, how low can someone go to get publicity for a bunch of paintings? As my friends pointed out at the time, if he was making a genuine gesture of selfless goodwill, then he would have phoned *me* directly and not the newspapers.

That finished it for me.

Charity You're a Star

Speaking as someone directly involved in the show, I can honestly say the editor of the three *Charity You're a Star* series deserved the Victoria Cross for charitable editing. Behind the scenes, which was also filmed for the show, saw a considerable amount of celebrity bitching and refusing to do things. Despite the fact that they were all singing on television for the first time, some of them immediately adopted a know-it-all attitude, the infamous kind normally exclusive to teenagers. Fortunately, those with more pleasant dispositions made my job as vocal coach and mentor a rather joyous one.

Looking back, I genuinely loved being a part of that programme and I adored going into rehearsals each day to work with the contestants, or at least those who were willing to work. Unfortunately, each series had its fair share of ego trippers, and my God, what unjustified egos they had. The one person everyone expected to be genuinely good fun, turned out to be the greatest pain. Sweet Jesus, he was the epitome of a smartarse and couldn't take an instruction if you were to slap him across the face with a list of them. One of the band members christened another contestant 'Mariah Carey' as a nod to her diva tendencies. Despite the fact that she had never sung in public before, this public face walked in with an attitude that would have made even the real Mariah blush. Her voice was like that of a bird … (if the bird in question was Dustin, that is!).

To be fair, anyone who watched the show could tell you that Seán Bán Breathnach was not the best singer. He never sang one note in the same key as the backing band and, to make matters worse, he never started on time with them either. When he sang, everyone was in hysterics including the crew. The thing is, it was so bad that people assumed he was doing it deliberately – that he was acutely aware of how out of tune he was. Well I can tell you now, Seán genuinely thought he could sing. He was convinced he had a great voice when in reality there was more air in a politician's promise than in his lungs. But he was always great craic!

There was another celebrity contestant who took himself so seriously that any time he walked into rehearsals, his ego would arrive in first. There was no guiding him in terms of singing, as far as he was concerned he knew everything there was to know about the field of entertainment.

Ironically, the egotistical people were always the ones with the least talent. It's the self-effacing ones that turn out to be the best. A few in particular stand out in my mind. Síle Seoige, for instance, had the most incredible voice. She was a dote, blessed with a set of pipes with a rich dark velvety tone.

The stunning model Vivienne Connolly likewise was another incredible star. When she walked out on stage wearing a white shirt, black belt, knee-high boots, and launched into the Shania Twain hit, 'Man I Feel Like a Woman', I think the jaw of every man in the Helix Theatre immediately hit the floor. She was breathtakingly beautiful in both looks and personality.

Despite being very shy, the rugby player Shane Byrne managed to summon the confidence to unlock his Meatloaf-style voice and enthral the viewers. He too was also as amazing to work with as he was to listen to. As for my darling Dáithí Ó Sé, I was so tough on him but God love him, he took everything with such good humour. I lost count of the number of times I had to take him to task and say, 'Dáithí, it's a good job I'm so in love with you because you're breaking my heart with your routine … if you do that on television you'll look like a pillock!'

He was such a pet that I could never stay angry at him for long, not even when he was acting like an absolute plonker, albeit a gorgeous one. I love that man to this day!

'Ah, Jaysus there's Twink!'

I find it hysterical when a magazine places me on their front cover simply because I never thought I would be a sixty-year-old cover girl. Then again, I never thought I would be 'spotted' by a certain Colin Farrell either – a memory that makes me very proud and my daughters very jealous! Our extremely brief encounter occurred one day a few years back as I was bringing a number of children to an audition in the Courtyard Film Studios in Sandymount. Colin was leaving a nearby pub with a cigarette in one hand, a girlfriend on the other and a signature woolly hat on his head. I didn't even realise it was the boy himself until I heard his familiar voice shout over, 'Ah Jaysus, there's Twink!'

My hump-smartner

I never wanted the headlines.

My 'cancer scare' was my business and not that of anyone else. Unfortunately, despite my best media intrusion-prevention efforts, the story escaped my control and promptly made its way to the nearest printing press. The story regarding my scare came about as I was giving an interview to a journalist about the *Dirty Dusting* show. In the middle of our conversation, a high-ranking member of the crew walked in and casually asked, 'Did you tell him about your cancer scare?'

With that, the reporter's eyes lit up, while my jaw hit the floor, shocked by the nonchalant nature in which a very private trauma had been introduced to a press interview without my consent. Even though I then went on to quickly clarify the story, the reporter was already envisioning his byline beside the big headline that would grace the front page.

❖

The scare in question occurred a few years ago when I was on tour in England with the smash comedy play *Dirty Dusting*. When we were playing the Kingston Theatre in Hull, I was experiencing a dreadful searing pain around the top of my left breast and underarm. A few weeks earlier, it had been more of a niggling pain that came and went. In Hull, however, it had somehow progressed into a deep, burning agony. The lump was so painful, it would keep me awake at night. Sleep would only ever come about as a result of exhaustion.

I always maintained a brave face, afraid to tell anyone about what I was going through. I know that sounds ridiculous, but looking back, I think I was terrified that they might confirm my worst fears by daring to mention the 'C' word.

You console yourself with the thoughts that maybe the situation only seems worse in your head because you have continuously mulled over it. You just know that the moment someone else puts voice to those fears, you will be presented with a very real and harsh reality of the future that could potentially await you. As horrendous as the pain already felt, I seriously dreaded the possibility of such agony being multiplied by a cancer diagnosis. In the end, it just seemed emotionally easier to ignore the problem than to confront it. Physically, however, it was hell.

I always walked to the Kingston Theatre because it was only a short distance from my hotel, however one particular night, the pain became so bad that I had to break the short journey by sitting down on the footpath. The severity of the pain escalated to a point where I found myself stalling a second time. When I eventually arrived at the theatre, the stage manager Roz voiced her concern over how distressed I appeared to be. I initially brushed it off, insisting I was fine, until something inside me snapped and I found myself in a distraught heap. I admitted everything to Roz. The physical pain, the emotional anguish and my own self-diagnosis that it must be breast cancer. I still don't know how I managed to go on stage and perform that night. I can only assume that once I was in costume, I fell into character thus causing all other concerns to drift away until the curtain came down.

The following day, Roz made an appointment for me in the hospital in Hull. The oncology nurse explained that there was not a lot they could do for me as I didn't live in the area, but she did ask for the name of my nearest hospital in Dublin and set about phoning them to make an appointment for me. The conversation she had with the person on the other end of the line still puts a smile on my face today. After explaining that she wanted to make an appointment at their clinic for an Irish woman called Adèle King, she looked a bit perplexed as she listened to the woman on the other end of the phone. I remember hearing her say, 'Pardon? Um … ok, I'll ask her. Eh – are you Twink?'

An appointment for a mammogram was arranged for the following Wednesday. This was then followed by a two-week wait for the results. I can honestly say that for every minute of those 336 hours, I was in torment. When the postman dropped off a letter from the hospital requesting that I attend a meeting with the consultant, I was sure the end of the road was nigh. Surely, if everything was fine they wouldn't go to the trouble of calling me in for a meeting?

When I stepped inside the consultant's room, the first thing I saw was my mammogram up on the screen. I was convinced she was going to start pointing out tumours; instead she pointed to a piece of fractured bone. When I was fourteen, I suffered some broken ribs following a horse fall on a beach in Wexford. It seems a piece of fractured bone had moved over the years before lodging itself in a muscle, thus causing the searing pain. What I didn't realise at the time was that there is no pain with a breast cancer lump. I was crying with relief when she told me the news. In fact I was so relieved that I literally jumped up and kissed her.

I'm not a pessimistic person by any means but the pain was so bad that I couldn't but help envision the worst possible scenario.

Even though I was crying with happiness at the revelation that it wasn't cancer, I also found myself crying in pain for all the women who had sat where I was and been told the opposite. I can't even imagine what it must be like to have your worst fears confirmed, nor can I imagine what it must be like for a nurse to have to break such news. In a way, 'the scare' was the best thing that ever happened to me as it forced me to become more aware of my mortality.

Paddy Cole's great name for a health scare is a 'hump-smartner'. After all, there's nothing like a brush with serious illness to straighten your hump out and stop you moaning and groaning about every little mundane thing that goes wrong.

Regardless of where I am performing in Ireland, every week without fail I receive notes either asking me to say hello to a woman in the audience who is suffering from cancer and only has a certain number of months left to live, or to give a shout out to a woman who recently got the all-clear from her doctors and is out celebrating with the girls. Sometimes, I will receive a note asking me if I would mind taking the time after a show to meet a woman who is suffering from terminal cancer. One night, I met a beautiful woman who told me that her daughter was getting married the following year but that she wouldn't live to see it as she was 'fading fast'.

I was absolutely devastated for her. So virulent and heartbreaking are the effects of that disease that I have often found myself in tears over a woman's story long after I have left the theatre.

9/11

August 2001, a month before the terrorist attacks on New York, David, Chloë, Naomi and I were standing on the roof of one of the Twin Towers. Our trip to the World Trade Center was made all the more special by a visit to my very dear friend Pat, who was involved in a restaurant near

the top of Tower One. Even though he started out as a fabulous dancer, Pat eventually decided to make a full-time career from his talent as a pastry chef, a move that certainly paid off as his business became phenomenally successful.

During the afternoon of 11 September 2001, I pulled in to Notre Dame in Churchtown to pick up Naomi, when Helen Connaughton, the mother of one of Naomi's best friend's Niamh, pulled in beside me and asked if I had heard the news about a plane crashing into one of the Twin Towers.

Immediately, I thought of Pat.

Like everyone else, I set about making frantic phone calls, trying to determine the whereabouts of friends. To my horror, I later found out that Pat and his partner had been in the restaurant that morning and had died during the atrocity. That attack on New York was a decimation of every semblance of humanity known. It was the most disgusting, revolting, evil act anyone could possibly do to innocent people; an act of the most gross violence.

I have worked in the Middle East all my life, so I like to think of myself as very much an arbiter.

I speak a smattering of Arabic and am fluent in Turkish; I adore the Arabic culture, the food, and the people. I have many wonderful Arabic and Muslim friends in the Middle East who will always have a special place in my heart. Likewise, I have worked extensively in America; I have many friends there and I love the different aspects of *their* culture. As such, I never try to weigh one culture against the other, but rather see them separately for what they are. Sadly, their differences are simply too vast to ever give hope to the idea that a solution may appear on the horizon in the near future.

I have worked with these people so I understand the differences. In my opinion, the trouble between the two cultures has stemmed from that age-old curse, religion. To quote the Nobel-prize-winning theoretical physicist, Steven Weinberg, without religion, 'you'd have good people doing good things and evil people doing evil things, *but*, it takes religion for good people to do evil things'.

Eileen Colgan is an actress I have admired all my life, so much so, that I was bowled over when the opportunity arose to work with her in **Dirty Dusting**. From day one she and I hit it off and have been best friends ever since. I truly adore her on stage and off.

Here's another LOL

There was this woman who had an artist paint her portrait covered with the most amazingly beautiful and expensive jewels. Her explanation: 'If I die and my husband remarries, I want the next bitch he marries to go mental looking for the jewels!'

'Mistress: something between a mister and a mattress' ~ Anonymous

Whenever an affair is taking place, someone on the outside is always left tackling that age old dilemma, 'Should I tell their wife/husband?'

When David and Ruth began their affair, it was common knowledge to everyone except me, and truthfully, I would have preferred if someone had told me the moment they knew. In the end, my darling Brian Merriman was the one who sat me down and told me the truth. He explained that a few of my colleagues had met up in the RTÉ canteen to discuss whether or not I should be informed. They were utterly torn over what to do as they were so afraid that I would end up despising the person who broke such news to me. They simply didn't know how to tell me.

Even though they knew what David was doing was dreadful, a part of them probably felt that maybe he would end the affair and that I would remain blissfully untouched by the trauma of yet another cheating episode from a man clearly bereft of the will to make a marriage work. Good intentions perhaps, but unfortunately the situation didn't run its course quite as smoothly as they had hoped.

❖

When I first learned of their affair that day in 2004, it really hit me that David's pattern in life had all but changed and, with that, I became immersed in the most excruciating pain, anguish and disbelief. It's one of those things that you have to experience to understand. While at first I was crying with the thoughts of *not again*, the blade of the knife really sliced me when I discovered that *this* particular affair had been taking place over a two-year period.

Immediately, your mind goes through all the things we did together during those two years. All the smiles and memories we had created in that time were suddenly reduced to nothing. I would think about all the times I had brought Chloë and Naomi to watch their dad play in the National Concert Orchestra, when at the same time that 'wan' was up on stage with him. Chloë's precious memories likewise have been unforgivably tarnished.

When Chloë was recording her first Celtic Woman DVD in the Helix, Ruth was playing the clarinet. In fact, she and David were sitting together while Chloë was singing on stage. That recording was the beginning of Chloë's career and, by rights, it should have been a treasured milestone for her. Thanks to David and his 'bit on the side', however, Chloë looks back on that night with great disdain and has never been able to watch the recording since. At one particular rehearsal, the two of them sat together on their own in the empty bleachers of the Helix watching Chloë practise. Naomi also later recalled Ruth helping her with her homework backstage in the concert hall.

When I made discreet enquiries with people I knew in RTÉ, I was met with the general response, 'Yes we've seen them together. They don't hide it; they've been seen kissing on the steps of the radio centre'.

I really felt that such a blatant vulgar display of infidelity in the grounds of RTÉ was particularly callous towards me considering that I had worked there from the time I was a child. In fact, most of the people David worked with would have been colleagues of mine long before he ever met them. They couldn't *but* have known of his affair and to be honest, it was an awful position for David to have put *them* in.

❖

I have never met Ruth Hickey, nor do I ever want to.

Admittedly I was made aware of her, long before I knew of the affair, as several people had subtly hinted to me about her on more than one occasion. She and David were both in the wind section of the orchestra, and to be honest, wind was the only thing I presumed they were capable of creating between them. You see David always hated the clarinet. There's a pecking order in every orchestra with oboists usually considering themselves to be the royalty of the room. As such, they tend to look upon certain other instruments with an air of contempt. In David's case, he always referred to the clarinet as the 'poor man's oboe', primarily because he felt it didn't take half the skill to play a clarinet as it did to play the oboe. I myself only ever enjoyed listening to the clarinet when it was in the truly gifted hands of Paddy Cole (jazz) or John Finucane (classical).

Looking back, I realise he was in the middle of his affair with Ruth, and his supposed hatred of the instrument she played was like a deliberate attempt to make me believe he loathed anyone associated with it. It was like his way of removing himself from any link with her.

❖

When David left his family in the autumn of 2004, the reverberations were nothing if not life changing. While a nicer term for such an experience would be to call it 'character defining', a more realistic term would be along the lines of 'soul crippling'. When the Yuletide season

came around, David arrived out to the house on Christmas morning, looking like the cat that got the cream. He was smug, arrogant, viciously sarcastic to me, not to mention downright rude to his daughters. He also made no secret that he was flying off to Prague that day with Ruth. In fact, all throughout his visit, he would repeatedly look at his watch and say, 'I can't stay, I have to fly somewhere'.

He kept going on about it to such an extent that Chloë eventually told him to leave as none of us were interested in hearing about his plans with that woman. As he stormed out, she and Naomi slammed the door shut. David retaliated by opening up the letterbox and shouting in, 'I don't want to be here anyway'.

The girls didn't hesitate to let him know he wasn't wanted, at which point, he fired back with the spiteful remark, 'I don't want to spend today with you, I'd rather live in a hovel than live here with you lot'.

To say that to your two young daughters on Christmas morning as you leave to join your mistress on a holiday, requires a degree of animosity I will never understand. That day was so miserable for us, certainly one of the blackest days of our lives. David's mother, who was there at the time, was also crying over what had happened. We had enjoyed some of the most magical Christmases, but this one was definitely the worst.

❖

At one point during another argument, David accused me of poisoning the girls against him. Naomi, at just eleven years of age, hit back, 'Don't worry, Dad, she didn't have to do a thing, you did a good enough job yourself'.

The one thing I always did was allow the girls the freedom to make their own decisions. I never once told them they couldn't speak to their dad, and, as for poisoning them against him, I wouldn't dream of it. David and I may have had our problems but as far as I was concerned, he was still their father.

In the early stages of our separation, the girls wanted to see him. He was missing during those crucial years when they really needed a father figure in their lives. I remember on one occasion, Naomi was in tears when she said to him, 'Ruth *wants* you, she doesn't *need* you. We *need* you. We're *your* girls'. David, rather callously, replied, 'Well Ruth lost her father at seventeen'.

My heart broke for Naomi when I heard her say back, 'Well, I've lost mine at eleven'.

David's departure was horrible for all of us, but it was particularly hurtful for Naomi as she had always been so close to her father until Ruth interfered.

❖

Naomi was like David in that she was a fantastic athlete. Every school picture I have of her in relation to sporting victories is of her standing on the middle podium holding the gold medal. Netball, basketball, sprinting, tennis, swimming, skiing, horse riding – you name it, Naomi had the gold for it.

David likewise had a collection of All-Ireland medals for cross-country and sprinting that merited a display cabinet of their own. I think Naomi felt that because Chloë had always been a mammy's girl and she a daddy's girl, David's exit meant he had chosen his 'bit on the side' over her.

There was also a huge element of embarrassment involved because the entire ordeal was so public.

Whenever any of her friends went through the trauma of a parent leaving the family, they didn't have to see the other partner if they didn't want to. Naomi was confronted with it on a daily basis. For a teenage girl to see her father posing for a magazine shoot alongside the 'other woman' was just disgusting, so, understandably, her pain was entwined in a mixture of hurt, anger and humiliation.

Around that time, I had begun to notice that she had scribbled over her name on her school copybooks, replacing it with Naomi King. Her teachers also began phoning me to see if I was aware that Naomi was insisting on her name being changed from 'Agnew' to 'King' on the roll call. They too were quite worried for her and took the matter seriously. I told them to allow her be referred to as Naomi King as I sensed it was an anger phase that would pass; it was her way of dealing with what was happening. Sadly, I don't think David was even aware that all of this was taking place in his absence.

❖

It's natural for kids to blame somebody when a marriage breaks up, and with Naomi having idolised her dad, her instinct was to blame me. We were both snappy and irritable around that time, so, of course, we exchanged a lot of cross words. Adolescents are hard to talk to as it is, but in trying times such as these, relations with this particular teenager were, at best, frayed.

When we went to see Chloë perform in America, the entire six-hour flight was spent in silence. We didn't speak a word. We had a few days to wait before Chloë arrived into the city, so I think we were both dreading being in the company of each other's foul moods. Communication had completely broken down between the two of us. Chloë had cried so much over David leaving but

Naomi hadn't shed a tear. Even though she was only eleven years of age, she internalised it all and became very withdrawn. I remember seeing her one evening sitting on the floor with her back to the Aga, completely lost in thought to a point where she wasn't even aware I was in the room. The poor thing looked so tortured that I could only wonder what was going through her mind.

When we were in the airport that day, however, I noticed she had changed her luggage tags from 'Agnew' to 'King'. When I pointed out to her that she couldn't have her luggage tags in a different name to her passport, a row ensued, which resulted in her admitting that she had been actively enquiring about changing her surname via deed poll. She pointed out that if she went ahead with it, she would be allowed to change her name on the passport. I tried to bluff her by making out that once a name was changed by deed poll, it was irreversible, but she genuinely didn't care. At that point, Naomi was adamant on severing all obvious connections with her father.

❖

In Ireland, any problem can be solved with the words 'put the kettle on'. In America however, the solution for an effective outcome is 'let's go for a Starbucks'. Well Naomi and I can absolutely verify the authenticity of the latter as Starbucks was precisely the place where we reached a turning point in our relationship. We had arranged to meet with Moya Doherty in her magnificent Columbus Circle penthouse, however as she had been held up, we decided to pass some time by going for a coffee. I still don't know how the topic arose, but somehow Naomi and I began talking about philosophy and religious beliefs. As the conversation grew deeper I just sat there in amazement, listening to her talk about the subject with such educated authority. She had clearly

devoured a phenomenal amount of reading material on the topics. We ended up sitting in Starbucks for exactly four hours and ten minutes absorbed in the most amazing conversation and, to be quite honest, I felt I knew my child for the first time as a result. Naomi had a tendency to internalise everything, whereas Chloë would tell you absolutely everything in a heartbeat.

Following Starbucks, Naomi and I went on to enjoy the most incredible day together which ended with us ordering some amazing food from one of her favourite restaurants and watching the most hilarious movie, *Religulous*.

Naomi, who knows her way around New York almost better than Rathfarnham, brought me to a variety of places the following day such as Madame Tussaud's, little knick-knack shops and the Hershey's chocolate shop where we made savages of ourselves. She and I have always shared a flair for anthropology, so of course our

trip to New York was not complete until we had spent a day inside the Natural History Museum. Some evenings we would catch our favourite shows on Broadway and on one particular occasion, even found ourselves in the Ripley's Believe It Or Not Museum before finishing the night in an Italian restaurant on 46th Street. We would then usually head back to the hotel where we would hire out another film to laugh at. It was just the most incredible quality time together and we have never looked back ever since.

❖

Fortunately, the name change phase fizzled out not long after she began attending Alexandra College. Chloë was always known by her friends in Alexandra as 'McAgnew', and on Naomi's first day in the school, the group presented her with an Alex hoodie on which they had emblazoned the name 'Mini McAgnew'. She adored it and from that point on was affectionately known in Alex as 'Mini McAgnew'.

Letters of love

After David took off to his new life of sex-and-not-much-else, I was left paying the mortgage, household bills, school fees, and day-to-day living expenses. He didn't offer a cent in child support.

I often found myself having to explain to the building society that I was a single mother, earning RTÉ fees, as opposed to Hollywood fees, and that the bills required two people working flat out. Coping on my own was virtually impossible, and selling the house was not an option because of the collapse in the property market. The girls were already heartbroken at losing their father to some woman, and truthfully, I didn't want them losing their family home as well. Fortunately they were blessed with a wonderful coterie of

Of course, Naomi and I still have our mother-daughter rows, particularly when *she* acts like the mother and treats *me* like the daughter. I swear I gave birth to my own mother. She is exactly like her in personality and will say things like, 'That dish isn't clean! You know, if you're not going to use the dishwasher at least make the effort to clean them properly.'

To annoy her, I would often reply, 'Ah, sure, I'm such a crap mother, it's a wonder you survived this long at all!'

Naomi has a great sardonic wit that has been evident from the time she was three years old. The boyfriend of her babysitter would always address her with 'Howya Blondie', a nickname she absolutely loathed. Eventually, she got so sick of it, that she walked right up to him with a killer attitude and a look to match. All of two and a half feet tall and two and a half years old, she stood before him with her hand on her hip and sternly replied, 'Hey, you, I don't like "Blondie"!'

supportive friends and, as for me, I can honestly say I would have swept the streets to pay their school fees before even so much as entertaining the idea of removing them from such a secure environment. They had already suffered enough disruption in their lives, they didn't need to be without their friends as well.

I believe in exorcising my demons not internalising them. That's precisely why I vented my anger when I needed to. I'm the better for it, because as time rolled on – I looked at David with more sympathy than anything else. The girls and I may be the losers financially in that we're crippled trying to pay him off to keep our house (a house that was bought thanks to my parents selling *their* house, I might add) – but emotionally, we're the

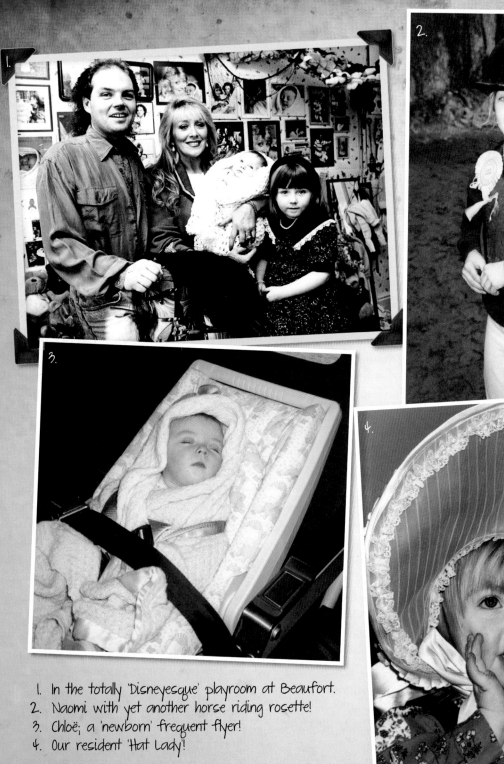

1. In the totally 'Disneyesque' playroom at Beaufort.
2. Naomi with yet another horse riding rosette!
3. Chloë; a 'newborn' frequent flyer!
4. Our resident 'Hat Lady'!

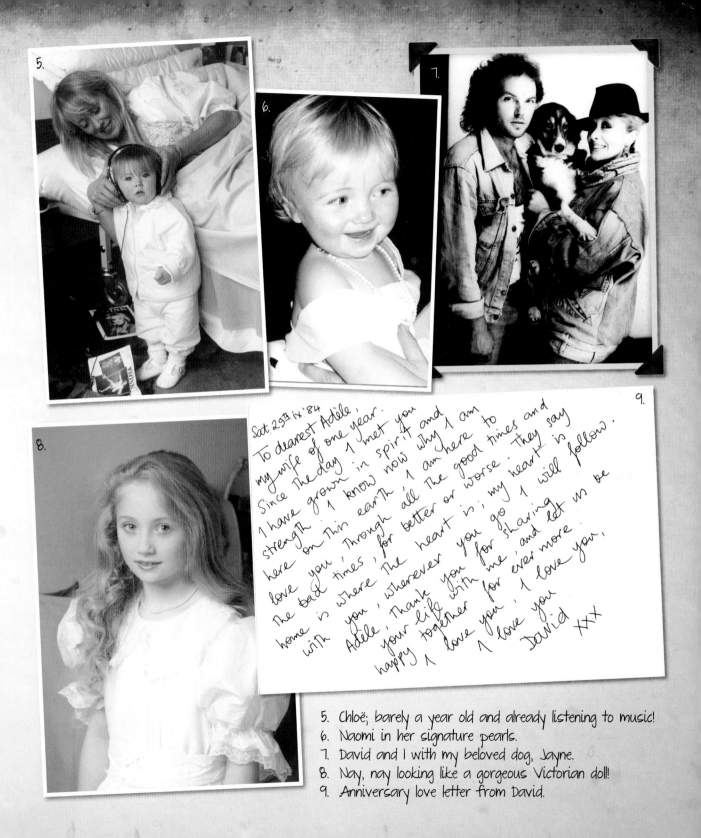

Sat. 29ᵗʰ ix '84

To dearest Adéle,

my wife of one year.
Since the day I met you
I have grown in spirit and
strength. I know now why I am
here on this earth. I am here to
love you. Through all the good times and
the bad times, for better or worse. They say
home is where the heart is; my heart is
with you, wherever you go I will follow.
Adéle, thank you for sharing and let us be
happy together for ever more.
I love you, I love you,

I love you
David xxx

5. Chloë; barely a year old and already listening to music!
6. Naomi in her signature pearls.
7. David and I with my beloved dog, Jayne.
8. Nay, nay looking like a gorgeous Victorian doll!
9. Anniversary love letter from David.

winners. We have survived the crap that was thrown at us, but, saying that, we really couldn't have come through it fighting had we not had the support of the women of Ireland.

When news of David's affair emerged in the media, the response was overwhelming. I received (and continue to receive) some of the most unbelievably beautiful letters and cards from women all over Ireland reassuring me that things would work out for the better and that I was strong enough to see through the storm. Even women I met in the shops or on the street were always there with a smile and a kind word; some of them even embraced me in a hug.

One card that cheered me up immensely was sent from a woman in Tipperary. She had obviously read about my mortgage troubles in the press and in her card included two twenty euro notes and three lottery tickets accompanied by the most beautiful words of comfort, all of which I still treasure to this day. When I read her letter and saw what she had included, I cried for ages, completely taken aback by such a sweet gesture. I couldn't believe that a woman had gone to so much trouble to write a letter and send money that she could have easily spent on herself and her own bills. She is a true lady with a twenty-four-carat gold heart and definitely gets my all-time trophy for kindness and goodwill.

Through the letters, I realised that so many women identified with my situation. They had been through the same experience and, like myself, were struggling to cope, be it emotionally or financially. It was after I received such letters that I decided to start giving interviews about my marriage break-up. I wanted other women in the same situation to know that they were not on their own in their struggle. Above all, I wanted women to see that even though they had been left behind to pick up the charred remains of their lives, they would come through it fighting and be all the stronger for it.

Zip it

Some years are filled with such a rotten roll of luck that you can't help but question if someone has a voodoo doll with *your* face on it. (Although if anyone really is thinking of creating a voodoo doll of me, would you mind carrying out some liposuction on it? I'll happily endure the pain if the prospect of being thin awaits me at the end of it!)

2005 was one such year.

One day, I was sitting in my bedroom with my two beauts enjoying the comfort of what we call a 'three girls and a cuddle' day. It was one of those horribly low days where the only place to seek solace is under the duvet.

I know from talking to women who have been through a marriage break-up that sometimes they feel as though they should smile for the sake of the kids. Look, when a marriage ends, your children will feel the pain every bit as much as you do, so rather than ignoring it, sit down together and share it. If nothing else, the therapy of talking it out will bring you closer as a family.

While I was chatting to Chlo and Nay in the room that day, David's number flashed up on the screen of my phone. Call it female intuition, but I immediately guessed what he was phoning to tell me. Stepping outside the door of my bedroom, I answered the call, bracing myself for the inevitable. He began with his usual gruff manner. 'Um, Adèle … I wanted … um to be the first to tell you …'

As soon as he said those words, I knew my inkling was correct. 'It's all right, David,' I interrupted. 'I know what you're going to tell me.'

'Ruth and I are pregnant!'

He said it in a tone of voice that suggested he was expecting a congratulatory response from me. His expectation was somewhat too high.

'So who is going to break this charming piece of news to your children?' I asked. 'I'm presuming you won't have the balls to do it yourself. Another piece of shit news I'll be left to deal with. You're full of it! Goodbye!'

The moment I walked back into the room, Chloë looked at me with tears already welling in her eyes and said, 'She's going to have a baby with him, isn't she?'

Both girls were absolutely beside themselves with grief. It completely crushed them and I think that was the news that really welded the door shut on their relationship. David always managed to time things perfectly. There was always something important happening in our lives anytime he would decide to turn the fan on and let the shit hit it.

Ruth had the baby on Valentine's Day 2006, the same day as the opening night of *Dirty Dusting* in Limerick University, the start of a sell-out tour. It was also the day before Chloë's concert in the Point Depot now called the O2.

I later heard they named the boy Jessie Isaac Agnew. David's mother Bernadette and sister Brenda have often babysat for them. Naturally, they are going to feel loyal to David, but I did feel it was *slightly* insensitive to me and the girls, particularly given the way he had treated us. As a mother myself now, if I had a son who asked me to babysit the child he'd had with his 'bit on the side', I wouldn't think twice about slapping the face off him and reminding him that he had a wife and children in his marital home.

Keep the cuffs handy

The grief that pair imposed on my girls left me absolutely seething. Chloë and Naomi were inconsolable over the idea of their father leaving them to begin a family with this other woman, so in a rage one day, I decided to phone her, basically to remind her of what a bitch she was (and that's putting it lightly). I left a message on her phone and painted a very grim, though accurate, picture of the devastation she and David had left in their wake. I told her in no uncertain terms what I thought of her, and I admit a few descriptive profanities may also have been mentioned. Yes, David and I were having marriage problems, but these were problems that required a marriage councillor, not the involvement of a spare wheel. The following day Blanchardstown Gardaí called to my door. Ruth Hickey had reported the phone call and was accusing me of harassment. What's more, David was backing her up.

At the time, he was so besotted with her that he defended everything she said and did. In his eyes, I was the bitch. In fairness to the Gardaí, they were already aware of our situation though the media and so were incredibly understanding about the whole matter. I told them straight out that I would rather be arrested than apologise for the message I'd left. In fact, I actually advised them to keep the cuffs handy because if the mood struck me again, I would be making another one or two calls.

I kept my word on that, and if you want proof, just Google the phrase 'zip up your mickey'.

A bit too Social, a bit too Personal

Ruth's friend P.J. Gibbons took it upon himself to mentor the Hickey/Agnew partnership. At a time when the media were portraying David as the arsehole he was, P.J. decided it would be a great PR exercise to not only hire Ruth as a columnist for his magazine *Social & Personal*, but to feature her and David in the accompanying photographs. They also appeared in the social pages attending one mundane launch after the next.

I presume P.J. had deluded himself into thinking that the more they were photographed together, the more people would like them. Well it backfired, because if the letters I received were anything to go by, people felt quite the opposite. I honestly don't know what P.J. is like as a person, and I couldn't care fucking less, but anyone with a heart would not have rubbed salt into the open wounds of two young teenage girls.

Unfortunately, within months of my children losing their dad, P.J. in his *wisdom* decided to arrange a photoshoot in which David and Ruth would pose together in a health and beauty spa. The photographs were accompanied by a detailed article which highlighted the following quote: 'My partner David and I opted for very different treatments, but he described his Ki Massage as extraordinary, life-changing.'

A life-changing massage? When I read that line, I couldn't help but think of the life-changing experience his daughters went through when he abandoned them. At one point during the piece, Ruth also recalled their ballroom dancing lessons not to mention her 'most difficult' decision of whether to choose aqua aerobics or an energetic run. Well if it was exercise she was after, she could have saved herself the hassle of

a spa and called over to my house where a good run would have been guaranteed. Ironically the headline that graced the article was 'Falling For a Dancer'.

Yes, seriously!

This was to be the very shoot that prompted the now infamous 'mickey call' to David. I thought it was disgusting that he chose to flaunt the relationship while clearly giving little or no thought to the feelings of his two heartbroken daughters. Every magazine you flicked through, they were at the opening of some venue, usually accompanied by the caption 'Ruth and her partner David'. While he was out being a social butterfly, I was at home consoling his children, trying to explain why their dad was choosing to attend the opening of every toilet lid alongside his 'partner' instead of spending time with them.

The spa photoshoot, however, was the final straw. The persistent humiliation he was intent on causing his daughters ignited a fiery rage within me and in a fit of anger, I picked up the kitchen phone and dialled his number. Ever heard of the Latin phrase *carpe diem* – seize the day? Well, I was intent on bloody strangling it.

I'm not going to delve into detail here but let's just say that during my two-minute voice message, I told him a few home truths before concluding with the point that it was high time he zipped up his mickey.

One morning, not too long after the call, my then-accountant and still friend, Frances Brennan phoned to tell me that a tape of my voicemail had been aired on the *Ian Dempsey Breakfast Show* on Today FM. She was even able to tell me that there was 'something about you saying "zip up your mickey"'.

The word 'shocked' doesn't even remotely compare to how I felt that morning. In fact, my mind was in a contusive mess trying to figure out how my message had suddenly become the property of a public audience.

I have *always* stood over every comment I have made, regardless of whether it's in person or on some answering machine, and I can honestly say, with hand on heart, that if I had to make that phone call again tomorrow, I would – happily. The only thing I regret is not capitalising on the merchandise.

A friend of mine in America who had obviously heard the call on YouTube, told me to have a look at the website cafepress.com on which they were selling Zip Up Your Mickey memorabilia. To this day, I wish I'd had a share in that business, because apparently they made a small fortune from it. For the fun of it, and partly to see if the merchandise was actually real, I bought several items from the site. Two weeks later, a big cardboard box arrived at my door but by that stage I had completely forgotten about the order. Bemused by the package, I tore it open and almost began crying with laughter when I saw the various items inside: a t-shirt, a g-string, a clock (which is on the den wall), a cushion (which is on the chair in the back lounge), a tile box (in which I keep scrabble pieces), a mug, key rings, pens and badges, all with the 'Zip Up Your Mickey' catchphrase printed on the front. On some of the items, there was even a picture of me accompanied by the slogan: 'Do as Twink says … Zip Up Your Mickey!'

Chloë and Naomi didn't find it a bit funny; I, on the other hand, thought it was hysterical. The phone call was a terrible embarrassment to my children at the time, but in comparison to what David did, it was piecemeal. Now that they are slightly older, the girls agree that my reaction was more than justified.

So many women, from the very young to the very elderly, have patted me on the back for that message, with some even going so far as to say how much they'd wished they'd had the balls to have delivered a similar message to their own cheating husbands at some point. That's enough to confirm for me I did the right thing. A glorious moment of achievement for scorned women everywhere! It's just a pity the recordings of my voice messages to Hickey hadn't been leaked, because I can assure you they would have made for far better entertainment!

That aside, a part of me is still angry about the fact that it *was* leaked. When I left that message, I never envisaged it being aired to the world, I saw it as a private message from an angry wife to her gobshite husband.

That voicemail was left on David's phone – so who was the PR-minded person that decided to leak it to the press? I certainly know who I'd place my money on – and, before you ask, it's not David. I believe that whoever released that message did so with the intention of trying to make Ruth look like an angel by comparison to me. Well their plan went somewhat awry. Apart from the odd 'oul prude, everyone enjoyed a good laugh from it and the phrase 'zip up your mickey' will be remembered long after Ruth what's-her-name is gone.

In the George, Dublin's best-known gay venue, they have a tape of the phone call and on certain nights, different guys will get up on stage complete with their wigs and costumes, and lip-sync the call to perfection! From what I'm told, they put on an absolutely hilarious show.

Gary Kavanagh, hairstylist to the stars, also once told me that every time the George does a 'Zip Up Your Mickey night', everyone stands up and toasts me! I have received so many heart-warming letters from men and women in the gay community. In fact, when I was in hospital in 2010, a lovely young man sent me a copy of the *Gay Times* in which he had written the most beautiful piece about me. On another occasion, two guys stopped me in the street and gave me a great laugh when they told me that my picture was on the wall of the George with a Sacred Heart Lamp underneath it! I have never seen it, but I have in the past witnessed their hilarious (not to mention hugely flattering) tradition of holding up my picture and having the whole crowd bow to it.

Needless to say, when I was invited to partake in a surprise gig there, I jumped at the chance. It was arranged that I would make my grand entrance by walking down the staircase that leads on to the stage where I would then perform alongside my dancers. I felt like Cher! It was an unbelievably memorable night and I don't think I ever experienced a reception like it anywhere in my life. I treasure and love all the wonderful support I have enjoyed from the gay community of Ireland.

When I was being interviewed by journalists in the aftermath of the 'mickey' phone call, a lot of them would broach the subject with great trepidation, almost too afraid to ask. They would teeter around the issue until I would usually stun them by saying straight out, 'You mean the 'zip up your mickey' phone call? Best thing I ever did in my life, dear!'

❖

I think what people saw in Ruth and didn't like, was behaviour akin to Camilla Parker Bowles. Frankly, it gained her little, if any, popularity. To this day, I receive letters of support from women who identify with my situation.

One woman wrote me the most incredible letter in which she told me that the 'zip up your mickey' call had put a smile back on her face. She outlined how she had gone through a separation after discovering her husband had been conducting a ten-year affair. She recalled how her sister had agreed to keep a lookout for the 'other woman' after she revealed her initial concerns that he might be playing away. She later discovered that the 'other woman' had, in fact, been her sister all along. My heart broke for her. Not only had she lost her husband, she had lost her sister as well. I could identify with her in more ways than one!

In my case, I had established a wonderful friendship with a businesswoman called Jackie, who was also my neighbour when I lived in Beaufort. Her then-husband owned the Old Orchard Inn right next door to us. At the time, Jackie owned a boutique in the Mount Merrion Shopping Centre and would often ask me to model the clothes for her latest fashion shoot. In turn, I invited her to appear on *Play the Game,* as I always did my best to give Irish businesswomen the widest possible publicity for their ventures. Jackie was superbly intelligent, glamorous and popular with the viewers, and also one of *my* personal favourite women guests. In the years that followed, she graduated to being one of the more frequent guests.

When she and I had become quite good friends, she began to quiz me about David and the health of our marriage. I, like an idiot, would pour my heart out to her. I remember confiding in her my suspicions that he was having an affair, but what I didn't realise at the time was that Jackie was in a relationship with Bill Cullen, Yvonne Clifford's uncle.

Yes that's right, I'm referring to Jackie Lavin.

I could never figure out where Yvonne was sourcing her information about what was going on in my marriage, but I soon discovered the 'Jackie connection' and concluded that she must have been keeping her informed on every Agnew update.

Bill Cullen with his niece Yvonne Clifford and his partner Jackie Lavin.

I was surprised and annoyed that Yvonne seemed to be armed with the same information about my marriage that I had previously shared in confidence with Jackie.

In 2010, one newspaper quoted a 'source' as having said that I was very upset over Ruth's decision to sue the newspapers. Not so. In fact, I honestly didn't give a fiddler's what that woman did. I think sleeping with my husband and becoming pregnant with his child was about the extent of upset she caused me. I was impervious to anything else she did after that. To be honest, I was actually quite surprised she was suing the newspapers. If I'd had an affair with a well-known married man, the last thing I would do is sue the newspapers that reported it, thus reminding the public yet again of what I had done. From what I can gather, Ruth took umbrage with being referred to as 'a whore'. Interestingly, the judgment of Judge P. Kearns on 8 October 2010 stated that 'in the context in which it was said in the newspaper, such an expression did not constitute a serious defamation'", and so her claim for damages against the newspaper was dismissed.

On a previous occasion, when she learned that Gerry Ryan had interviewed me for *Ryan Confidential*, she immediately slapped RTÉ with an injunction which resulted in the episode never being aired. She swore she would sue to the hilt if it was televised.

Here's the gas bit! For all the hurt Ruth has caused my family, she and David are no longer together. Yes, she became involved with another person and it was left to me to break it to him – what a turn up for the books, eh? She now has a second child with that man. In fact her partner is the CEO of St Joseph's Centre for the Visually Impaired in Dublin.

Ah now ladies, no cruel jokes please!

Ironically, David is now on better terms with me than he is with Ruth, Yvonne and all the others. Then again, they do say there's nothing like a dose of a man's mistress to make him appreciate his wife.

Unfortunately, his appreciation has come too late. Of course I still love David, I always will. There was a special spark between us from the moment we laid eyes on each other, and even after all these years, it has never left. That said, there is absolutely no chance of us reuniting. While a part of me enjoys being single far too much to want to be restricted, another part of me is head over heels in love with a very important man in my life – a man I have rarely spoken about in public.

Until now!

Returning visitor

When one of my favourite composers Verdi opened his grandest libretto *Aïda* in Cairo on Christmas Eve 1871, he set pulses racing with a creation that would be forever woven in the threads of operatic history. Egypt was the scene of this unusual love story and 127 years later, it would also become the scene of mine.

Rather fittingly, *Aïda* is an Arabic term meaning both 'visitor' and 'returning'. I say 'fittingly' because a returning visitor is exactly what I became after my path crossed with that of a certain gentleman.

It began in 1998 when David and I flew to Egypt with the girls for the inaugural Children's International Song Festival in the Cairo Opera House. Chloë had been selected to represent Ireland in the competition and for her performance, her godfather John Sullivan and I had created the first draft of a song called 'The Friendship Tree', which was then transformed and arranged into a proper piece of music by the gifted pianist Frank McNamara.

When we arrived at our hotel in Egypt, it was outlined in our itinerary that we would be collected from our hotel at midday and brought to the opera house for the first rehearsal. Before I go on, I should point out that the Egyptians are without doubt the most eccentric-but-lovingly-disorganised race in existence. I honestly don't how they ever managed to build the bloody pyramids. Sure enough, two o'clock came and went with no sign of our translator or our bus. Upon phoning the representative I was assured, 'Your translator will be with you in a minute'.

Before I knew it, my watch was reading four o'clock and we were still no closer to the opera house.

I phoned once again.

'Eh … your translator will be with you in a minute, Miss King.'

With the kids' threshold for boredom now having long past, I decided to bring them for a swim. By five o'clock, we were back in our hotel rooms getting changed, not to mention trying to dry Chloë's hair which was almost down to the back of her knees, when a frantic phone call came through from an irate Egyptian.

'You're late! You must come down to the lobby right now!'

'We'll be down in a few minutes when we are finished changing,' I snapped back.

'No. Come now!'

'The children's hair is still wet. I've just told you we will be down when it's dry. Get it pal!'

Throw a hot temper and a few dozen expletives into that last sentence and you will have yourself a very subtle version of what I really said to him.

Ten minutes later, we arrived down into the lobby only to be greeted by the same man I had spoken with on the phone. Turns out the voice on the phone belonged to a very tall handsome man called Ahmed.

'You're holding everybody up. We are going to be late for the rehearsal.'

Here was a man who had been late by five hours, attempting to blame *me* for holding everyone up by ten minutes! What a fucking nerve, I thought!

Unfortunately my inner-Arian had long since trampled my inner-Buddha, and as a result I let fly, quietening him pretty quickly in the process. When we eventually arrived at the opera house, David went backstage with the girls while I remained out front so I could hear the quality of the acoustics. As I was taking my seat, Ahmed arrived in and sheepishly made his way over to apologise for his behaviour back in the hotel. He seemed genuinely regretful, although he did admit it had been a long time since someone had spoken to him like that. Twenty minutes later, he was back over.

'Black coffee, no milk, no sugar.'

'How did you know?'

'I made it my business!'

It was killing me to admit it but he was slowly winning me over. We started chatting and with every passing minute, he grew more and more charming. At the time, I was not in love, or even 'in like', with David. There was always yet another affair, another woman for him to hide, another heartbreak for me to endure.

In fact, the week before we travelled to Egypt, I discovered a roll of undeveloped film in one of his bags. Suspicious, I decided to have the pictures developed, however as I looked through them, I began to relax, realising that they were just pictures of me in hospital, pregnant with Chloë. Unfortunately, however, that was merely the calm before the storm. A number of the photographs included close-up shots of a newborn child, one that definitely was not Chloë, while another picture showed a woman smiling as an out-of-shot figure stroked the face of the baby she was cradling.

The figure in question was David, as was evident from the visible gold bracelet, one I had bought for him in Turkey. It was at that point I realised his other child had been born *just weeks* before Chloë. I had begged him so many times to tell me if Chloë had been his first-born. Each time he said to me she was.

It really made me realise I was no longer at the end of my tether with David, but rather well and truly past it. At the beginning of the trip, he was quite cool towards me. He knew he had been found out *yet again* but didn't quite know how to deal with the situation, so he resorted to his usual tactic of keeping the head down and ignoring it. Fortunately, there was too much going on for me to either notice or care.

The festival itself was enormous. The participants were brought on trips each day to various places such as the pyramids, theme parks and so on. Egypt has always had a very press-hungry culture so almost everything the contestants did was filmed and broadcast on a daily basis, thus resulting in the kids becoming mini-celebrities.

Gradually I began to notice that Ahmed would seek me out whenever we were on the tour bus. In fact, I knew I was really falling for him when I realised that my mood would plummet any time he wasn't sitting next to me. I didn't care about not being with David. To be quite frank, I didn't give a damn about him right there and then. Ahmed had obviously done his homework on me because he knew about my profession in Ireland. I, on the other hand, was still learning more about him. On the coach one day, I asked him if he was a tour guide or an interpreter, to which he smiled and replied, 'Neither, I am a doctor!'

Ah well that was it, I was smitten. Sitting in front of me was perfection in human form. He went on to explain that any time a major event was being staged in Egypt, people who could speak several languages were always called upon. As well as being well-read, I discovered he was also well-travelled, having studied for some time in Germany and other European colleges before eventually deciding to carve out his career in Egypt. He is Egyptian to the core with a family tree that boasts links to the pharaohs.

❖

One evening, a dinner was held in a beautiful restaurant for all the parents of the contestants. David, however, chose to stay behind in the hotel, a decision I certainly didn't object to. When Ahmed and I sat beside each other on the coach to the dinner, we held hands for the first time, playing those very sensual teasing hand games. For the entire meal, we were completely engrossed in conversation. Following the dinner, he brought me to a beautiful little café that was literally situated at the top of a mountain. It was the kind of place that had a small bar in which the local men could play backgammon, and a small alfresco area for the couples, filled with beautiful Egyptian camel rugs and incense. So there we were, Ahmed with his hookah pipe, me with my mint tea and the beautiful Egyptian moon shining over us. That was the night we shared a very passionate first kiss. It actually happened after we noticed a jet approaching nearby Cairo airport. We realised the plane had no landing lights on, and so in jest, I cupped my hands and roared 'Put … your … landing … lights … on!'

No sooner had the last word left my mouth, when a blinding flash hit us as the pilot suddenly turned on every light on the aircraft. Of course it was just a fluke but it was still quite funny as it really seemed as though he had heard me. Joking, Ahmed said, 'Well done!' and leaned over to give me a congratulatory kiss. It was at that point that all the mocking and laughter transformed into the passion that had been building between us from the moment we met. We were utterly smitten with each other and it wasn't too long before I found myself falling hopelessly in love.

Chloë guessed what was going on and, at that time, didn't take kindly to Ahmed. I was always very careful around the kids, but she noticed the way he was looking at me and instinctively knew there was something between us. David also sensed it.

The irony of the situation was that Ahmed ended up saving David's life on that trip. He had fallen ill with a gastric stomach bug which admittedly doesn't sound like anything serious but trust me, you could have the Turkey droppings, the Montezuma's revenge and all the holiday stomach illnesses at once, and you *still* would have no idea what pain is like until you have had a dose of the 'Tutankhamun trots' in Egypt. I experienced it once before and I swear to God I wouldn't wish it upon anyone (well maybe I'd make the exception for a journalist I call the 'Bunny Boiler'. You will see why when you read about her later).

The cramps are far worse than labour pains and that's speaking as someone who has been through labour twice. You become so ill that you're shivering with the cold while sweating at the same time. I'm not trying to be vulgar, but it's a sickness that leaves you in need of two toilets because it's literally coming out both ends.

In Egypt, the water is the most likely culprit source. Even eating a salad that was rinsed in tap water can result in you subsequently becoming closely acquainted with Armitage Shanks. David contracted his gastro virus from ice-cream. The kids didn't like theirs so I had Naomi's and David had Chloë's. An hour later, it hit us. While I managed to overcome my sickness that night, David was effectively twice as sick as he had consumed his own ice cream dish as well as Chloë's. The following day, I had to bring the kids to the theatre for another rehearsal. I was very uneasy leaving, as David was still feeling extremely ill. Differences aside, I was genuinely concerned for him.

When I arrived back at the hotel room a short while later, he was lying motionless on the couch, his lips blue, his once sallow skin now ashen white. There were black circles around his eyes and his entire body was freezing. He was conscious but unable to talk. I was frantic. Fortunately, our girls didn't witness any of this as they were in a different part of the hotel enjoying an afternoon tea that was being held for the contestants. I ran downstairs to alert Ahmed who immediately ran to the room where he took David's temperature and checked his pulse. He phoned a colleague who had medical supplies in his car and when he arrived, Ahmed administered the necessary injections and medication. It was the most incongruous situation. I heard myself repeatedly pleading, 'Ahmed, please don't let David die'.

There was my husband gravely ill, and yet here was my new love saving his life. To say we were all very confused is an understatement. Bit by bit, the colour returned to David's face and his condition gradually improved. I later learned he had been about an hour away from death when I found him.

When Chloë's godfather John Sullivan flew over to Egypt for the competition, I didn't have to tell him about Ahmed, he guessed it quickly enough. While he gave me a bollocking about it at first, I swiftly reminded him of the old adage about closed doors and not knowing what goes on behind them. David's philandering had trampled all over my self-esteem and I can't say I was enchanted by the lonely, loveless place I was currently in. I was fed up with his 'lifestyle' encroaching on our marriage. I most certainly did not ask to develop feelings for Ahmed but when they did happen, bloody hell they felt wonderful – too wonderful to want to let go.

As soon as I admitted to John that I was falling in love with Ahmed, his exact response was 'don't be ridiculous'. He brushed it off as a fling that would soon dissipate once the real world kicked in. That was fourteen years ago, and today I can honestly say that Ahmed and I are even more in love now than we were back then.

❖

On the night of the competition, there were prizes from sixth place right through to first, however the Grand Prix was the highest accolade every participant coveted. I can still remember us standing backstage, our hair practically greying by the second with the nerves. As they called out the different ranks of finalists, our hopes for the big win began to slightly wane as we figured the main prize would be awarded to one of the children who had made it to the top three. The newspapers had long earmarked Chloë as a favourite to win the Grand Prix but, by this particular point, she had resigned herself to the notion that she would not be taking any silverware back to Ireland. By the time the host was ready to announce the main winner, my hopes were down and my blood pressure was up.

'And the Grand Prix goes to …'

I looked over at John. The golden tan gifted to him by the Egyptian sun was in the process of being replaced by a stress-induced pallour.

'Ireland! Chloë Agnew and "The Friendship Tree"!'

Not even when I was giving birth to Chloë did I scream as loud as I did that night. If there was a level above euphoria, we definitely surpassed it when she took to the stage to receive her plaque from the president's wife along with a papyrus from the Ministry of Arts and Education in Egypt. When she subsequently appeared on *The Late Late Show* to sing her winning song, Pat Kenny carried out the most charming interview with her. When he asked her what she had bought with the $6,000 prize money, I can still picture her face as she innocently replied, 'I bought a Gameboy, Pat'.

❖

The day we were leaving for Ireland, I had to tear myself away from Ahmed. As I produced my passport for customs later that day, it rather poignantly dawned on me that it was on the 29th September, the date of my wedding anniversary. Long after I had left Egypt, he and I constantly exchanged letters and spoke on the phone. On the occasions when David and I would hit a particularly bad patch, I sought solace in Egypt. I might only go for three days, but it was enough to give me a spring in my step.

When you are with a man who cannot be faithful and who is forever rowing with you, why shouldn't you seek love, comfort and kind words somewhere else?

It doesn't matter how frequently he embarked on his affairs, every time he began a new one it was as soul-crushing as the first. Knowing he

was with other women reinforced my own belief that I wasn't enough for him. Being with Ahmed however strengthened my faith in love. You know that saying *'to the whole world you may just be someone, but to someone you may be their whole world'*? Well, let me tell you, those words are very truthful, and my situation with Ahmed was indicative of that.

Ahmed's mother unfortunately didn't see it quite so romantically. Understandably, she was worried about the relationship, mainly because I was slightly older than him, I wasn't Muslim, and I wasn't Egyptian. In fact on one occasion, she wrote me a beautiful letter in which she politely explained that she wanted her son to have a Muslim wife and pleaded with me not to deny him that. In her letter she wrote: 'Please don't have him fall in love with you.'

I replied and reassured her that she had no reason to worry as I wasn't going to stand in his way of getting married to a Muslim girl. I thought the world of Ahmed and I still travelled to Egypt to see him, but I didn't need a Tarot session with Fergie to know that marriage was never going to be on the cards for us. Unfortunately, our religious differences cemented that. Following an exchange of letters, my brief correspondence with his mother ended with her thanking me for my understanding. She was relieved that I had no intentions of ruining her vision of him finding a Muslim wife.

As much as it pained me to do so, I literally had to force Ahmed to go out to meet other women. We were living different lives in different parts of the world and I genuinely didn't want to be the reason he couldn't find someone with whom he could start a family. I won't lie, I was heartbroken when he got married – so too was he. But I just felt it was something he had to experience in his life. I had been through it and I didn't feel it was right for me to stand in his way.

Once he was married, I made sure not to interfere or influence; I didn't want to be the 'Camilla' of their relationship. He and his wife went on to have two children together, although the marriage itself didn't last and they are now long separated. He later told me he made a mistake going ahead with the marriage in the first place.

I Sphinx Square

You cannot but create wonderful memories in a place like Egypt. When I first visited its sandy soil, I was fortunate to experience the most amazing train journey alongside the River Nile. This was followed by a trip to the pyramids during the day and a jaw-dropping sound and light show that night. It was during the show that I made a wonderful lifelong friend, who was also called Adel. Any time I'm in the country, I visit him. That's right, *his* name is Adel! Unfortunately for me, Adel is a man's name in Egypt.

Adel's address is, in my opinion, possibly the best one in existence. It reads:

> I Sphinx Square,
> The Pyramids,
> Giza,
> Egypt.

I challenge anyone to find me an address as romantic as that!

Adel owns a little shop directly across from the entrance to the pyramids, which sells everything from camel rugs to perfumes and every kind of Egyptian artefact in between. On the upper floor of his shop, there's a bockety little balcony where you can sit and enjoy some Egyptian tea while you watch the spectacular view of the sound and light show. If our own Harry Crosbie got his hands on it, he would turn it into a gold mine! Adel however doesn't see it quite like that. He sits outside with a cigarette and a cup of tea, and thinks of it as home!

Religion? Bad case of OCD or my Duchess of Cambridge moment?

Muslims. Not big on nudity that lot.

Even though the heat is sweltering, some will hiss and yell at you if you dare wear a T-shirt or a skirt out in public. Even though you're clearly a tourist and not of the same religion, they will look upon you in a degrading manner.

When I am in Egypt, I always prefer staying in an apartment block rather than a hotel simply because the security rules in hotels are so archaic.

Inviting Ahmed into my room for a drink would be completely out of the question as men and women are not allowed share a hotel room unless they are married. There's even a security man on each floor checking to make sure the rules are adhered to. Public signs of affection are also frowned upon. On one occasion, Ahmed and I were on a beach in Sharm el-Sheikh and as he handed me an ice-cream, he gave me a kiss. Almost immediately, two security men were over shouting at us in Arabic that kissing in pubic was strictly forbidden.

Well if they thought kissing was bad, they were certainly in for a shock.

During another one of my trips to Egypt, I was staying in an apartment that had a tiny balcony. Considering I was more than twelve floors up, I saw no harm in sunbathing topless. Absolutely no one could see me and, as there was just one other building a good distance away, privacy was a certainty. If I learned anything from that trip, it was that *nothing* in life is a certainty. As I was relaxing *sans* bikini top, some movement on the roof of the other building caught my eye. At first I could see only one figure on the rooftop, however he was then swiftly joined by a second and a third man … until suddenly a swarm of men appeared to be rushing out onto the roof to join the first three. Something about their behaviour seemed aggressive and I got the distinct impression they were angry.

Then I realised they had binoculars and a camera.

Shit!

It turns out the building in question was a government one and the men on the roof who had spotted me sunbathing were actually security men. It wasn't any of their bloody business what I did in my apartment, but then let's not bring logic into a situation involving people who see no wrong in stoning you to death over something as simple as a disagreement.

Within minutes, they were banging on my apartment door. I was terrified, too terrified to answer. As far as I was concerned there was no pacifying them and I wasn't going to be the fool to try. I immediately packed my bags and left them ready for collection inside the door hoping Ahmed would pick them up later. Wearing a long coat and a scarf wrapped around my head to disguise all traces of blonde hair, I cautiously made my way to the lobby where I spotted 'them' skulking outside the front door. It was obvious by their build and stature alone that they were government heavyweights. Fortunately, I managed to blend in with a group of people and left the complex unnoticed.

❖

The whole air of Muslim predominance in Egypt is so oppressive, it really rises my fury. Men are on their knees singing to Allah at six in the morning, not to mention out praying several times throughout the day, not in silence I might add, but in the same audible wail that woke you at dawn. Then there is the compulsive washing that takes place as part of their daily religious tradition. No I'm not intentionally singling out the Muslims. To be quite honest, I hate everything associated with *any* form of religion. The whole thing is like a bad case of OCD as far as I'm concerned.

Throughout the entire history of the blue planet, how many people have lost their lives or had their lives destroyed as a result of battles carried out in defence of a particular faith? While I find Catholicism particularly stupid, I do think the Muslim religion takes the Oscar. To see women wearing the full burqa, or being made walk five paces behind a man is, in my opinion, nothing more than a reluctance to leave the dark ages, and as a woman I find it very offensive. Although to be fair, Muslim men are not alone when it comes to enforcing that religion. In fact some of the women out there are just as bad, if not worse.

One particular incident that springs to mind occurred when I was browsing the stalls of a wonderful market in Cairo. Despite the weather, the women were out in the full garb with not a bead of sweat to be seen. I on the other hand, had barely a stitch on me and was sweating like a chicken in a chipper. Anywhere water could come out, it did. Wearing a string vest and a pair of Bermuda shorts, I was very obviously a tourist, however when I went to pay for a number of items, the woman at the stall refused to serve me. I wasn't fluent in Arabic but I knew enough of the language to know she more than disapproved of my attire. Rather than leave things be, she instead signalled at two other women nearby who suddenly began hollering at me. She stood there looking at me like I was a walking insult to the culture. The PC brigade will no doubt accuse me of not embracing the cultural differences but you know what guys, that's easier said than done

when they refuse to tolerate ours! I was dressed appropriately for their climate, not their culture. I'm delighted to say, however, that I eventually enjoyed the satisfaction of revenge.

When I became very well-known in Turkey, I developed a pop star image which the people absolutely loved. As a result, I would usually make the effort to dress in accordance with that image. On this particular occasion, I was in Istanbul Airport about to board a flight to Ireland and was wearing a white leather mini-skirt paired with a crop top under a denim jacket. Not exactly on the same level as wearing a thong to a mosque, but then the hardcore followers of this religion are not exactly the most reasonable of people. Conscious that I was holding up the aircraft, I ran across the tarmac towards the plane. At that time however, a group of around thirty fully-robed Muslim women had just left *their* plane and were walking towards the airport when one of them spotted me and tipped off the others. Sure enough they followed her lead and began their high-pitched holler. Believe me, that distinctive piercing sound, when multiplied by thirty, is truly terrifying when you're the one on its receiving end. As I walked up the steps of the plane, absolutely mortified, they continued to holler at me, making gestures of disgust.

I have always been a woman of little patience and by this point I was pissed off at being treated with such horrendous contempt over my decision to bare a little skin in sweltering heat. When I reached the top of the steps leading into the plane, I turned around and, with a laugh that could be translated as 'can't get me now bitches!', I swiftly hiked up my top and flashed them, (I wasn't even wearing a bra!). Given that the pyramids are named Cheops, Chephron and Mycerinus, they were definitely treated to at least a C & C moment! I then high-tailed it into the plane and with that, the door was shut tight and the steps were lifted up. I'd say half of them had to be hospitalised with shock-induced coronaries.

Do I regret it? As if!

In fact, I consider it to be one of my life's greatest 'Up Yours' moments. I'd had enough of their interference. Even looking at their attire on the streets of Ireland I just don't get it, but I wouldn't dare be so ignorant as to heckle or intimidate them for their choice, so why on earth should they be allowed escape with harassing me?

❖

Religion is a bone of contention between Ahmed and me. Whenever we're together, we can talk for hours as we share so many things in common. We always enjoy discussing the same topics until, that is, he broaches the subject of religion at which point I could kill him. When he talks about religion, he transforms from being a doctor with a genius mind back to that of a Neanderthal. Despite being highly educated, Ahmed staunchly abides by the dated conformities of the Muslim culture. I often question him about the general 'Muslim refusal' to embrace change, and each time he will firmly insist that there's no need to change something that 'has been so good for the past two thousand years'.

Reality is that nothing stays the same, nothing stands still. Even the very coastline of each country changes shape over time. Unfortunately, Ahmed refuses to accept he has been brainwashed into believing that the views of his culture are ethical. It's as though he doesn't have the capacity to see outside the Muslim framework because it has been hammered into his psyche from childhood. I have often pointed out to him the length of time it took for the Irish to shake off the iron grasp of the Catholic Church, but he refuses to listen. Combined with his religious beliefs and my overall lack of them, we have shared many a row which, in itself, proves my point about religion causing disputes. It still amazes me the level of power religion has over some people. It can transform one person into a saint, another into a tyrant.

Vulgar displays of religion also set my blood pressure soaring. Even the pioneer pin riles me. Can someone please tell me why on earth alcohol has to come into the equation? I had an uncle who wore that bloody pin for his entire life, so out of curiosity one day I asked him when it was he decided to give up the drink in the name of Jesus.

'Oh, I never took a drink in my life, not a drop,' he told me, proudly. 'So exactly how is that a sacrifice?' I asked him. 'Surely, you have to really enjoy something in order for it to be a sacrifice when you relinquish it? You're giving up something you have never even tried!'

Despite presenting a valid argument, he wouldn't listen to what I was saying.

I brought my children up to believe that they were in charge of their own lives. To *need* a God or to *need* anything for that matter is a crutch and, frankly, I want them to live their lives free of such emotional crutches. I reared them to be respectful of people and animals, or as Linda McCartney once wisely said, 'Anything that has a face, a heart and a central nervous system'.

How nice a place would the world be if we all lived in accordance with that particular premise?

Even the most ferociously religious person should not die without reading Richard Dawkins or Stephen Hawkins – even simpler just listen to the lyrics of John Lennon's 'Imagine'!

The priest

My dislike for religion can be traced back to when I was a young teenager. The idea of a priest condemning someone's supposedly shameful behaviour from the pulpit was in my opinion nothing less than bullying. The hypocrisy is crippling to my mind! To be honest, I wish this was the only reason that inspired my dislike of religion. Unfortunately, it was an incident of a more sinister nature that sealed the lid on any chance of me being 'converted' in the end.

After school each day, I would get the 15B bus home and, on one particular evening, an African priest from the White Fathers' sat down beside me. Noticing the large portfolio I was carrying, he asked if he could see my artwork. At the time, I just wanted him to get lost, but he was a priest, so out of politeness I humoured him. Big mistake on my part, because from that point onwards, he seemed to make a point of being on the same bus as me every evening.

He then began giving me gifts such as boxes of colouring pencils, sketch pads and so on. Even though I was just thirteen years of age, there was something about him that made me distinctly suspicious of his motives. One evening when the bus reached my stop, he stepped off and insisted, much to my horror, that he meet my parents. My mother was already aware of him because she'd asked me where the new colouring pencils had come from. Once I mentioned that I had received them from a priest, she didn't mind. He was a man of the cloth and at that time in Ireland, they could do no wrong.

When he accompanied me into the house that evening, Mom courteously welcomed him in. Tea in the best cups, fairy cakes on the best plates, the whole works were brought out for him, all because he wore the collar. He sat there for ages going on about how his parents had died pagans and how his greatest wish had been to convert them before they passed away. I was already going off religion at the time, but Christ Almighty, this yo-ho certainly finished it for me.

Suddenly, he started dropping in on his way to mass to give the family a blessing and to be quite frank, it was beginning to rile me.

One day, however, after seeking the permission of my mother, he brought me to a large art gallery in town. As he was showing me the different paintings and explaining the significance of each one, he then brought me upstairs to where there was a gargantuan painting depicting the Blessed Virgin breastfeeding the baby Jesus. He dwelled on this one picture for ages, asking me the most awkward questions about what was happening between the mother and child. Several times, he referenced 'the beautiful breasts' of the Virgin Mary, and even though I felt so uncomfortable, absolutely nothing prepared me for what he did next. While he was talking about the Virgin Mary, he suddenly shot his hand down my shirt and groped me, telling me what beautiful breasts I had. I remember being so shocked by what was happening that I could barely scream. Without any hesitation, I turned and sprinted from the building, continuing until I reached O'Connell Street where I knew I would be able to catch the 15B bus home. I was literally shaking with shock. As I stood at the bus stop, immersed in every anxious emotion you could think of, I suddenly felt a tap on my shoulder. There he was standing over me with two ice-cream cones in his hands and my school bag thrown over his shoulder.

'Here, young lady! What are you being a silly girl for? Have a nice ice-cream!' he smiled.

After slapping the ice-cream out of his hand, I ran onto the bus, where I immediately made for the upper level. After a few minutes, just as the bus was pulling off, he appeared on the top deck and sat beside me. Placing his hand on my knee, he said in his broken English, 'You must not be silly about this now. I can explain to your parents. Don't be telling them anything that would upset them. I can work this out with you. This is a silly reaction! I was just explaining the painting to you.'

In the past, I have more than defended myself. When I was nine years old, a man reeking of eau-de-vodka attempted to attack me on a roadside late one evening. I responded with a punch that broke his jaw in two places followed by a kick that unquestionably destroyed his marriage prospects (a two-piece suite instead of three if you will!). This time however, I was so frightened that I could barely even move. I was also conscious of the fact that if I ran to the other passengers on the bus for help, chances are they wouldn't believe my allegations. He was a priest, for God's sake! This was a time when people practically bowed to the clergy. Who on earth would believe the accusations of a teenage girl? All I could do was endure the journey while he continued talking and talking.

I vividly remember looking out the window and willing every bus stop to fade into oblivion, I just wanted to be home so badly. When the bus finally reached my stop, I ran out so fast that an oncoming car had to swerve to avoid me. Calling my name, which he always pronounced 'Adela', the priest ran up the road after me shouting at me to stop. As I burst in the door of the house in tears, my poor mother looked horrified by the state I was in. Without saying a word, I ran up to my bedroom and locked the door. Almost immediately I could hear his voice downstairs telling my parents that 'Adela was upset over something'.

Shortly afterwards, my father was up knocking on my door, insisting that I come out from my room. I don't know why, maybe I feared I would destroy their faith, but I didn't want to tell my parents what had happened. I remember Dad scolding me through the door over my disgraceful behaviour and how it was an absolute insult to remain in my room while a man of the cloth was in the house. I, however, was hysterical and steadfastly refused to emerge until the priest was gone. Would you believe that scumbag sat in our living room for hours that evening in the hope that I would eventually appear?

Following that day, I did everything I could to avoid him. Even though I never told my father, I only shared the full story with my mother years later when I was an adult. She was always such a gentle woman who never even raised her voice, let alone use profane language. But the moment I revealed what that priest had done, her first response was, 'Well that son of a bitch! I'd have smashed the door in his face if I had known!'

Last time I checked, the 'son of a bitch' in question was still alive ... having run back to Nigeria!

❖

The Restaurant

People often ask me what Stephen McAllister was referring to when he wrote: 'I'll take you up on that!' on a card that the chefs had all signed for me. It actually stems from an arrangement we made in the kitchen during the filming of RTÉ's *The Restaurant*. Anyone who knows Stephen knows he makes a killer champ. It's a dish to die for. In fact, I would go so far as to say that whoever insisted chocolate was better than sex had clearly never tasted Stephen McAllister's mashed potatoes!

Unfortunately for me, his recipe didn't come from a cookery book but rather his brilliant culinary mind. As a barter, I promised I would teach him how to make sugar roses if he promised to show me how to make McAllister-style mash. He agreed, hence his comment, 'I'll take you up on that!'

Despite having been looking down the barrel of a television lens from the time I was a child, *The Restaurant* was singularly the most nerve-racking thing I have ever done (well that is until I participated in *Celebrity Head Chef* with Conrad Gallagher!).

I adore cooking but had never cooked for a restaurant of one hundred people before, and so, felt very much out of my comfort zone. For my starter, guests had a choice of Coulibiac, Christmas coddle or Tarragon pears with blue cheese on a salad of baby spinach leaves. The main course boasted a brochette of seafood served with risotto, or braised venison with juniper and thyme served on a bed of sage and chive mash. The dessert menu, my favourite by far, consisted of winter spiced mini-muffins on top of a garibaldi slice. This was served on a roof slate onto which I had sieved snow (icing sugar) over a pair of tiny boots belonging to Naomi's *Bratz* doll, thus giving the impression of Santa's footprints in the snow.

My feature piece for the room was a beautiful Christmas cake, which I had iced and decorated with sugar crafted embellishments. The inspiration for the cake occurred to me one evening when I noticed the late autumnal berries on the trees as I was out walking my dogs. I took home a few pieces of the foliage, photographed them and later made exact replicas from sugar. Other sugar features of the cake included little choristers holding prayer books, an old-fashioned street lamp, and the vision of a church in the background. I also made a number of candles for the top layer of the cake and on each one, I piped a drizzle effect which I then glazed so that it would look like real melting candle wax. When I brought it into the restaurant on the day of filming, the chefs were smitten with it. It took me ages to convince them I had made the bloody thing.

When judging time rolled around, no fault was found with the food. The wine, on the other hand, let me down. I had chosen the most perfect red and white wines to accompany the meal. On the day of recording, however, I saw the waitress present the guests with a completely different brands to the ones I had chosen. It seems the wine merchants didn't have the ones I requested, so a person from the show picked different ones in their place without telling me. Rather annoyingly, I was awarded four stars out of five, with one star deducted for wines I didn't even choose. Pain in the butt, eh?

My top 100 favourite restaurants

Some of my fave eating places on the planet ... No 'CUISINE SNOBBERY' here folks – just places I have REALLY liked to eat in over an entire lifetime of my travels.

There are hundreds of superb restaurants in Ireland alone that I have not only never eaten in ... but haven't even discovered yet ... Shame on me!

So, until I do, Here are my 100 best!

Outside of the Troc – 'MY GLOBAL No. 1' they are in no particular order ... just as they occurred to me!

And forgive me those wonderful eateries I love ... that temporarily escaped my memory!

Favourite Restaurants and 'Caffs'

Trocadero, St Andrew's Street, Dublin 2.

Residence, 41 St Stephen's Green Dublin 2. Opulence and excellence!

The Al Muntaha Restaurant at the Burj Al Arab, Dubai – On my 'bucket list' to return to!

The Italian Connection, Kilkenny. (Superb Superb!)

Atwood Cafe, (corner of Washington and State Street Chicago, USA ... do not die without eating here!)

Cafe Trio, London (Wonderful Turkish and Med, Cuisine), 15 Wigmore St. South, Welwyn Garden City, UK. (Tell the boss 'Ibo' that Twink sent you – and say Merhaba (Hello) from me!)

Renvyle House Hotel, Connemara, ... (With THE chef ... that I want to be when I grow up ... the brilliant Tim O'Sullivan.)

The Indian Brasserie, Rathfarnham, Dublin. (My super Indian take-away.)

Zanzibar Restaurant, London, UK. (Sshhhh Micheal B ... I won't tell if you won't!)

Chez Slah, 14 Bis Rue Pierre De Coubertin, Tunis, Tunisia. (Hard to find ... but keep walking ... well worth it!)

Chlo and I in Cipriani's NY on opening night of Riverdance.

Good old Captain America's, Dublin, a family favourite.

Colm Wilkinson and friends in a Chinese restaurant.

Captain America's, Grafton Street. (My children's favourite from infancy to today!)

Gladstones, Malibu Beach, Los Angeles, California. USA … (SOMEONE take me back here Pleeeeease!)

The Dining Room at Waterford Castle. (Mmmmmmmm!……then we stroll back to our little house on the island… 'heaven on earth'!) P.s. I wish it was our house!

Topo Gigio's, Greenside, London. (Old Favourite)

Ananda, Dundrum Shopping Centre, Dublin – 25 star Indian Restaurant!

L'Officina, (Italian) Dundrum Shopping Centre, Dublin. (Luverly – and sweet staff)

L'Ecrivain, (The consistently amazing Derry and Sally Clark) Dublin.

Fatso's Pasta, London. (So many 'post show' laughs with Siobhan McCarthy and UK colleagues over the years.)

The Dining Room at La Stampa, Dawson St., Dublin. (Happy Happy memories of winning CELEBRITY HEAD CHEF 2011 for TV3.)

Mesazul at the Doral Country Club, Miami, Florida. USA. (Scenic, Scenic, Scenic … Divine!)

L'Escargot, 48 Greek Street, London UK. (Many fun lunches with Hubbards.)

Harvey Nicholls Restaurant, Dundrum Shopping Centre, Dublin. (Happy memories of filming a super fun and laughter filled lunch with lovely Lucy Kennedy.)

The Little Owl, Solihull, Birmingham (a little 'world treasure' restaurant and my fave eatery after a long day's judging in the 'Cake International' show in the NEC each November.)

Mandarin Inn, Rathfarnham, Dublin. (My super local Chinese take-away.)

Cava Spanish Tapas Restaurant, Galway. (Every smart actor's late night eatery in Galway.)

Great Miami food!

Dining in Cyprus.

In the much missed Eastern Tandoori, Dublin.

Great friend Barbara McKenzie and I in the Four Seasons, Dublin 4.

Anywhere **Conrad Gallagher** happens to be cooking!!!!

Schilthorn-Piz Gloria, Revolving Restaurant, at the top of the Swiss Alps ... (Yes ... the James Bond one ... prepare to lose your mind with the view ... from the cable car ride ... right to your table!)

The Sunday Carvery at The Glenview Hotel, Glen of the Downs, Co. Wicklow – Ireland at it's loveliest!

Vis aan de Schelde, a MUST for seafood in Amsterdam, Holland. (Part of the fabric there, though VERY out of the way.)

Howard's Way, Churchtown, Dublin. (One of our staples.)

Taverna Azzurra Ristorante, Grotto Azzurra, Marina Grande, Sorrento, Italy. (Found this whilst filming *Bon Voyage* for RTE in 1993 ... excellent!)

Cornstore Restaurant, 19 Thomas Street, Co. Limerick. Class!

Gallagher's Irish Bar and Restaurant, London, UK. (Memories of nights out with the Hubbards.)

The dining carriage on the **Venice Simplon Orient Express** 'One of my greatest life experiences' ever. (Did we have fun Colin Connaughton or did we have fun?)

Mario's, Terenure, Dublin. Another Agnew family favourite.

Peppermint Park, London, UK. Happy memories of working in London and bringing my babies there for Sunday lunch.

Chapter 1, Parnell Square, Dublin. Michelin Star restaurant. ('Nuff said!)

Gotham City, 8 South Anne Street, Dublin – Great Craic!

Felfela, 15 Hoda Shaarawi St. Cairo, Egypt. (Love love Love!! ... When is our next dinner date Ahmed?)

Fire Restaurant, at The Mansion House Dublin. (Best big chunky 'cheffy' chips ever!)

Patrick Guilbaud and **'The Cellar'** at The Merrion Hotel, Dublin. As posh as it gets folks!

Chlo and I share a 'heart' pizza in Austria.

Johnny Fox's, The Dublin Mountains – such great fun!

The Fireplace Inn, 1448 North Wells Street Chicago USA ... (Best ribs on the planet!)

Son'z Maui at Swan Court, Maui, Hawaii. (You'll have to pinch yourself hard to believe the setting ...unreal ... like a movie backdrop!)

Paparazzi, Templeogue Village, Dublin. Super food and service – great prices.

Union Oyster House, 41. Union Street, Boston, USA. (Great, great seafood.)

Dunbrody Country House and Hotel, Wexford ... (BRILL Head Chef/Proprietor Kevin Dundon ... Love ya Kev!)

Bijou, Bistro/Restaurant, Highfield Road, Rathgar, Dublin 6. Little Rathgar Gem.

Villa Masianco, St. Johann (Ski resort) Tirol, Austria. (One of my kids 'Ski-zer' favourites.)

Jewel of the Nile, Luxor, Egypt. (AFTER you've seen the Sound and Light Show at the ancient ruins ... trust me ... you won't run out of dinner conversation – a must!)

Domino's Pizza, Ballyboden, Dublin – Young people's fave takeaway back in our house, after a 'tired and emotional' night out!

Joe Allen's, Covent Garden, London, UK. (Celebrity spotting.)

Joe Allen's, New York, USA. (Even better celebrity spotting.)

Adele's Hühnergrill, Tirol, Austria (treat yourself to their Apple strudel with a mug of hot Glühweine... Oooooo ... you won't notice the cold – I promise!)

Puddleduck, Luxor, Egypt (or this one for post Sound and Light show ...equally Fab!)

VM Restaurant at Viewmount House, Longford ... (with GENIUS head chef Gary O'Hanlon ... how could you POSSIBLY go wrong?)

The exquisite dining room at **Hotel Muerice,** Paris ... (Dining room a master class in good taste!)

Pullman Restaurant, (Train Carriage) at Glenlo Abbey Galway. (Another must before you die ... wait till you hear it's history ... incredible!)

The Aku Aku, Las Vegas. (Watch out for the Mai Tai's there LETHAL ... after two ... yer knees go missing!!!)

Heron's Cove, Goleen, West Cork. Ireland. (Finest fish dishes on the planet! Tell Sue Buswell-Hill I sent ya!!!!)

Restaurant Spruengli am Paradeplatz, Zurich, Switzerland ... (Champagne and chocolate heaven eh Chlo? and that's only breakfast LOL!)

Abruzzi, Rome, Italy. (Wonderful memories of great times with baby Chloë and 'great fun' genius Cedric Culliton, head of the film crew.)

Chlo and I in London.

Family 'dine time' in Israel.

Chatter's Restaurant, in the stunning grounds of the Gabarone Sun Hotel, Botswsana, Africa. (Four year old Naomi's favourite restaurant.)

Journey's End, Crookhaven, West Cork. (Sadly Ina and Peter have retired to their Restaurant in Spain.)

Caffe Noto. ... corner of Frances Street and Thomas Street Dublin ... (Scrumptious home made soups, breads, etc.)

Dokuz Bucuk, Çeşme, Turkey. (Roof comes off at dawn – amazing!!!)

The Eastern Tandoori, Cork City. (Opposite the Cork Opera House) Consistently lovely Indian Food.

Hafiz Mustafa, 1864, Istanbul, Turkey. (Baklava & Coffee to die for!)

Luigi Malones, Cork City. (Also opposite the Cork Opera House) Fab Spag Bol, plus nicest wine glasses ever!!!

The Dining Room of the **Intercontinental Hotel,** Haile Selassie Avenue, Lusaka, Zambia, Africa. (But you DO need a tie ... AND a booking Andy O'Callaghan ... LOL!!!)

The Tea Rooms in Harrods, Knightsbridge, London, UK. (Crumpets, jam and clotted cream, yummy! ... Naomi's favourite treat when in London with me.)

Fitzpatrick's Hotel and Bar, Dundalk ... picture postcard wonderfully Irish setting ... bring all your 'tourist' friends there!

Roly's, Ballsbridge or Dundrum, Dublin. Either/Or – both fab!

Pagoda Floating Restaurant, Honolulu, Hawaii ... (Ahhhhhh ... Don't get me started!)

Bistro du Vin at Hotel Du Vin, One Devonshire Gardens, Glasgow, Scotland. (They always put me in Simon Cowell's suite ... puts a whole new meaning to 'suite dreams' eh?)

King Sitric, East Pier, Howth, Co. Dublin. (One of my first introductions to great seafood in Ireland.)

The Metro Café, 200 W 57th St (between 7th Ave & Broadway), New York, USA ... Great great DIY food ... (make up your own combinations ... cooked freshly in front of you.)

Marco Pierre White, 51 Dawson Street, Dublin. (The Fitzer family have always known their stuff!)

Gordon Ramsey at **The London Hotel,** N.Y., USA. Very posh, very pricey, worth a treat though!

Bel and Bellucci, Ballsbridge, Dublin 4. (Wonderful attentive service.)

Dunne & Crescenzi, 6 Frederick Street, Dublin. (A regular Fave when in town.)

Pasta Fresca, Chatham Street, Dublin, (Chef/ Proprietor … Long, great reputation … Lifelong pal … the beautiful May Frisbee.)

Vapiano, Rämistrasse 8, Zurich, Switzerland. (Dermot Kiernan will forceably DRAG you there even if you want to go elsewhere – worth the struggle though, ha!)

Villa Tiberio, Carretera Cadiz Km. 185, Marbella, Spain. (Sit in the garden area – you can easily pretend you are an ancient Roman here … timelessly beautiful.)

Little Caesars, Rathfarnham/Chatham Street, Dublin. (Many happy memories of the Agnews as a foursome.)

Le Riad Monceau, Marrakech, Morrocco……. OMG! Decor as fantastic as the food! (Had just bought two VERY big ornamental Ibis and Crane birds in the market … had to bring them to dinner with me … highly embarrassing!)

JP's Steakhouse Restaurant, 28 Dominick Street, Mullingar, Co. Westmeath, Ireland. (J'sus … Great big Shlabs of Shooper Shteak!)

Cipriani's, 110, East 42nd. Street (between Lexington & Park Avenue New York USA), OMG … John & Moya … The greatest opening night 'after party' dinner for *Riverdance* NY in the history of the entertainment business!

The Great Room in The Merchant Hotel, Belfast … (Magnificent building.)

Ruth Chris Steakhouse, in ANY country … (particularly USA … obviously!)

Killakee House, Hell Fire Club, (Just up the road from me – can't believe it's gone – miss it so much!)

The Eucalyptus, 14 Hativat, Yerushalayim, Jerusalem, Israel. Sit outside … (even if I was bitten by insects) it's worth it for the food and the amazing amazing view of old Jerusalem.

Brambles Café, Knocklyon Shopping Centre, Dublin 16. Great oul' tuna corn n' cheese sambo, to munch when you're in Scruples Hair Salon next door!

Although I haven't had the pleasure of eating there (yet) Chlo will *not* speak to me if I don't put *her* favourite rest on the list and that is … (not counting these two are they are not mine … cheat!)

    Neven Maguire's MacNean House and **Restaurant Blacklion,** Co. Cavan.

… And again … I haven't been, but Naomi will *not* speak to me if I don't mention *her* fave restaurant … and that is (she is our Sushi Queen) …

    Fukuzushi, 5-7-8 Roppongi, Tokyo, Japan.

The best breakfast spreads anywhere on the planet are to be found in:

    Tau Game Lodge, Madikwe, South Africa,
    Adams Beach Hotel, Ayia Napa, Cyprus.
    Hotel du Vin Glasgow … AGAIN!!!!
    Ria Park Garden Hotel, Vale De Lobo.
    Almancil, Portugal.

and finally … last but definitely not least!

Café Angelos, Camden street, Dublin.

Burdocks (ANYWHERE!!!!!)

The Roma Café, Marian Road, Rathfarnham, 'best chippers ever'!

Ever the comic - Naomi decides to 'wear' her dinner as a hat!

At the mercy of Liza

Most women leave their hairdresser with a gorgeous new 'do'. Thanks to a young stylist working in the Dublin branch of a well-known hair salon, I left with the bare remnants of my hair still intact. The stylist's handiwork occurred after he left my hair colour in too long, although if his earlier conversations with me were anything to go by, I can safely assume he got held up while regaling another client with his incessant stories of how he planned to make it in showbusiness. He was convinced of his ability to be the next Liza Minnelli. When a salon girl reminded 'Liza' of my hair colour, I knew immediately by his look of sudden panic that he had completely forgotten, although this was nothing compared to the panic that shot across his face when he removed the foils from my hair and rinsed it.

My hair was falling out by the fistful while the ends of what little hair remained were also frazzled and burned from the bleach. The salon issued a litany of excuses, even suggesting that I go to one of their trichologists who would decide if it was the bleach that had caused the damage. A ridiculous suggestion considering that anyone on their payroll is hardly going to talk themselves out of a job by siding against them.

Having been a long-time customer of theirs, I genuinely wasn't interested in suing or having the case turn nasty. I just wanted them to repair the damage they had caused so that my hair could be restored back to its original quality. I would have been happy even if they had issued me with a disclaimer stating that while they were not taking responsibility for it, they would in good faith carry out the necessary treatments to rectify it. Instead I received a letter in which they claimed that coloured hair is more fragile, and so, it's pretty much the luck of the draw each time you dye it. In hindsight, I should have insisted that they take one of their own stylists who had no colour in her hair and have them leave the bleach in for the same length of time as it had been left in mine. It would have proved my point perfectly, but as I said, I didn't want things to turn bitter, I just wanted a solution. Following my trauma at the hands of Liza, a good friend of mine recommended I go to Scruple's salon. Elaine, my stylist, has since literally brought my hair back from the dead through a series of treatments.

I never proceeded any further with my case against the offending salon but then the statute of limitations has not yet expired, so if the mood takes me, who knows?

Oh she's a diva, that one

Theatre, like everything else, may not be recession-proof but it is without doubt, recession-resilient. Robert C. Kelly's entrance into my life is one of the best things that ever happened to me. He has been my producer for shows such as *Menopause the Musical*, *Dirty Dusting*, *Mum's the Word* and *Grumpy Old Women*, all of which have been huge successes. I'm convinced the man is a distant cousin of Cameron Mackintosh.

Prior to meeting with me, however, Robert was repeatedly warned that I was 'difficult' to work with. Look, the only people who say I am difficult to work with are those who have either never worked with me or those who have been so bloody useless while working with me that I confronted them about it.

Theatre has always been known as the land of hot tempers and cold coffees; it's no place for someone of a delicate disposition. Directors don't placate you; in fact a pat on the back is never given unless you really deserve it, and, as both Dáithí Ó Sé and Mick McCarthy once rightly pointed out, 'It's only a few inches away from a kick in the arse!'

If rumours are anything to go by, I'm made out to be a much bigger diva than I actually am. Yes I have had my fair share of 'words' and 'exchanges' with different directors who insist their ways are better, when in fact, I know that my way of delivering the line would have more impact. We'll argue the toss, but I usually prove to them that it's best to trust my instinct as I am the one performing the role. Let's face it, if I don't know how to instinctively work a part at this stage in my life, then there really is no hope for me.

I set extraordinarily high standards for myself and whatever about being a diva, I can certainly be a demon when I feel people don't deliver to that standard. This is why I have always been so specific about those I work with. Some production companies phone me regularly but I refuse to even take their calls because I know they will lower the bar. When I work with people who are unprofessional and who have low standards, I become a problem for them because I always demand the best from people in terms of work, production, quality and whatever else may follow.

When this knocks a few egos out of joint, they brand *me* a diva! Why? Because I want to get the production 100 per cent right? Because I want it to be amazing?

I have never in my life let down a production, primarily because I don't stop rehearsing from the moment I get the job. Following rehearsals with the cast from around ten o'clock until six, I arrive home and continue to rehearse my future performance until it shines like the top of the Chrysler Building. I then go to bed with my earphones on and listen to the various songs that I have to learn. RTÉ's shelves are full of excellent shows I've done for them and if that's the result of being a diva, then so be it. I call it 'not settling for second best'.

As part of my role in *Mum's the Word*, I had to learn a song called 'Momsense'. This has to be sung at a very high speed to the tune of the William Tell overture. I rehearsed that song so intensely that I ended up with a slight paralysis of my lower jaw for a couple of days. YouTube the song and you'll see what I'm talking about!

Robert and I.

One of the advantages of donning a wig on stage is that I can wear a good conditioning treatment underneath it. Beneath my wig is a mass of leave-in conditioner covered with a plastic bag which I secure in place with the crotch section from a pair of tights! The heat of the layers gives my hair a really good conditioning, and as the wig is well pinned in, absolutely nothing moves! On one or two occasions in Dirty Dusting, I felt a trickle of conditioner run down my face but, fortunately, my character had to carry around a cloth with her while she worked, so I just nonchalantly wiped it away as though it were perspiration and no one was any the wiser!

Eileen Colgan

Áine Ní Mhuiri

Eileen Gibbons

Flo McSweeney

Nellie Conroy

Anna Fox

The show *Dirty Dusting* was another 'bitch' of a learn. As well as learning your own lines, you had to know everyone else's simply because the script moves so fast that you need to know exactly where to interject. A momentary lapse of concentration and you were finished. It is without doubt a mentally exhausting show, although fast-paced comedy, by its very nature, will always be difficult to play. It doesn't matter how many times you rehearse, an intricate play will forever be intricate. On the upside however, it does keep you mentally sharp.

A girlfriend of mine, who made the decision to return to the classroom and study medicine, once remarked that 'learning how to learn again' was the one thing she found most difficult. In the average job, you are typing or reading but how often are you actually learning? One of the big advantages to acting is that you are always studying new lines and thankfully this helps keep the brain active and the cells well-oiled. This is of some comfort to me as one of my greatest fears is dementia. Stripping a person of their memories is, in my opinion, the cruellest end to a life. A movie scene that never fails to make me cry is the wonderful portrayal by Judy Dench of the writer Iris Murdoch, when in a brief moment of lucidity, she says 'I wrote books!'

Jim Broadbent's wonderfully sensitive answer to her was, 'Oh, yes, my dear, wonderful, wonderful books!'

To think that a mind once so sharp and gifted was now in darkness is just so profoundly sad. This is why I have always said to my girls, 'If that happens to me, go out and get the shotgun or please feel free to slip me the pills'.

I don't want to be in a state that prompts people to remark, 'Ah, sure, there's no point in going to see her, the poor creature won't know who you are'.

Media

I once read somewhere that the Shubert brothers, who were big-time theatrical managers and producers, barred the *Times* critic Alexander Woollcott from their productions because they felt he had too much power and liked too few shows. The modern day Woollcott-equivalent is Frank Rich, the former 'butcher of Broadway', a man whose witterings have the power to close an entire show. Why anyone would give any weight or credence to a critical pen-pusher, is truly beyond my understanding. Be the review good or bad, you certainly won't find it amongst my reading material. I'm long enough in the business to instinctively trust *my* own judgement of the production and not that of some young fella from the local tech with a notepad and a chewed up biro.

Most people are often surprised to find that I don't even read the good reviews. My reasoning is simple. Where are the critics when my mortgage is due? They don't pay my wages; the members of the public who pay in to see me perform, do. As far as I'm concerned the audience are the only critics worth listening to.

I have no animosity towards journalists, absolutely none whatsoever. In fact, it would take something rather ruthless against my children before I would even consider suing. If anything, I genuinely appreciate the tough, pressured job that goes with being a journalist.

Every day, the various editors take a look at the front page headlines of other newspapers and deride their staff for not having sourced the stories first. The reporters are then left with no option but to try to dig for more scurrilous material and in doing so, are usually forced to cast aside all forms of moral conduct. I think most journalists will agree that the moment the British tabloids arrived in Ireland, they brought with them their Fleet Street (lack of) ethics and, from that point onwards, it was a race to the bottom. While I have always found most Irish reporters to be extremely nice and easy to get along with, unfortunately, a tiny handful of nasty ones have given them all a bad name.

I'm not exaggerating when I say that one of the aforementioned 'handful' is the most evil-minded reporter in Ireland – a complete and utter insult to the ethics of the profession. God love her, she's as equally as talentless as she is malevolent. I call her the 'Bunny Boiler'.

I have never been interviewed by this woman, never even so much as shared a few words with her, but for some reason she enjoys sending me the most viciously hateful text messages.

On one occasion, she texted to say was going to write an article, regardless of whether or not I responded, stating that Paddy Cole, Louis Walsh and Feargal Quinn had given me money. It was completely untrue and as a result of her threat, my solicitor had to tip off the three men in question. They, in turn, had to send legal letters to the newspaper stating that they had never given me a cent and would sue, if her article stated otherwise. Honest to God, this woman experiences fanciful shit-epiphanies in the same nonchalant way the rest of us drink coffee.

If I'm on stage at eight o'clock, she will always tell me about the article at around ten to eight. That way, she ensures there's nothing I can do about it because by the time I'm off stage, the newspaper will have already gone to print.

On another occasion, she stood outside my house gates and rang the bell every minute for over an hour. The dogs were going crazy and I quite frankly nearly followed suit. In total, she

and the photographer waited there for almost three hours. One day, she even parked across the path directly outside my gates thus blocking me from leaving my house. I phoned the Gardaí to report her for harassment, but they legally couldn't remove her because technically she was on a public pavement.

If I had done something to offend this woman in the past then at least I would understand exactly where her bitterness stems from. Unfortunately it appears to be a random act of hatred. When I was seriously ill in Mount Carmel Hospital two years ago after having collapsed with my asthma, some journalists would arrive into the ward bearing gifts under the guise of being friends of mine. Marion, the matron, used to work in New York and, as the 'Bunny Boiler' herself soon discovered first-hand, she had no tolerance or time for any of the media.

One day, as Marion was walking down the corridor, she spotted the bitch going from room to room, blatantly looking inside each one before moving on. When Marion confronted her, she began by explaining that she had an appointment, before suddenly changing her story midway through and saying she was visiting a friend. She became so shirty with Marion that in the end, security were called to remove her. The woman in the room next to me was dying, and here was this bitch imposing on gravely ill people such as her all for the sake of a bloody photograph.

The journalists that did their homework discovered that the maternity ward was on the same floor as mine, and so, would arrive in carrying baby gifts in the hope that they would be able to sneak over to my room unnoticed. In the end, none of them succeeded, although one did make it as far as the desk before he was caught. The hospital staff were incredible. In fact, when the doctor allowed me outside to see how my lungs would adapt to the pollen in the air, two nurses went out ahead of me to make sure no journalists were waiting to pounce from the shrubbery.

Following my hospitalisation, I appeared on *The Late Late Show* to plead with the press to give me some breathing space as I tried to recover from what had essentially been a near-death experience. Unfortunately, my request led to me being on the receiving end of a nasty backlash, and suddenly, the papers were describing my interview with Ryan Tubridy as 'a lunatic rant about the press'.

Normally, I am very controlled in my interviews, but at the time I appeared on the *Late Late*, I was so incredibly ill and distressed that it just got the better of me. As well as having been placed on a heavy course of asthma medication, I had also experienced one of the worst weeks of my life, in which I had lost my best friend Gerry Ryan. Theoretically, I should have thought twice about going on air; the reality however, is that I felt it was very necessary for me to go ahead with the interview. I wanted to put a halt to a number of vicious rumours surrounding my hospitalisation. But most of all, I wanted to ask for the media to give me space to grieve the death of one of my closest friends, and to recover from my illness. I never intended for it to sound like a rant. When I asked for the journalists to leave me alone, I wasn't targeting them all, just the vicious relentless ones, the rat-pack so to speak. Unfortunately, the media people I was *not* getting at were the very ones who took umbrage.

With some reporters, there just seems to be no line of decency in the sand. Regional journalists,

on the other hand, tend to be very fair as they're not relying on salacious gossip to sell their newspapers. When I give an interview to a regional, I know they will print exactly what I have said rather than twisting or embellishing it to make it sound like something else. Despite my chequered history with the *Sunday Independent*, they are one of the few national newspapers that will always print my words in the nature in which they were intended.

I love it when Robert C. Kelly phones me with an idea for a new show – my mind starts buzzing with ideas, thinking about how great it will be. Unfortunately, my excitement quickly diminishes the moment I think of all the interviews I will have to give in order to promote the show. It wrecks my head. The journalists don't want to know about the show, all they want to know is what shit has hit the fan that week. A large number of them will create an article filled with gossip before attaching a footnote that reads something like: 'Twink will be appearing in *Dirty Dusting* in the Gaiety Theatre this weekend.'

To give you an idea of how some journalists create their stories, envision the following scenario.

A journalist asks me what I think of Ruth Hickey's decision to sue the newspapers. My reply might contain just one sentence such as, 'Oh I thought it was ridiculous, but anyway I'm here to talk about the show I'm performing in next week'.

The following day the headline will be: 'Ruthless Twink Slams Hickey's Case'.

The sub-editor will then accompany the article with the most horrendous picture they can find, usually one of me looking like I'm shouting. Refusing interviews is not an option unfortunately, as it is almost always part of an actor's contract that he/she has to carry out pre-show publicity. It's almost akin to press prostitution. I can think of only one actor whose contract firmly stipulates limited interviews and that's Robert Di Niro.

In my early days of working with Robert (C. Kelly, not Di Niro!) David would phone up with the sole intention of antagonising me. He would accuse me of being 'in bed with the media' which was utterly preposterous, particularly considering that he of all people knew I had only ever phoned a journalist on two occasions, both of which were to help generate publicity for worthy charity events. He knows full well that I'm the last person to phone a journalist with a story, but then that was typical of him, always batting the ball back into my court. I could never understand the level of audacity he possessed. After all it takes a fair oul' bit of neck to phone the mother of your children and berate her for giving interviews to promote shows that are effectively putting food on their table.

❖

Sometimes the new brats in the journalism industry are far worse than those who have enjoyed a lifetime of bylines. They're fresh out of college and trying to prove themselves, armed with nothing more than an attitude and a pen. Regardless of whether they're novices or veterans, I don't know why any of them bother repeatedly returning to my gate because I never talk to them.

As for the genius who decided to go one step further and climb up onto the roof of the tree-house in our front garden, well I could think of two possible words I'd like to have said to him. This particular incident occurred around the time David left. The press had all but set up camp outside my house in the hope of snapping a photograph or gleaning a detail from whoever passed them by.

We didn't have the gates at the time so some of them were actually parked in our driveway. One evening, I was in my bedroom when a sparkle of glass on the roof of the garden tree-house suddenly caught my eye. There was nothing in that part of the garden that was reflective so I knew immediately it had to be a camera lens. Sure enough, the bright flash that followed proved it was a photographer. It later transpired that he had sneaked into the grounds of the neighbouring house completely unbeknownst to the owners. He then walked through their shrubbery before setting up a long, expanding steel ladder against the wall so that he could gain access to the roof of my children's tree-house. It was there he sat with a telescopic lens trained on my bedroom window. The moment I spotted him, I immediately phoned the police. Naturally, he scarpered as soon as he saw the squad car approaching but at least the neighbours got a nice new steel ladder out of it!

That night, I made dinner for the children in the kitchen which was almost pitch dark with the exception of two candles. I wanted to make sure they didn't get a shot if they managed to sneak around the back of the house. As they beamed the headlights of their cars into the front hallway, we slid the trays along the floor and crawled up the stairs. We had the shutters closed upstairs and ate in total darkness. I remember thinking how mental it was that we were being forced to do this in our own home.

One morning, members of the press took up residence outside Alexandra College where my girls were in attendance at the time. This resulted in me receiving a rather curt phone call from someone in the school asking if I could remove the journalists from outside. The reality however was that even the Gardaí had no power to remove them because they were on public property.

I feel as though I'm at the same stage Mike Murphy was when he bowed out of the industry. He couldn't endure the invasion of privacy and, as I reach the autumn of my years, I too have found myself becoming far more reclusive, not to mention more regretful, that I ever entered into this business in the first place. The promise of privacy is so tempting that I would consider moving to another country but, to be honest,

I genuinely don't want to have to go to that extreme. I have lived in other countries in the past but I have always deliberately returned to Ireland because I love living here.

These days I try not to allow myself become bothered by crap in the newspapers; yes its upsetting when it's happening, but it passes. I'm in the business long enough to know that the same article that had caused so much hurt will end up at the bottom of my bird cage the following day, although if I may paraphrase Mike Royko, no self-respecting canary would even bother defecating on a Murdoch rag.

Lisa Lambe with two-year-old Chloë. When Lisa performed with me as a child, we had the most amazing chemistry on stage. I still love her like a daughter. Her beauty as a performer was rivalled only by the beauty of her personality. She now sings alongside Chloë in Celtic Woman.

Favourite shops

1. Sharon Creagh Interiors, Rathgar
2. Yankee Candles (any branch)
3. Kadee Boutique, Athlone
4. The Anvil, Bray
5. O'Conaill Chocolate, Cork
6. The Gift Shop, Rathfarnham SC
7. Kitchen Complements

No sympathy for the pilot

I'm a quiz junkie. I have always loved general knowledge, you know, the kind that raises your brows in surprise. For instance, I know that the area code for Antarctica is 672; that the Germans tried to copy Coca-Cola and instead came up with a drink called Fanta; that in *Silence of the Lambs*, Anthony Hopkins never blinks when in character; or that Uri Geller was once sued by a pregnant woman who claimed that he had bent her contraceptive coil after she watched him perform on television. Now, I bet you raised your brows at least once while reading that!

I think I inherited this insatiable thirst for knowledge from my beloved uncle Chris, a man with a most marvellous outlook. His ability to converse on any topic laid before him meant I always thought of him as my philosopher uncle. The man was scarily intelligent. When I was a teenager, he would regularly hold Trivial Pursuit evenings. Of course, you would all but bribe your way on to Uncle Chris's team because, with him at the helm, you would be guaranteed to win. Only a week before he died in 2010, he was recalling memories of a school quiz where he successfully answered the winning question of the buzzer round, 'The word Laser is an acronym. What do the initials stand for?'

Even at eighty-nine years old, he was still able to remember that my answer was Light Amplified Solar Emissions of Radiation!

Naomi never knew my father, while Chloë only vaguely remembers him. Likewise, I never knew my mother's father, so, in a way, uncle Chris became almost like a surrogate grandfather to us all. After his funeral, my wonderfully witty Uncle Jack (his brother) said to me, 'Well, you've lost your favourite, you only have to suffer me now!'

Uncle Chris had lived a fantastic life and was blessed in that he enjoyed the full capacity of his senses right up to his dying day. If anything, he would be the one reminding *me* of stories! Not long before he died, we had a discussion about our mutual fear of flying. I theorised that we're all born with a blueprint and that the moment we enter the world, a day is on the calendar for us to leave it.

'So, here's what I'm thinking, Uncle Chris,' I began. 'These days when I get on a plane, my philosophy is, sure if today's the day my number is up, then so be it, there's nothing I can do about it!'

Ever the sharp wit, my Uncle Chris immediately quipped, 'Well, my darling niece, that's a very valid theory. My problem however, is getting on a plane the day the *pilot's* number is up and we all have to go down in sympathy with him.' Brill!

My beloved Uncle Chris R.I.P.

All together now! Naomi, Chloë and myself with Mackie, Jilly, Sykes and Yazmina.

Vintage shot from my teens of Tiutti, Mowglii and O'Malley.

Pets: The Pack

Teddy Bear – a Yorkshire Terrier who believes he's a Rottweiler.

Peanut Sheridan – has my shrubs killed from peeing on them.

Rosie Kinnitty – so human I'm convinced she's going to walk into the kitchen one of these days and say, 'Howya, Ma.'

Mary Christmas – a Deerhound Lurcher completely unaware of how big she is. She has no brain, just two hearts.

Bertie Ahern – has the body of a pit bull and the personality of a kitten.

J.J. McNamara – has the cutest face and literally no idea how to harm even a fly.

Rita Kelly – the newest hard-luck-case from Dunboyne Pound.

Timby and *Poppy* – non-stop talking cockatiels who live in the company of twenty-one canaries and finches.

All of us live in Idrone House at the discretion of our cats, Esther and Taj, both of whom rule the roost. In fact some days they bring to mind the very appropriate quotation, 'Thousands of years ago, cats were worshipped as gods; cats have never forgotten this!'

There's a photograph of me aged fifteen months walking along the beach. One hand is clasped in that of my father's, the other is stretched out towards a nearby 'oul mutt. For as long as I can remember, my parents maintained that I could never pass anything with fur on it. They were right! If it had a coat of fur, I had to kiss it. I'm telling you now, if there really is an afterlife, then there had better be a place for the animals, because otherwise I'm not bloody going. I have had every animal-related injury imaginable from broken limbs to broken ribs, a massive horse bite to the shoulder and a near-severed finger, yet I doubt there is any injury that could possibly make me love them any less.

To give Linda Martin her dues, she presented me with one of the most novel presents for my fiftieth birthday. She sponsored a donkey for me (which she called Twinkles) and paid the bills to feed and keep him in the Cork Donkey Sanctuary. I received some beautiful and unusual presents for my fiftieth but, given my passion for animals, that gift certainly stood out. It was just the sweetest gesture.

Anytime I am asked about my dogs, their names inevitably prompt a few questions. Funnily enough, we never had to work at finding names for our pets; the right moniker always just seemed to come about. On one occasion for instance, we rescued a gorgeous dog, and as the girls were doting on him they suddenly remarked, 'Look at his little face, he's so cute! He's cute like ... a like J.J. McNamara!'

So that's what we called him! His tag now reads 'J.J. McNamara', an homage to the amazingly talented (and cute as a button) son of Frank McNamara and Teresa Lowe. We then rescued a pit bull who had been knocked down underneath a poster of Bertie Ahern so, of course, from that day forth, he was known as Bertie Ahern.

One year, I went up to the DSPCA on Christmas Eve to collect a beautiful cat called Esther, however while we were there, Naomi spotted the most gorgeous dog, a Deerhound Lurcher. She gave me a signature pleading look, the kind exclusive to teenagers when they're about to start begging for something.

Immediately I cut her short and said, 'Naomi forget it, we are not getting another dog! We only came here for a flippin' cat!'

'Aw but Mom, look at her! All she has is a small cuddly toy ... and it's Christmas Eve!'

I took one look at the dog and it looked back at me as if to say, 'I would be so easy to love!'

Clearly working me to a tee, Naomi asked if we could take her out of the cage 'just to hug', which I refused point blank, because I knew if we held her for even a second, she wouldn't be going back in. Twenty minutes later, we were on our way home to Knocklyon ... with the bloody dog in tow. We decided to call her 'Mary Christmas'.

Gerreh'?!

Aw shit, here he is!

For all his affairs, David is now on his own with nothing but memories of scattered lives. Yvonne Clifford is still living in France but now goes by her married name Yvonne le Quément.

Meanwhile Hayley, the child Yvonne had with David, lives and works in Ireland. I don't know if Hayley is in contact with David, but I think she would probably know better than to try to make contact with her half-sisters. I know it's not her fault she was conceived as a result of an illicit affair in a shop, but my girls have no desire to know her.

Ironically, when I was pregnant with Naomi and trying to choose a name, one of the suggestions I singled out from the baby book was 'Hayley'. Of course, David almost had a conniption when I mentioned the prospect of calling our newborn, Hayley Agnew. Immediately he said, 'No, no – no way, I *hate* that name.' Oh, how little did I know!

To give David his dues, he never failed to remember birthdays and wedding anniversaries. Although for as long as I can remember, red roses always formed part of his gift despite me dropping countless hints about how much I detest them. I always associated red roses with guilt because the only other time he would give them to me was after he had buggered off for a few days to be with his 'bit on the side'. That said, there is a redeeming feature to be found in everyone and despite all his infidelities, there was no denying that David was a fantastic family man when he *was* with us. When Chloë was looking at the video montage of her life which I had made for her twenty-first birthday, one of the first things she remarked on was how wonderful a father he had been when they were growing up.

It has been a struggle to do the job on my own, but it wasn't too long ago that he admitted I had done a great job with the girls. David being David, he couldn't just say it straight out to me. It had to be in his usual gruff manner with every second word interspersed with an awkward cough.

❖

When he and I were so in love, we saw other couples fighting and confidently thought 'that will never be us'.

There's a Peggy Lee song about a young couple Jack and Jill who turned into an old couple Darby and Joan. During the early days, David and I always joked that we would turn into Darby and Joan and that no matter what, nothing would break us up. In a curious way, nothing really has broken us up completely. Yvonne Clifford didn't split us and while, admittedly, Ruth Hickey caused irreparable damage, she is now nowhere to be seen. In fact, once the novelty of her wore off, he was back spending time with the girls and me.

When he served me with the separation papers during the height of his affair with Ruth, I asked him how long it would be before he would be filing for divorce to which he replied, 'You needn't worry. I won't be serving you with divorce papers. I have no intention of ever getting married again and you can take my word on that.'

Not too sure how aware Ruth was of this.

When I initiated divorce proceedings on the day of our separation, however, I do think he was genuinely shocked. It clearly wasn't something he had ever envisaged happening.

I remember asking David why in the seven years he was with Yvonne, he never admitted the affair

Tunisia.

In Planet Hollywood, USA.

In Israel.

to me. The reason which dictated his decision was simple. It was never the right time. There was always something going on in our lives that he felt he would ruin if he broke the news.

He recalled how there had been one moment during a working holiday in Israel when, after we had made love on the balcony of our beautiful suite in Jerusalem, he had come close to revealing everything to me. At the last minute, however, he succumbed to silence, afraid to destroy the memories of the beautiful time we had just shared together.

❖

In recent years, David has resumed his yuletide role of serving drinks to the neighbours on Christmas morning. As he welcomes the guests, he's full of smiles and convivial banter, a stark contrast to the pompous-bastard behaviour he exhibited during what we now refer to as the 'Black Christmas'. We still haven't spoken about that incident, but then we have never really had the opportunity to. David doesn't really do apologies anyway, so I imagine if I ever do talk about that morning, it will be met with a gruff, muffled response.

It was clear that the man who had once swanned into the house with his blunt sarcasm and his I'm-having-sex-twenty-four-hours-a-day attitude, had since discovered a new-found grace. It brings to mind a great metaphor my mother often used, 'Give him enough rope to hang himself … and he will'.

I have noticed that with each passing Christmas, he becomes a bit mellower. For Christmas 2010, he brought us a pudding he had made and even offered to help with dinner before then exchanging gifts. He seemed genuinely happy to be around the house. In fact when he was leaving, there was a palpable hesitancy. I really think there was a part of him that wished he was the one saying goodbye to the guests as they left the house, rather than him being one of the guests leaving. He was the complete antithesis to the man who had roared through the letterbox that he would rather live in a hovel than spend the day with his family.

He and I may have exchanged some harsh words in private, some in person, some over the phone(!) but I have never talked rudely about David in the media. The only comment I ever made about him was that he had problems; problems I wish he had sought help for. I loved and adored him. I took care of him, I was his lover, his friend, his confidante, and if his words to Chloë on the night of her twenty-first birthday were anything to go by, I think he realises now that he never had a better woman in his life.

When I read back on all those letters, cards, and notes David and I wrote to each other, I can only wonder exactly where along the way our love and promises evaporated? It's just so hard to believe that words as beautiful as those we once shared would one day turn into a venomous screaming match. He will always be the first man I fell hopelessly head over heels in love with and that will never change. Despite the pain and the tears, there will always be a special place in my heart for David Agnew.

The minute we saw each other, we both knew we would be together; something unique happened when we caught each other's glance and to be honest, I think there will always be that 'something' between us. No two people could possibly go through everything we have been through and not still feel something for each other.

On 4 August 2009, there was a moment when we looked at each other in court as our divorce was being finalised. He looked crushed and I could clearly see the tears welling up in his eyes. In that moment, when we caught each other's glance, countless feelings surfaced. It was as though we were both thinking back on all the happy memories we had created throughout our years of marriage and were now simultaneously wondering how we ended up arguing in a courtroom.

I can still remember the moment I realised I was over him. I was driving over Portobello Bridge when out of nowhere his name shot into my mind. I realised it had been four days since I had given him a second thought. Considering how I used to think of him every minute of every day, those four days were not so much a break but rather a breakthrough.

People often ask me if I would ever go back into a full-time relationship whether it be with David or someone else. Hand on heart, I love being single far too much to want to be in a relationship. Not even if Aristotle Onassis himself got out of the grave and begged me to live on his yacht, would I trade the independence I'm enjoying now. If I were to change my mind, Ahmed would be the one but, unfortunately, the religious divide is like a ravine. Anyway my idea of bliss is being at home with my girls and my animals, working on my tapestries and cakes and listening to Classic FM. With the exception of Ahmed, a man doesn't come into the picture. I think if I were to hear the words, 'I'm home dear, any dinner?' my first response would probably be, 'Aw, shit, here he is!'

David has an obsession with forbidden fruits – what he can't have is all the more appealing. A demon he battles with to this day.

August 2009
Dear Adele, there was no pleasure taken in anything that happened last week, just nearly 30 years of mixed emotions, as always, but crammed into one day. I hope we can draw that line in the sand and find the positive things that existed between us again.

May I wish you, as always, every success in your show and health and happiness for now and the future

David x

The card I received from David on the night our divorce was made final.

Word of advice

Women often ask me for advice on how to cope when a husband calls time on the marriage in favour of another woman. All I can say is walk willingly through the eye of the storm and when you emerge the other side, you will be all the better for it. Compose yourself, get your life together, and you will soon realise what you're *not* missing.

If you start using a more reserved mellow tone of conversation with him, suddenly the mistress will look like the fishwife! Keep it civil. He will soon begin to wonder why he left and when he comes crawling back, you will have the pleasure of saying, 'Not a chance dear!'

My boy Stephen

Sometime around 1993, a group of young teenagers sat before me in my living room in Beaufort House waiting to be educated in the techniques of being interviewed for television. The small, black-haired boy with the cutest face imaginable immediately became my favourite. Introducing them, Louis Walsh turned to me and said, 'Adèle, this is my new band … Boyzone'.

The small black-haired boy was Stephen Gately.

There was so much charisma wrapped up in that Disney-esque voice of his, that from the moment I heard him sing, I told Louis he was destined for West End and Broadway. My prediction turned out to be accurate, and some years later, I found myself sitting in a major London theatre watching Stephen perform in *Joseph and the Amazing Technicolor Dreamcoat*.

When we went out for a meal afterwards, we chatted for hours about everything from life in general to the tough industry we were both embroiled in. I remember at one point trying to convince him to do an album of Disney songs. Everything about Stephen was so boyishly lovable and sweet that Disney seemed like the perfect avenue for his talents. Regardless of whether you were a fan or a friend, the 'Stephen treatment'

would consist of the brightest, warmest smile followed by a big hug. The boy genuinely didn't know how to see anything other than the good in people. The moment I heard Stephen and Ronan were going to be appearing on the *Lyrics Board* Christmas Special alongside myself and Linda Martin, I practically begged the producers to let me be on the same team as Stephen. Never cared much for Ronan, to be quite honest. When I look back at the photographs, I can still remember the wonderful fun Stephen and I enjoyed that night. Jesus, you couldn't but love him. On the morning of Sunday, 11 October 2009, I ran over to Superquinn to pick up some things for breakfast. As I was making my way into the shop, a local man on his way out stopped me and said, 'God love ya, Twink, you must be stunned. Awful sad news about poor Stephen.'

Thinking he was referring to someone in the area, I nonchalantly replied, 'Stephen who?'

'You mean you haven't heard? Stephen Gately is dead.'

As you know by now I'm not remotely religious, but as I made my way back to the house, I prayed and prayed that the story was nothing more than an internet rumour conjured up by someone with nothing better to do. To my sheer horror and devastation, my worst fears were quickly confirmed by colleagues. I couldn't take it in.

A crack across the legs

My father's style of parenting is one I adopted when I became a mother. If one of the girls pushed me too far, a crack across the legs warned them from doing it a second time. I make no apologies for it, because, to this day, my children praise me for how I reared them. They know they were only ever slapped when they really deserved it, and whereas I am not a believer in physical punishment, I do think political correctness with children has gone completely off the rails.

The young boy who had sat in my living room all those years ago, eager and excited by the thought of being on television, was gone forever.

I never asked my girls to be saints because let's face it, saints were very boring people to begin with. However I always let them know that if they crossed the line, there would be repercussions. The better they behaved, the more freedom they were given, and the clip around the ear so to speak, was only needed for a very short time. As a result, both girls have now turned into very well-mannered young adults.

Fingers crossed it lasts!

Chloë and Naomi.

Some of Naomi's artwork.

Nay

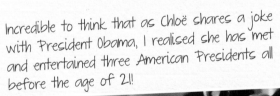

Chlo (as herself).

Incredible to think that as Chloë shares a joke with President Obama, I realised she has met and entertained three American Presidents all before the age of 21!

LOL time!

Two very elderly women were playing cards one day when one suddenly turned to the other and said, 'Please don't get mad … I know we've been friends since childhood, but for the life of me, I can't remember your name. What it is?'

Her friend glared intensely at her and continued to do so for at around five minutes, until finally, she replied, 'How soon do you need to know?'

'Stercus accidit' (Latin: Shit happens)

So, why did I choose to call Linda Martin a c**t that night in the hotel?

Well that's rather simple. There are remarkably few insults in the English language that are capable of compounding as much anger into one syllable as that particular word, so it was either that *one* word or the twenty others I had in mind.

Do I regret calling her that? Absolutely not!

I told you before, I stand over everything I say.

❖

When I was outlining the topics I wanted to include in this book, I was adamant that Linda Martin was not going to be a part of it. The history between us goes back much farther than people realise. For legal reasons, I cannot delve into detail other than to say that I have had to live with the scars.

Literally.

The following letter, which I received last year, wasn't long changing my mind however:

'This week I read about what happened to the unfortunate Linda Martin and how she overheard your going on at length about her. What crime did she commit to your cowardly Menopause colleagues who didn't stand up and tell you to stop.[sic] I had sympathy for your situation before this but it needs to be said that you were out of order, and it was in the media how hurt and shocked she was. I believe it. Twink, my dear, you can be too proudly tough for your own good. It wasn't nice or fair what you did.'

That one letter made me realise that so many people had formed their opinions without knowing the full truth. Well, I would like the woman who wrote that letter to know that there are two sides to every story. Everyone heard Linda's side after she went running to the nearest journalist, well now you're going to hear mine.

❖

The icon Bette Davis once said, 'The best time I ever had with Joan Crawford was when I pushed her down the stairs in the film *Whatever Happened to Baby Jane*.'

Even though Linda and I were quite good friends in our twenties, I think even she will agree that two particular incidents back then led to us sharing a similar relationship to that of Bette and Joan.

That said, I still recommended her for a role that stood to earn her quite a lot of money. When Robert C. Kelly set his sights on bringing *Menopause the Musical* to Ireland, he phoned me from his base in Scotland to ask if I could recommend anyone for the part of 'Faded' Soap Star. Every other part had been cast except for this one role. I told him I would give it some thought and get back to him with my suggestions but to be honest, I found myself struggling to think of an actress that would fit the necessary look of the role. One evening however, as I was going though an old edition of the *RTÉ Guide*, I spotted a photograph of Linda on the *Lyrics Board*. That's when it occurred to me that she would be ideal for the role. The many unresolved issues that lingered between us at that point didn't influence my decision in the slightest; if I felt someone was right for a particular part then I would recommend them, regardless of our personal differences.

Shortly after forwarding Linda's phone number to Robert, he contacted me to confirm she had been given the job. He also mentioned in passing that Linda was aware she was being given the part on my recommendation. Four weeks later, we all met up in the rehearsal room. During our first day working together, a few members of the cast approached me during a coffee break to thank me for having recommended them for the roles. Linda, on the other hand, never uttered a word.

Quite the opposite in fact.

When she first began rehearsing, she openly admitted that she was not a dancer or an actress, but after a few days, she began to get a tad overconfident. To put it mildly, working with Linda became rather challenging. Even though I was the dance-captain, whenever I issued a dance call to go over the steps with the girls, she would stand there and refuse to move.

I had also been appointed as the show-captain, which meant it was my responsibility to keep the show in shape when the producer and director went back to England. One of my responsibilities was to run through the dialogue with the cast and tweak it where necessary to make sure it was being delivered in the most appropriate tone. When it came to the dialogue-call, Linda would immediately walk over to the nearest chair, sit down and start playing with her mobile phone. Even though I had been appointed by the producer to do all these things, Linda didn't like to take any form of direction from me. It was infuriating because some nights on stage, she would mess up her steps and dialogue, leaving the rest of us to pick up the pieces. In fact, she would be so busy talking about the latest goings-on in *Coronation Street* that when it was her turn to go on stage, umpteen times she forgot her opening line.

The rules of theatre I learned as a child are now so ingrained in my brain that I still religiously abide by them today. For instance, you will never see me sitting down before a show. Once my costume is on, I am perpendicular until the curtain falls. When I was a kid in the Gaiety, if you were caught sitting down in your costume you were fined half a crown. You were only allowed so many black marks before you were let go from the show. It's small elements like these that make it easy to distinguish between the actresses who were theatre-trained and those who had probably never set foot backstage before. Linda was the latter and this was glaringly obvious.

While she was waiting to go on stage each night, she would put on her dressing gown and slippers (she's always cold for some reason) and then sit on a chair which she had placed at the top of the stairs. On one occasion, she even went out on stage in her slippers, a sackable offence in theatre.

As we were waiting to go on one night, Linda was sitting back like a lady of leisure talking and talking about nothing of relevance. At this point, I approached her and quietly explained that I had been instructed to remove the chair as there was to be no sitting down before the show. She was angry and shouted, 'You touch that chair and I will wrap it around your fucking neck'. She then stormed off into the dressing room, leaving us there with no clue as to whether or not she was going to perform that night. She eventually arrived back out on stage and believe me, I have seen women in labour with less pained expressions on their faces.

There were scenes in the play where we had to address each other, but she wouldn't make eye contact with me, preferring instead to look directly past me. As I mentioned earlier in the book, off-stage occurrences should remain off-stage and never at any point interfere with the performance. In the middle of the song, 'No Business Like Showbusiness', the lyrics very fittingly read, 'There's no people like show people, they smile when they are low'.

It makes absolutely no difference if you are in the depths of a depression and can't stop crying, you still have to get up on that stage and flash those gnashers like you're an ambassador for dentures.

One particular night that springs to mind occurred back in the early 1980s when I was in a show with Mike Murphy called *Olympia Carousel*. A great friend of mine was flying over from England to sell a horse and had arranged to catch the show while she was here.

Her plan was to be in the theatre for six o'clock, but she assured me she would phone when she arrived. Six o'clock came and went with no sign of a phone call. I took no notice and assumed she had been delayed. By seven o'clock however, there was no reply from her phone and I was becoming slightly concerned. Five minutes before I was due on stage, I had a deep-seated feeling of uneasiness and angst. At the time, there was a truly awful woman working on the show. She was tyrannical at best. She lived near my parents' house, and even when I was a child, I remember hearing her scream at her kids in the backyard. She was volatile, tactless and, as I was to find out, not remotely sensitive either. That evening at five to eight she knocked on my dressing-room door.

'Adèle, this is your five-minute call. Oh by the way, your friend Judy won't be here. She's been killed in a car crash on the motorway in England. Now, this is your final call, OK?'

I couldn't believe how nonchalantly she'd said it; like it were some general off-the-cuff remark. I later discovered that my friend's horse box had jack-knifed sending her car sliding across the motorway and into the path of an artic lorry. Needless to say, that was one of the most difficult times I have ever had to go on stage. Once I was in character though, I performed in the same manner as I had done each night before, and not one person in the audience would have guessed there was something wrong. In fact, even my colleagues on stage didn't know until afterwards.

It's not the kind of job where you can take the night off because of a personal matter; the reality is that hundreds of people have paid to see a show in the hope that it will make them laugh and forget about their own troubles. After all, it wasn't their problem that a close friend of mine had just been killed – I could cry my eyes out when the show was over.

This is one of the benefits of theatre-training, you must leave all personal issues aside an go on stage to entertain the audience. If a British or American theatre bore witness to such attitude, the actor would be replaced immediately.

When *Menopause the Musical* was brought back for a second run, Flo McSweeney and Ellen O'Grady were brought in alongside Linda and me.

Flo and Ellen are possibly the nicest people you could meet and we clicked immediately. Linda however developed a tendency to single herself out. Whenever we were on tour, she would travel with the crew and reside in the same hired house as them, rather than be with her colleagues. There was a great sense of camaraderie between the actresses. Some nights we would pile into one of our rooms and just have a couple of scoops, a laugh and a chat.

Women are the greatest problem solvers in the world; throw a bottle of wine or two into the equation and we could probably solve the nation's problems. Had Linda joined us on our nights out, she would have realised that we were there for each other. Unfortunately though, she never gave this potential friendship a chance. No matter how many times we invited her, our offer was met with a refusal. I admit that I didn't give

a toss whether or not she joined us. If she wanted to be on her own, then that was her prerogative. To quote a famous director to an equally famous actress, 'You like to work alone? Then go work in a fuckin' lighthouse dear, this is show business.'

Flo has a heart of gold and would often phone Linda to ask if she wanted to join us for dinner. Her offer was always spurned in favour of dinner with someone else. A culmination of events eventually led to a flare up between Linda and I in the rehearsal hall one day in 2010. She had voluntarily taken it upon herself to use the parking space that had been provided for me by management. It was all very childish in that she would deliberately arrive early just so she could take the space. One night, however, someone had *cúpla focal* with her about the parking space. Clearly this didn't sit well with her, because she roared at me at the top of her voice the moment I walked into the rehearsal room the following morning. She then went on to deliver what can only be described as a tirade of verbal abuse. I asked her if we could take it outside; she refused.

As she stood up to look at the clock, she roared back at me, 'And furthermore, you're late!'

My call was for 11.30 a.m., it was now 10.45 a.m. As I had a wedding present to collect around the corner that morning, I was deliberately early. More to the point, it was not the job of a cast member to give the lead actress a time check. If I had turned around to Maureen Potter when we were working in the Gaiety and roared, 'Furthermore Maureen, you're late!', I guarantee you my next port of call would have been Mount Jerome Cemetery.

Without saying a word, I immediately upped and left. Never before in my life have I left a show, which I think in itself is a testament to how infuriated I was by the long-term grief she had been causing. I was adamant that there was no going back. The history between us was not so much water under the bridge, but rather, muck bubbling in a swamp and, frankly, I'd had enough.

Upon looking into the various incidents that had occurred during rehearsals, Robert concluded that an apology from Linda was justified, and with that, a meeting was quickly arranged between all parties. When Robert pointed out to Linda that my name was the one selling the tickets, she responded by adopting quite a shirty stance against him. She wasn't long quietening down when Robert reminded her that if he had to choose which one of us he wanted in the show, she would be the one receiving her P45.

Against the absolute guidance of my heart and head, but out of courtesy and respect to Robert, I returned to the show. I don't think I have enjoyed working with anyone as much as I have enjoyed working with Robert C. Kelly. Naturally our relationship is not without its thorns but we always get over it and work on. Even my own daughters and Robert's beautiful wife Jennifer all joke that Robert and I are like an oul' married couple because when we're not killing each other, we're the best of friends.

At this point, relations were becoming more than strained behind the theatre curtains. Some members of the cast suffered the sharp end of Linda's comments.

The penultimate night of the tour took place in the Theatre Royal in Castlebar, a spectacular venue I have always loved working in. Following the show, the girls invited me up for a few end-of-show drinks, however I had to go to the shop to pick up some food for my dogs, Teddy and Rosie. In the end, the girls decided they would meet up with me after I returned. As I was making my way over to the twenty-four-hour Tesco, I was descended upon by a group of high-spirited teenagers coming from a party. Some of them whipped out their phones for a photograph, others whipped out their buttocks for an autograph. All in all I spent about an hour chatting with them. After twenty minutes in Tesco, I was walking back to the hotel when a car carrying a number of women swung around. They had just come from my show and had ordered the driver to turn around when they spotted me. I was on my way again following half an hour of chatting, taking photographs and signing personal messages, including one on a handbag that read: 'From one old bag to another!'

When I reached the back door of the hotel, I was greeted by about ninety post-show, post-wine women boarding their huge coach, and after about an hour and a half of chatting, I was still nowhere near my room. All in all, a six-minute trip to Tesco had taken almost three hours. Once

I made it into my suite, the girls called over with a few bottles of wine. As it was a hot May night, I opened the windows slightly, and, with that, we sat down to enjoy a chat and a laugh. Flo told me how they had invited Linda but she refused, saying she was going to bed early. A short while later, when Flo went downstairs to get a corkscrew, there was Linda sitting with the crew enjoying drinks.

'Can you fuckin' believe Linda?' one of the girls piped up.

At this point, I remember replying, 'You shouldn't have wasted your time even asking her. Why do you bother with her? She always rejects you! Forget about her! She's a c**t. I've had a traumatic lifetime with her, and I'm over it now.'

It was then that I poured my heart out about the long history between Linda and me, a history that stems back to when we were both in our twenties. When I told them about a certain incident that had occurred a number of years earlier, one that resulted in a vicious scar on my forehead, Flo and Ellen asked me why I had never confronted Linda about it.

I swear to God, my exact reply was, 'Because with some things in life, you just need to wait until that right window of opportunity is open.'

Little did I know at the time that Linda was hanging out of a window listening to us. Following my story, every single woman in the room contributed her own negative experience with Linda and assured me I wasn't the only one who was fed up with her behaviour.

The following night, prior to our final performance in the INEC in Killarney, I was in my dressing room when I heard a frantic knock on my door. It was Flo, Ellen and Grace, their faces white with fright.

'Jesus you three look like you've seen the devil,' I laughed.

'No but we had an appearance by him! Oh, Jesus, Twink, she heard it all; she heard everything we said last night.'

'Who?'

'Linda! She had the window open. She heard everything we said about her. She's written it down and she says she has phoned Louis Walsh and Robert Kelly.'

I burst out laughing at the idea of Linda hanging out her hotel window at two in the morning, and, believe me, she had to have been hanging out very far in order to have heard us.

In mock cockney, I replied, 'You're 'avin a lawf!'

'No! She really heard everything!'

'So what? I'm delighted she heard! Now, she finally knows how much of a misery it's been working with her. Girls, if anything I feel relieved. The only thing I'm angry about is that there was never an occasion for me to say it directly to her face. Apologise? Over my dead body!'

To be perfectly frank, my attitude could have been summed up with the Latin phrase '*stercus accidit*'. In other words, 'shit happens'.

Our friendship was superficial. If I had a row with Flo, we would overcome it because we love each other, but I don't love Linda – and Linda definitely doesn't love me.

That night, Linda blanked the whole cast. When poor little Grace made a genuine attempt to apologise, Linda roared at our company manager Ray Tizzard, 'Get this fucking understudy out of my room before I fling her down the stairs'.

How can you work with someone like that?

While I was getting ready for the show, Linda walked into my dressing room without knocking. At the time I was changing so I was pretty much standing there wearing nothing but a microphone belt. She muttered something and turned to leave but I threw on a dressing gown and beckoned her back in.

'Well, I heard your little party with your friends in the cast last night,' she began. 'I had the window open. I heard everything. I wrote it all down.'

'Good for you, Linda.'

'So that's it?'

'Are you looking for me to say something? Because I'm jolly glad it happened. For me, it has put an end to a lifetime of misery with you. I meant everything I said. I want to tell you right now Linda that the only thing I'm really angry about, is that I didn't get the opportunity to say it to your face and that you had to hear it through a window … mind you, I have no idea what you were doing hanging out of a fucking window at two in the morning. I'm tired of hearing you saying "my friend Twaeg". You and I will never be friends, Linda, we're a match made in hell.'

At this point, she turned and walked away. She was the one who walked into my dressing room to have her say, but yet wasn't ballsy enough to let *me* have mine, so I followed her up the stairs.

She turned her back to me and said, 'I'm finished!'

'Well I'm not, Linda' I replied. 'Now, you will have time to reflect on all the things you heard me say about you last night. The crap is over.'

I brought up the 'incident' that occurred all those years earlier.

'I don't know what you're talking about,' came the reply. I lifted back my fringe to show her my scarred forehead. 'I think you do, Linda. My mental and physical scars with you go back a long way. '

Afterwards, some cast members told me that Linda spoke to them about 'the incident'. She remembers part of it, though not all of it. Wish I could say the same.

When I read in the newspapers that Linda complained I was 'loud to her', I could immediately hear my father's wonderful line, 'Those with the softest voices say the cruellest things'.

As I mentioned earlier, I cannot divulge the full history between us – oh indeed there is a history – and it has not all been doom and gloom. We had such wonderful times together when we were younger. Anyone who loves animals as much as Linda does can't be all that bad, but with regard to running into the arms of the media, I would like to remind her of the golden rule – what happens on tour stays on tour!

X Factor and the Emmett Spiceland

Whenever *X Factor* is on, the iPhone comes out and the texts to and from Louis Walsh begin! It's like a tradition at this stage. One night recently, however, I told him how much I loved the judge Tulisa and that I was so looking forward to meeting her at some stage.

'And likewise!' came the reply.

'What do you mean?' I asked.

'She said to say hello! She remembers her mother dressing her up in her best frock and taking her to see you in the panto when she was a kid! The best laugh of all is that you used to date her uncle!'

'I used to what?!'

'Mick Byrne from the Emmet Spiceland!'

I'm telling you folks, the world is a village!

Gerry

I began the book with a story about Gerry Ryan and so I think it is only appropriate that I end it on the same note. Boy, would he have loved that!

I can see him now, sitting up there with St Peter sharing a bottle of Hennessy and saying something like, 'Ah here, Pete, have a look at what Miss King is writing about me!'

A conversation with Gerry would never find itself reduced to banality; he was a *bon viveur* in every sense of the word. He was also lethal to go for lunch with. The pair of us would sit there for hours talking incessantly. I remember when we met to discuss plans for a show in the O2. Following our lunch, we went into the Shelbourne for a few drinks and ended up talking for so long that we decided to head back into the dining room to have dinner. Naturally, we gravitated back to the bar once our meal was over and pretty much stayed there until two in the morning.

And that was just *lunch* with Gerry!

He was so articulate that it's really no surprise he enjoyed the career of a solicitor before the airwaves seduced his interest. During a conversation about the legal profession one night, he admitted that he had always felt he would have made a fantastic barrister. The paperwork, however, was the one element that deterred him from pursuing his dream. He loved the drama of a courtroom and God knows if anyone had the capability of winning over a jury, it would have been Gerry. He and I were very similar in that we had to keep moving; we needed jobs that stimulated us, not stifled us.

I know deep down he was heartbroken at being overlooked for *The Late Late Show* job. Ryan Tubridy, an absolute darling, had begun his career in RTÉ as Gerry's tea boy and after his new position as host was announced, Gerry joked to me on the phone, 'If I had known the little fucker was going to do so well, I'd have thrown him out years ago!'

Truth be told, he was living for that September when he would finally take over as host of the *Saturday Night Show*. He was adamant that everything was going to be a success.

'D'you know what, King?' he said to me on the phone one night. 'I'm goin' to be in the gym every day. They won't fuckin' recognise me when I walk out in September. I won't even have any pictures done beforehand, I'm just going to arrive on the set! I'm going to lose three, no, four stone.'

'You will in your arse, Gerry!'

'Yeah, there as well! I'm going to be in the gym every day!'

'And where do Dr Hennessy and Dr Cigars fit into all this?'

'Don't be such a Debbie Downer! You're killin' me fuckin' impulse here, King!'

❖

During the last week of Gerry's life, a topic that frequently made an appearance in our conversations were 'the suits'.

They were the bane of his life; God how he hated them but, then again, who didn't? I think anyone who has worked in RTÉ will agree with me when I say, the bigger the talent, the more the suits hate you. They can take moderate talent, controllable talent, the ones who ask, 'How high do you want me to jump today?'

But talents like Gay, Gerry, Dermot and myself, all of whom have no problem saying, 'Go fuck yourself', yes they have a real problem with us. We have a voice and they don't like it. Some of the suits have degrees in subjects like civil engineering but what on earth does that have to do with running a television station? Where is their expertise in broadcasting entertainment? All their presence ever does is simply reinforce the famous line, 'You will always find a few Eskimos ready to tell the Congolese how to cope with the heat'.

Gerry Ryan fought with the suits on a regular basis to be able to offer his true opinion on the radio. The week before he died, he very memorably proclaimed, 'We were already thinking we were knackered, but then yer man came on the airwaves to give us the great news that we were totally, completely and utterly *bollixed*!'

Only Gerry Ryan could tell the listeners of morning radio that we were all 'totally, completely and utterly bollixed'.

I have no doubt that following the show that morning, he was hauled up into the office and given a slap on the wrist over his remarks. Did he give a fiddler's? Not a chance. Did he give them the two fingers? Knowing Gerry, more than likely!

I was lucky in that I have never signed a contract with RTÉ. I have never had to suffer the indignity of presenting a rubbish show because they had to find some way of using me until my contract expired. I have always maintained the control in that regard.

When I hosted a Saturday morning radio show for RTÉ, it was phenomenally popular with listeners. One morning, however, I noticed the topic of hare coursing in the newspapers and decided to talk about it on my show. I voiced my honest opinion about it being an utterly vulgar activity before then drawing a comparison with the disgusting bullfights that take place in Spain. From what I can remember, I pretty much told my listeners that the day the matador – a pompous little bollix in a glittery suit – gets the bull's horn right up the arse, is the day I will cheer, 'Yeah! Let's hear it for the bull!'

I then pointed out that the barbarian attitude of the bull run was being brought into Ireland through coursing. A few days later, I was hauled up to the office of the suits and told to apologise to the nation for my remarks. They informed me of the many letters they had received from the coursing association before warning that my show would be pulled off air unless I apologised. My response?

'Fuck you. I'm not apologising to anyone!'

I pointed out that I had nothing to say sorry for, and that I would happily take the axe before apologising to any committee of shits who voluntarily slaughter innocent animals.

While I was allowed finish the remaining five weeks, I never got the show back again. I think the suits always felt the need to take down the big talents because they didn't want anyone thinking they were bigger than the suits themselves.

❖

When I collapsed as a result of an asthma attack last year, I really believed my death was imminent. Only for Naomi, it probably was. I couldn't even talk, but she immediately knew what was happening and managed to find the number to phone my consultant for help.

As the ambulance crew tried to make me comfortable a short time later, I remember looking at the house through the back windows of the ambulance as we drove away, genuinely convinced I was leaving for the last time. The strength of the attack had been so severe, like nothing I had ever experienced before.

Despite having their own busy lives, Gerry Ryan and Maxi never failed to phone me first thing every morning and last thing at night for the length of time I was in hospital. Flo and Moya became my regular mammies while my agent/ hero Noel Kelly called in on a daily basis to assure me that my children, mutts and house were all taken care of.

David also phoned to see how I was feeling, although his main reason for calling was to ask when I would be ready to go back into court to resolve the issue with the house.

All week, Gerry ate the face off me for not slowing down.

'Now Ms King, look at where ya are now, ya dopey bitch! In a fuckin' hospital! Why? Stress, worry, media, all those stupid things that we let get to us, but look at where it got ya!'

This was my pal Gerry a few days before he died lecturing *me* on *my* health and *my* stress levels, ordering *me* to take it easy!

The Wednesday before his death, he told me about a huge row he'd had with a bank official. During the meeting, the bank man had informed Gerry, the nation's leading broadcaster, that he was a 'has-been'.

Gerry recalled for me how the man then went on to say, 'You're finished, you're washed up. It's over for you.' That from a banker? Stop me from accidentally spelling that 'incorrectly', would you!

I knew he was very upset by it though. The thing about Gerry is that he was never one for moaning in public. If anything, he would have had the tendency to bottle things up. He was always naturally upbeat by nature and would have talked to the nation in the same way he would have talked to a friend. To quote Morah's beautiful sentiment to all his listeners 'You were his – and he was yours'. There wasn't a huge difference between 'real Gerry' and 'radio Gerry'.

Compounding the sting of the bank official's comments, was the row he'd also had with the suits in Montrose. It had been a tough week for him. Ironically, a senior female 'suit' told newspapers not long after his death that Gerry was not stressed. That's RTÉ for you. Diss your own at all costs, never defend them. It always amazes me how quickly they forget the millions that the likes of Gerry made for them in advertising revenue.

❖

I could be wrong, and I apologise in advance if I am, but I don't think Morah Ryan likes me very much. Part of me thinks she always suspected there was something more going on between Gerry and me, when in fact there was never anything of the sort. He and I had been good friends since childhood but that was the extent of it. Gerry was a flirtatious maggot by nature, but Morah was the woman he truly loved. He was crazy about her and when they separated, I know he was terribly lonely. Gerry told me himself how much he missed the buzz of the home environment. He missed saying things like, 'Rex, turn that fuckin' music down' or 'Babette, get off that bloody couch and stop answering your mother back!'

I think any parent can understand that. When my two girls argue over something ludicrous like shoes, I end up walking out of the room with a wrecked head. When they're both away, however, the house is like a mausoleum and after about two days, the peace and quiet is no longer a novelty but a nuisance. It's the empty nest syndrome. You miss caring for them, catering for them, chauffeuring for them … all the personal services teenagers assume they're entitled to.

Gerry was *such* a devoted dad; he idolised his kids. Who could forget him stopping mid-sentence as a member of his staff informed him that one of the kids had phoned to say they needed money for something? Most presenters would have pushed the note aside and dealt with it that evening. Not Gerry. Gerry was a father first and a presenter second.

❖

When you look back in life, you sometimes find yourself having to review that yard of old rope. In this particular situation, it was my first encounter with Melanie Verwoerd; one that didn't exactly endear us to each other.

My wonderful friend, Alma Carroll, who has devoted her life to UNICEF, often invited me to the organisation's famous Mothers' Day Lunch as her guest. Around the time of that event in 2009, Alma's mother Sheila, whom I absolutely adore, was a little unwell so as a token of goodwill, I made her a small cake. The cake, which looked like a miniature wedding cake, consisted of handmade pink sugar roses surrounding her name which I had piped on in icing.

When I arrived early at the venue, Alma was already there fastidiously arranging the place names on each table. As I presented her with Sheila's cake, Alma immediately took it from the box and placed it on the table to show her friends. While they were admiring the details of the cake, Melanie joined us at the table. With one look, she remarked, 'What is this thing? Is this a wedding cake for children? What will they think of next?'

She was blatantly making a laugh of my work which I thought was rather rude, considering it was the first time we had ever met.

However, shortly after the event, I received a thank you letter which I actually laminated. It's quite rare to receive such a letter of gratitude for giving up your time free of charge for an organisation or cause.

It read:

March, 26th 2009
Dear Twink,
I would like to take this opportunity on behalf of UNICEF, to offer my warmest thanks for your incredible performance at our Mothers' Day brunch at L'Ecrivain last week. You had the whole restaurant in tears of laughter. The energy and authenticity you bring to your performance is amazing and we are grateful to have had you as part of our lunch. As you know the event has been an important one for UNICEF over the past twelve years in terms of generating vital funding. This year was no exception. Funds raised from that day will go towards UNICEF's safe motherhood programme which works worldwide to combat infant mortality. Thank you so much for kindly lending us your time and doing such a fantastic job.
Warm regards,
Melanie Verwoerd

Maybe she was having a bad day when she made that remark about my work; fuck it, maybe we were both having a bad day and needed to vent. Either way, I'm holding my hands up now and admitting I made a snap decision about her. After all, first impressions can be everything, especially misguiding.

In the months following Gerry's death, an envelope arrived in the post containing a photograph of myself and Gerry performing in the panto *Sleeping Beauty, Sort Of* at the Point, a picture I had never seen before in my entire life. The accompanying note read:

Dear Adèle,

I know that you and Gerry were close for many years and you must have many happy memories. He was very concerned about you the week before he died and I know he spoke to you a few times. I hope you are keeping well and in full health. I include a photo I found amongst his papers. I thought you would enjoy it.

Kindest regards

Melanie Verwoerd

While at the time I thought it was nice of Melanie to have sent the photograph to me, it does beg the question, why was she going through Gerry's papers and lifelong possessions? Surely that was Morah's place, not hers?

❖

Around lunchtime on Friday, 30 April 2010, still lying in my bed in Mount Camel, a number of missed calls from my agent Noel Kelly registered on my phone. No sooner had I spotted them when a frantic call from my daughter Naomi came through. Absolutely distraught, she broke the news to me that Gerry had been found dead in his apartment that morning. I couldn't get my head around it at first. I had only just spoken to him the night before.

Gerry dead? No way!

Someone had to have their bloody wires crossed because the Gerry I knew was surely on the radio making wise-cracks while single-handedly rising the blood pressure of the suits.

When I realised it was true, I sank into a cold, raw, almost mind-numbing devastation, the kind you can't see any way of recovering from.

I think anyone who saw Gerry laid out in his coffin found themselves at a loss for words. He was never still, never quiet, always the vibrant one, and yet there he was so motionless with his trademark GR effervescence now reduced to silence. It wasn't right; in fact it was cruel.

Marian Finucane and I shared a long chat at the wake, both of us trying to comprehend the reality of what we were experiencing. It was just so completely incongruous to see Gerry lying there in a coffin. He would have been the one going around having a few drinks and making people laugh. I couldn't take it in – to be perfectly honest, I still can't.

As a funeral takes place, you're almost in too much shock to realise the full extent of what has happened. It's only as the weeks and months pass that it really hits you. You begin to notice your mobile is unusually quiet without his calls or texts. If something amazing happens in your life, you immediately reach for the phone to tell him about it only to hear your inner voice remind you that you can't do that anymore.

I miss him terribly.

❖

At first, the doctors were understandably very hesitant to discharge me from hospital so that I could attend Gerry's funeral. I didn't care; I was going to be in that church with or without their consent.

Gerry and I shared the same agent, Noel Kelly, or to give him his full mafia title, as I rechristened him 'Don Kellyone'. On the morning of the funeral, Noel arranged for a car to pick me up from Mount Carmel Hospital and bring me to the breakfast banquet he had arranged for

Gerry's colleagues in the Four Seasons Hotel. He also provided coaches to transport both his own coterie of artists and others to the funeral service. The organisation he invested into making sure the whole affair ran smoothly was so unbelievably professional and efficient, that I swear to God it would have put the Obama election campaign to shame.

To get into the church, your name had to be on the list as everyone had an assigned seat. A joke went around on the day that if someone bombed the church, the entire entertainment and broadcasting industry in Ireland would have been wiped out.

Gerry would have *loved* that one!

Outside, there were thousands of people behind the barriers, good-natured members of the public who had come out to pay their respects. As Naomi and I were making our way inside, I suddenly spotted Louis Walsh, Carol Hanna and Linda Martin standing behind these barriers, so I approached Noel and asked him if they could be brought into the enclave, a request he happily obliged.

The mass itself was beautiful. Lottie Ryan surmised her father perfectly when she said during her eulogy, 'the star that shines twice as bright, burns twice as fast'.

That was Gerry all right.

At the end of the mass, when Morah so eloquently addressed the congregation, there wasn't a tearless eye in the church. I was sitting beside Ryan Tubridy and the poor lad was distraught. My heart absolutely broke for the boy.

❖

Outside the church MCD Promotions arranged for a special platform to be constructed for the congregated media. The Ryan family also allowed the press to set up their cameras outside the house on the condition that there were no shots to be taken inside the house or at the cemetery. Of course, there's always one fucking person who has to ignore the boundaries. It transpired that Brian Whitehead and his security team had found a photographer hiding in the graveyard. At the time, I had a cannula in one arm and bandaging on the other from where a second cannula had been.

As I reached out to Gerry's former agent Carol Hanna, (a woman I have the height of admiration for), a journalist spotted the bandaging and swiftly pulled aside my agent Noel to ask if I had tried to commit suicide. Can you see now how stupid rumours start?

So there I was hugging Carol when I spotted Linda behind her. Of all the opportunities for a reconciliation, this was it. There was such an air of vulnerability around, that a peace offering seemed appropriate. As I leaned over to hug her, she forcefully smacked my hand away. Unfortunately in doing so, she caught the cannula, leaving my hand roaring red. A number of people nearby witnessed what had happened and immediately approached me to see if I was OK. Linda's rebuttal inspired one wit amongst the crowd to christen her 'the Red Hand of Ulster'.

While Gerry's passing made me so aware of the depths of a good friendship and how much one person can mean to another, Linda's presence made me realise that life is just far too short to waste on negative people you don't want in it.

Dory Previn once said, 'Kick a person when he's down and you can break his spirit you know, but kick a person when he's up and all you break is your toe'.

She was right. Having just lost one of my closest friends, I was already at my lowest ebb when

Linda decided to run to the newspapers with her 'Twink is a bitch' story. During the midst of this unspeakable grief, she didn't throw me a lifeline, she threw me a brick. Regardless of the animosity that was festering between us, you would imagine that somewhere inside her was an element of human compassion. Clearly not.

Even though she denied having spoken to the press, I can name journalists who phoned me to say me she had given them interviews about it.

❖

If your memories of someone make you smile, then that person deserves to be a part of your life. Gerry is the finest example I can think of in this regard.

One story that springs to mind is of the day Chloë received her Leaving Cert results. Due to studying on the road with tutors while on tour in the USA with Celtic Woman, she was terrified of what grades lay in wait inside that little brown envelope. The final years of schooling were a hard slog for her. For instance, when the other Celtic Woman members were enjoying a long break from work, Chloë was back in her Alexandra school uniform being a schoolgirl again. When results day arrived, she wouldn't let me drop her off at the door of the school, requesting instead that I park at the end of the car park. My heart broke for her as she cut a lone figure walking across the yard to the front doors. A few minutes later Naomi and I saw her emerging from the school, both of us trying to read her face in order to obtain some clue as to the contents of the envelope she was carrying. As she approached the car, she began crying. Like any mother, I got ready to console her.

As she opened the door however, she suddenly smiled and through the tears, said, 'I did fantastically!'

She got nine honours not to mention enough points to become a bloody doctor. She was ecstatic. I was never the kind of mother that heaped pressure on the girls to do exceptionally well. If anything I hate those parents that try to force their children into becoming high achievers – it almost always backfires with the child either resenting the parent or rebelling against their ideals. I remember seeing one mother in the car park that morning berating her daughter over the results she got. The poor child was hysterical. Surely a piece of paper with a few grades couldn't be worth that?

To celebrate, I treated the girls to lunch at the Shelbourne. No sooner were we in the door than we spotted Gerry Ryan walking across the lobby towards us. Upon hearing of Chloë's results, he got down on his knees in the middle of the Shelbourne lobby and started bowing to her while singing, 'Allah, Allah!'. The expressions on the faces of the American tourists were priceless. After all, Gerry had such sallow skin that they probably assumed he really was an Arab. Those who recognised him, however, were in convulsions laughing and knew he was just being G. Ryan.

As the girls and I took our seats in the restaurant, the maître d arrived over with a bottle of Bollinger champagne. As I thanked him, he said, 'I'm sorry, Miss King, but I have a message from Mr Ryan. It's not for you … it's for your daughters!'

Well did my girls laugh.

That was the mischievously fun side of Gerry I loved.

❖

Gerry always joked that he was going to continue with his 'morning check and evening check' until

I was out of hospital. After speaking with me each morning, he would then start his show with something along the lines of, 'Well, I was talking to Miss King last night and she's doing fantaaaaastic ...'

The night before Gerry died, he and I talked for about an hour and a half on the phone. He was in two minds about whether or not to attend some event he had been invited to.

'Are you going to go?' I asked.

'I might pass on it.'

'Ah for God's sake, it's sponsored by Hennessy's!' I laughed. 'At least the brandy will be good! Do you have a date to bring with you?'

'Probably Dave Kavanagh.'

Dave is Chloë's boss and a good mate of both Gerry and myself, which is why I then added, 'Ah, now, you're rightly scuppered if Dave is your date! Sure go! It'll only be a few hours.'

'Do you know what, King? I can't wait for tomorrow's show to tell them how much you have improved and how we talked the hind legs off a donkey tonight.'

He went on to ask me when I thought I would be discharged from hospital. I told him it would probably be the following week but that I hoped it would be sooner. The moment he heard this, he launched into a lecture.

'Don't be rushing out now! Knowing you, you'll be back doing things at a hundred fuckin' miles an hour. You'll be back doing cakes, racing here and there and dropping a child somewhere. While you're on your back, stay there and chill the fuck out.'

In the end, we agreed that if I was released when I hoped, he would come up to the house for dinner that weekend. Naomi is a phenomenal chef and was planning a seriously gorgeous meal for her uncle Gerry.

That night on the phone he and I also discussed a script for a show. I think if Gerry had made it into a theatre, he would have been a hit. He was theatrical by nature, all he needed was a stage and a spotlight.

When my producer Robert C. Kelly gave me a script called *Sexy Laundry* to read, I knew by the time I had reached page seven that there was one particular person for whom the male role would be ideal. I couldn't think who at first, but as I read on, it hit me. The part required a personality like Gerry's. From that point onwards, I couldn't envisage anyone else in the role. When I phoned Robert to tell him of my idea, he agreed it was a plan to consider, as did our agent Noel Kelly. In fact, when we broached the idea with Gerry, he was so excited about the project and was more than willing to meet Robert to discuss taking it further. I just know he and I would have been dynamic on stage, presuming of course we would have stopped laughing in time to make it through rehearsals.

When the topic of Melanie entered the conversation that night on the phone, Gerry paused and said, 'You don't like her do you?'

Bear in mind, I didn't know the real Melanie at that point and had based my judgement on our initial run-in at the UNICEF event. As a result, I replied, 'Ah, my jury's out on that, Ger!', thus prompting him to burst out laughing. For the sake of courtesy, I asked him if he wanted to bring someone with him to the dinner we had planned for my house.

'Like who?'

'Like a date!'

'I thought you were me date?'

'I mean do you want to bring Melanie.'

There was a silence.

'Ah … no, you're all right.'

'Look, Gerry, I'm not being nosy …'

'No … but you're *about* to fuckin' be!'

'I see an awful lot of pictures of you in the papers on your own … yes, you're right, I'm about to be nosy … is there trouble at mill?'

There was a hesitancy in his response.

'Ahhh, you know yourself, King. Time to think, bit of reflection on things in my life. Ah sure, I'll tell you about it on Saturday week. I'll tell you where my head is at.'

We talked a little more before calling it a night.

As I was to find out from two Garda detectives in my home recently (who had interviewed myself and a plethora of Gerry's friends in a bid to establish his frame of mind in the days prior to his death), I was the last person he ever phoned.

I can still remember our parting words:

'You're the best, Gerry! Love you!'

'Love you too, King … now put that *fuckin'* phone down and get some sleep! Talk to you tomorrow!'

'Bye, Gerry.'

❖

The Final Curtain Call

So here we are ladies! I can't believe it, we're at the end of the book (well, this one anyway!)

How are the blood pressure levels?

I hope my stories have prompted some reaction, be it one of laughter, tears, anger or shock … preferably anything other than a yawn or a heart attack.

Like everyone else, I have had my troubles, but thanks to you, the women of Ireland, I have seen through my difficulties and emerged the other side all the stronger for it. You have been my support and my saviours to a point where I dread to think what life would have been like without you. It goes without saying that short of having an Oprah Winfrey-style team on hand, I don't have the capacity to reply to you all. Having said that, I assure you that I have kept every letter, every card, every email you have sent me and whenever things get tough, I know that reading your beautiful words will put a smile back on my face faster than any amount of Prozac could.

You know, there were times when I was so angry David's philandering was upsetting his daughters that I genuinely considered running him and his mistress off the road? I was at such a low point that I felt life would be so much easier if they weren't around to constantly poison it. One of the things that kept me from such rash conduct were your letters of support assuring me I would see through the storm. What's more, ladies, you were absolutely right.

If you are going through a marriage break-up and are finding yourself in the depths of depression or in the grips of heartache, trust me when I say, bear with it. However painful it may be to think of him with someone else, the ache will eventually abate and before you know it, he will be the one whose heart breaks with regret every time he sees you in the arms of someone more deserving of your love.

For the days you are feeling particularly down, just remember the famous line, 'When a woman steals your man, there's no better revenge than to let her keep him!'

Loving and admiring you all so very much.

Twink XXXXXX PS Thanks for buying the book!

I am strong, because I've been weak.

I am fearless, because I've been afraid.

I am wise, because I've been foolish.

And I am loyal, because I've been betrayed.

ACKNOWLEDGEMENTS

I would not be here to write this book without two extraordinarily wonderful people, my beloved parents, Leopold (Leo) Frances King and Elizabeth Felicitas Condron.

I told you a million times during your life on this earth how undyingly grateful I was to you both for such a wonderful childhood, a great upbringing, and in the main, splendid parenting. The right amounts of discipline, love and honesty, to make a strong child, who grew to be a strong woman, who was always assured of her parents' trust and belief in her.

You both gave me this strength. You both showed me how, eventually, my own judgement on just about everything, was crucial to survival.

Of course, it was you who trained me to find 'the wind beneath my wings', so that when I eventually jumped out of the nest, I could fly, and boy did I fly!

I have tried to stay true to your wonderful philosophies to this day.

> Be strong ...
> Be honest...
> Say it like it is ...

Never have anyone hurt by something you said behind their backs that you wouldn't have the balls to say to their face. (Well in truth, I don't actually remember you using the word 'balls', but it was words to that effect ... LOL!)

My darling mom and dad, I would like to think I have done you proud.

I wish with all my heart you were here today to see who or what I have become, and would you approve? I kinda hope so.

I wish with all my heart you were here today to see how wonderful your granddaughters are.

It was you who taught me the parenting skills, which I am now hopefully passing on to them.

Daddy, you said it all in the last days of your life, when you said, 'I am honoured that we have given birth to you sweetheart, one child only, but by God, what a child! Who would have thought when I married Mom, that we would give birth to someone who would be in the entertainment history books of Ireland? I am so very proud of you bunny ...'

Thank you both for the gift of life, and then devoting your own lives to me.

I love and miss you both every day of my life.

ACKNOWLEDGEMENTS contd ...

My exquisitely blonde brainy beautiful nieces Kate, Líobhan, and my goddaughter Béibhínn Clancy and their smashing and gorgeous mom Brenda (Agnew) and grandparents Bernadette and Arthur Agnew. The wonderful Lana, Ross, Ben, and Scott Condron.

Dermot Kiernan, for being Dermie, and for all the love and care you show to Chlo and Nay and all the Idrone mutties (and stay well Mary and Phelim); Sophie Menton, Anna Mitchell, Ailis Mara, Nadia Cardillo and all the wonderful girls and boys who have been such great friends to my girls over the years.

I would like to thank my publisher John O'Connor, and my writer Tara King, for almost two years of work, and for coming up with the brilliant book title ... (that I bloody well wish 'I' had thought of) Liz, Claire and all at Blackwater Press for their help and support on the book, and particularly Paula Byrne who helped me jump the final hurdles, with laughter, craic, and down-home great 'womanliness' all the way to the print gate.

My beloved friend and colleague, and again, most supportive human being, Mike Murphy. Thank you so very much for your kind and witty preface Mike, you're the coolest!

Robert C Kelly (my theatre producer) for being not just a brilliant and intuitive producer who always manages to pick the right shows for me, but whose great, great, humour, friendship and generosity I have treasured for the past seven years. I love you, your beautiful wife and children so much. Thank you for all your wonderful words of support and encouragement to me during shows where I was at rock bottom in my heart during the painful years of my marriage break-up and subsequent media coverage. Friends for ever I hope Robert!

To my lifelong PR people, the brilliant Gerry Lundberg and Sinead O'Doherty at Lundberg PR for always being there for me with 'the right words'. Not forgetting the lovely Donna Fitzpatrick PR.

My brilliant and beautiful solicitor Pamela O'Loughlin at Actons for sorting out all the shit that happens in my life with a smile (and not forgetting you lovely chirpy Ali ... the phone queen of Actons).

My super accountant Randal Grey, who always tries to keep my head above the water line. Couldn't mention accountants without a big thank you to you dear Frances Brennan and Alan Duffy for all the years up to now!

If I were to do anymore 'thank yous', there would be no point in writing the book, but my penultimate thank you has to go to my dearest friend and colleague Paddy Cole, arguably one of my favourite people on the entire planet. He has been a friend, mentor to me for too long to mention. It was Paddy who encouraged me to pursue a path in comedy, and he is by far one of the wittiest, funniest people you could ever have the pleasure of knowing. Thank you for all the wonderful advice and support you afforded me in Las Vegas in the times I really needed it. You are simply the best, as indeed are your lovely wife, children, and don't get me started on those sensational sisters of yours, not to mention your darling much-missed mother, Cissy, and sister Sadie, for all the endless cups of tea and great craic in the kitchen in 'Blayney'.

Some of the happiest days of my life were spent around the extended Cole family. Love you always Cosy!!!!

And finally to the two most brilliant agents any artiste could be lucky enough to have.

The totally amazing Noel Kelly, and very beautiful and talented Niamh Kirwan at NK management. I would walk on hot coals for both of you. Your care and attention to my life and career is second to none, not to mention your endless patience with me when I am driving you both mental! LOL! Love also to the lovely Catriona, Leah, Naoise, and Abbi Kelly … who are 'da bomb'!!!!!

The people who make my world revolve … with as little pain as is humanly possible!

My dentists: Niall O'Connor and DN. Barbara, who keep me smiling, literally!!

My doctor: Doctor Edel McAteer and all the gals Emer, Aine, Mary … and super dep. Paula.

My animal doctors, who keep my beloved menagerie of furry friends in great shape.

Vets, Manfred, Amanda and Sarah Neale, at Fairways Veterinary Practice, Rathfarnham.

My bird vets, John at Charlemont Vets, and Dr Bairbre O'Malley, Dr Liz O'Malley and Elaine, at Bray Avian vets.

My throat specialist Mr Donald McShane at Charlemont Clinic.

My foot queen Chiropodist Dr Esther Batt.

Paschal, Pauline, Anna, Claire, Mammy and all the wonderful Mac Mahons at Knocklyon's No 1. Dry Cleaners. How many brilliant 'last minute' costume jobs have you saved my career with Paschal. A true gentleman!

Danielle at Danielle Dress Hire, Clontarf, for those special occasions!

Make up supremos: Lisa O'Connor and all the divine guys and gals over the years in RTÉ make-up room.

Show injury masseuse Brendan in Butterfield Health Centre.

My eye doctors: Dr Kate Coleman, Tom Egan Cork (Egans) and Gerard Brady Dublin (Bradys).

Cobblers supreme, old Mr Clegg repaired all my tap, ballet, Irish dance shoes, and to this day so do his sons, and grandson Brian Clegg RSC.

Security supremo Mervyn Rundle, (and Sean O'Connor).

The one and only Declan Hanley at Hanley storage, Newtownmountkennedy.

Paul and all the gang at Panda.

John my 'drains hero' (in an old Georgian house – a *very* important man!).

Eurotech Underfloor Heating Castleblayney, Gerry, Agnes and Co. who keep an old Georgian house well heated ... Brrrrrr!

The talented Melissa Nolan in Dublin's finest 'The Dolls Hospital'.

Hairspray ... Couldn't do a show without your fab hair 'stuff' Dolores!

My picture framer, Bernard, in Terenure Framers.

Exquisite lace maker and dear friend Celcie Deveraux.

The totally divine John Healy, *The Restaurant* RTÉ/The Four Seasons.

All my DIY needs: Brian and Pat at Knocklyon Hardware, plus all the fab staff at Woodies, Tallaght.

Super 'house looker afterers' Maria Popa, Valera Vitale, Constantine Denis and Dmitri ... and of course our beloved Anna Possderie.

Super parody writer Niall Jordan.

The totally professional and caring 'Safe Hands' guys n' gals ... for exercising my mutts when I can't.

All the countless drivers, roadies, taxi drivers and chauffeurs that have taken me safely through the day and night to gigs ... God bless you all!

Orla and Paddy Boland ... Only *you* know how brilliant you are!

All the fab staff at Knocklyon Xtravision.

Daryn (brilliant) Crosby, Paddy and Finola Whelan, the best neighbours any one could ask for. Úna and Damian Gibbons likewise. Not forgetting handsome Damian Jnr and beautiful little Lauren.

The magnificent Geraldine and Dermot Wagner, Gilda (Naomi's teacher) and all the Sisk family. Jackie Green. The 'other' Mary and Oliver Coughlan, Patricia and Paudric and the ever generous Mairéad Egan.

Myra and gals at Terenure Office Supplies.

Trimbles Gift Shop, Terenure.

Kathleen at Tesco Rathfarnham – the best!

Oliver and all the gang in Musgraves, Ballymount.

Mick at Power City and Jennifer and all at Harvey Normans.

All my friends in Newlands Garden Centre.

The Heffernan twins ... David and Gerard.

Vincent, Neil, Derek, and all the divine guys in Edmonstown Post Office ... y'all the best!

June and all my pals in Louis Vuitton in Brown Thomas.

Cian McGuirk, Brendan, Steven, Graham in BNC O2 Rathfarnham Shopping Centre.

Ireland's theatre bar queen boss – Maureen Grant.

One of the greatest stage door managers of all time – The Gaiety's James Fitzgerald.

Connolly Seafood Company, Rathmines … Fab shop!

The ever stylish 'Locky' at Carroll and Kinsella Motors, Churchtown.

The beautiful Amanda Brunker for just being FA! Love that gal!

Breffni Pets: (Dave Walsh) Windy Arbour and all my friends at Maxi Zoo in Tallaght and all over the country when I'm on tour, and dear Paddy in Rathfarnham Garden Centre.

Sullys Pet Shop, Cork.

Glass 'experts' Theresa and Joanne at Capitol Glass.

Mrs build it, paint it, fix it, Pam (The Painting Company) Gaffney.

Most talented carpenter in Ireland Mark Sheeran, if he would ever contact me!

Pat McGuirk, Castleblayney – one of the nicest people I have ever met and the finest chicken farmer in Ireland!

Pat Henry – The no 1. trainer on the planet!

Pat Trunkfield, Shailesh Patel, Jocelyn Balubar, Mel Finn, Lisa Slatter, Tony Warren, Gary Chapman, (my South African husband … LOL!) Neil Maythem, the brilliant Brian Taylor and all my wonderful friends in PME/GEM Sugarcraft, UK and South Africa.

Hollingsworths for all the great bicycles since childhood, and Maeve Hollingsworth for all the laughs at school.

Falks Lighting, likewise Vivienne Richardson, for continued school laughs.

Dodi, Kemal, Yumna and all my friends in the grand bazaar in Istanbul – the best costume jewellery in the world.

All my wonderful Irish friends in Gabarone, Africa.

Adel El Gabry and all my friends at Sphinx square in Giza, Cairo, Egypt.

To Fr Dermod McCarthy – thank you for your lovely story! Ahh the Young Dublin Three singing the wrong lyrics on the stage of the Rathmines parish hall! What were we like? You're right, the Banana Boat Song wasn't the same after us!

All the super managers and staff of Superquinn, Knocklyon, (especially Jim Herbage and all the brilliant butchers).

LX Supremo Eamon McConnell – *the* greatest electrician of all time!

Have to also mention Martin Kelehan (theatre & film) in the brilliant LX dept.

World class costumier, Synan O'Mahony.

Sound supremos Terry Heron (Ireland and EUROVISION) Tommy (Scotland) Gorman and Jim Doherty.

Restaurant supremo Robert Doggett, every entertainer's fave restaurant, Trocadero.

Adrian Rossetti and all in my beloved Waterford Castle, (our escape from all the madness!).

Stylist supremo, Mary Fay.

Sinead Sheehan, PR lady and all at O2 Phones.

Hair supremos Elaine (at Scruples … great hairdresser), Colin Connaughton and Gary Kavanagh.

Stage director Supremos: Áine Flanagan, George McFall, Fergal O'Doherty, John Brogan, Marie Breen.

Interiors supremo: Sharon Creagh (Sharon Creagh Interiors – the most beautiful shop in Ireland (Rathgar, Dublin).

My genius artist cousin Neil Condron (painter of Sinead O'Connor's sublime album cover *Upon Small Shoulders*), his wife, Ireland's premier milliner, Jean Condron (Hats by Jean) a gifted lady and the *only* person to buy a hat from!

Owen Connolly's touching book *Upon My Father's Shoulders,* not forgetting Susie Condron – Owen and Susie being the family shrinks!

Ireland's queen of the circus – ringmaster extraordinaire – Marion Fossett of Fossett's Circus.

Über pro theatre chaperones, Yvonne May, Phil Dempsey, Gay Ivory, Crona Byrne (another of my Fairy God children, you da bomb Crona!).

My favourite radio producer, Kevin Hough and all the talented Hough family.

World's number one choreographer and dancer – Belinda Murphy.

Ireland's number one tailor, 'the cousin', Louis Copeland, and most importantly my dear uncle Jack Condron of O'Connor's 'bespoke tailors to the gentry' 1930 to the late 70s and of course the irreplaceable, Viava Masalskiene.

Über efficient theatre school administrator, Annette Walsh.

Pasta queen – May Frisbee (Pasta Fresco).

Dave McClean and Niall in Dublin's finest food emporium Donnybrook Fair.

Weather forecast queen, Evelyn Cusack, who was kind enough to take my phone calls in RTÉ for every one of my children's birthday parties over the years, to give me the weather prospects!

Great theatre director and even greater friend, Brian Merriman.

The legendary Don Nugent and all his super staff in Dundrum Shopping Centre.

Inspiring Ideas, Blanchardstown Shopping Centre, Alma and Paul Donnelly, for all my craft/needlework and gift needs. Fab shop!

Easons in Dundrum Shopping Centre, a big thank you over the years to Sheila Baker and Jackie Tate.

Great nannies way back when: Anna Butler (the goddess of them all); Caroline and Tracy Comorford (salt of the earth); Dolores ... Wonderful Madeline from Malta! (R.I.P.).

Knocklyon Post Office heroines; the indefatigable and über brave, Louise and Joanne Donohue (we all love you in Knocklyon ladies).

My lifelong hero: Perry Como.

My bones king: Dr Maurice Neligan, at the Beacon Clinic.

My asthma king: Professor Steven Lane and the superbly efficient Jane.

My say it like it is HERO: Nell McCafferty.

My darling Alice 'Sugarcraft' Christie, UK.

Frances McDermot ... the woman I always wanted to look like!

Broadcaster and programme maker extraordinaire Brendan Balfe.

Brilliant female radio star, and favourite interviewer of them all – Marian Finucane; and in that category of brilliance as an interviewer, Derek Mooney, and lately, Nora Owen.

Lisa Kelly and Scott Porter and the beautiful Porter children: Cian, Jack, Ellie and the latest addition baby Harry-Scott Porter ... for your individual and collective great talent and all your kindness to my daughters, in particular Chloë.

Alan Murphy at AIB Baggot Street: the young, gorgeous, boy band-looking manager – Arrragghhh!!! Don't get me started!

All the beautiful gals of Celtic Woman past, present, and I've no doubt future – thank you for your kindness to Chlo.

Photographers whose pics I have loved: No. 1, Peter Orford; Tony Gavin; Colm Henry; Brian McEvoy; Barry McCall; Dermot Sullivan; Sarah Doyle (My cover shooter) Tony Higgins; Tom Collins; RTE Guide's terrific Eve Holmes; Roy Bedel and the irrepressible, John Cooney; Billy, and all in the Dublin Camera Exchange.

Lucy Johnston; Kevin McFeely; Fionn McCann; Mark McCall; All the best 'paps' – you know who you are – yes, yes, yes of course you're top of the list Mark Doyle!

Gerry Moorhead – my sugarcraft 'chocolate fixer'.

The amazing astrologer Fergie Gibson.

Gilda Turner, best dance captain ever.

Fiona at the Gleneagle Killarney.

John Murphy ... 'The Sounds" for first 'You Know What'.

Norcool's great John Fitzgerald – fridge genius!

RTÉ's Stills Library, my thanks to Emma Keogh, Natalie, Rajeep for all your help with RTÉ shots.

Washing machine genius Colm Jackson, and his assistant Robert Kordan.

Stereo Repairs in Rathmines, Sean Gallagher.

All the great gals in Pierce and Fitzgibbons Kerry.

Michael O'Doherty and the much missed, Emer O'Reilly Hyland and all the wonderful staff of *VIP* magazine.

Brilliant young journalist and articulate presenter Colette Fitzpatrick ... between herself the amazing (and terrifying) Terry Prone, Michael O'Doherty and the crossword, that's reason enough for me to buy the Evening Herald every night!

Paint guru's in Nash's Dundrum, and Farrow & Ball at MRCB.

Margaret Heffernan for her kindness to me during the panto years.

Likewise, Ben Dunne and old Mr Dunne for the Braemor Rooms and Old Jury's cabaret years.

Ben Frow TV3 boss: One of the classiest, sharpest, most clued in people I have ever met. They'll never replace you! (And yes, somehow, we will eventually work together Ben!)

Super TV people Jim Jennings and Bill Malone; Justin Nelson; Ted Dolan; Mike Kelly; Aiden Maguire; Ian McGarry; Linda McQuaid; Avril McRory; Larry Masterson; Joe and Tina O'Donnell; Mike and Maureen Kelly.

Great talent, great friend of too many years to mention Shay Healy and the amazing Dympna.

Great private educators of my time, Maeve Binchy, Mrs Kathleen McAllister-Doohan, Mine Gurekan, and all my Turkish tutors in the language centre, Trinity College – great times there, great memories!

Brilliant Georgian architects/experts Pat and Miriam Colclough.

My fave celeb chefs: Conrad Gallagher, Derry Clark, Kevin Dundon, Nevin Maguire, Stephen McAllister,

Gary O'Hanlon, Tim O'Sullivan, the late great, Noel McHugh.

Mega tour manager, Ray Tizzard.

Rubinesque Ribbons ... stunning shop!

Sahara Nuts – Declan and gang – best bar snacks in Ireland!

Superb jewellers, Adrian and all at Fitzgibbon Jewellers, Rathfarnham Shopping Centre; Audrey Lehane in the beautiful Azure Jewellers, Cork.

Fave florists Bill and all the crew at Knocklyon Florists, Frank and crew at Day by Day, in Rathfarnham Village, then in Cork, lovely Kamla at Kamla's Flowers.

The lovely gift shop in Rathfarnham Shopping Centre.

Brilliant pharmacists Donal and Maureen (not forgetting Eddie – we miss ya), Barbara, Bernie, Kathy, Jo-Anne Andrea, Niamh, the lovely Leslie and all the super gang at Doc Morris, Knocklyon.

The Banana Tree, Grammes Jewellers, Stephens Green Centre, and the wonderful and so so thoughtful Carol Magee, R.I.P., (That stunning coral and silver piece still worn and admired all over the world, even my daughters have started to borrow it!)

James Murphy and all at Life's 2 Good, for super work over the years.

Gerry Barnes at the Cork Opera House for introducing Robert and I – nice one Gerry!

Teresa Condron for loving Uncle Chris so well.

Pat Talbot at the Everyman Theatre Cork, for the wittiest cards.

All my pals in Unilever head office in Dublin, have *never* prepared for a show without the time-old, tested and wonderful Slim-fast.

John P. Burke and Julie, for super asthma "natural" help, Lyprinol capsules, and the brilliant 'Slim gum'.

Right up almost to print, the discovery of Irish Peat/Turf Incense, the best home or abroad burner ever! Buy it or miss out on 'Ireland – and the smell of home' big time!

My sugarcraft friends internationally … I will mention you all in the sugarcraft book ok?

Incredible friends, and people I have had the pleasure of knowing/performing/working with ...

Maxi (joined at the hip); Moya Doherty (long-term friend); Barbara McKenzie (the best of the best); Siobhan McCarthy (my buddy); Alma Carroll (friends since forever); Flo McSweeney (love ya); Margo Tracy; Eileen Colgan; Eileen Pearson; Mine Gurekan; Carol Kelly-Brandon (what a horsewoman); Sinead (Nothing compares to you) O'Connor; Katy Reddy; Brian Whitehead (Olympia Theatre boss); Gerry Sinnott (former Olympia Theatre boss); Louis Walsh; Bill (Riverdance genius) Whelan; Andrew (what's going on?) Boland; Lady Joan Bergen 'our Oscar winning' film costume designer; Andrew 'the beautiful bodyguard' Green; Adam (world talent) Lawlor; Carol Hanna; Celcie Deveraux; Dáithí Ó Sé; Anna Fox; Nellie Conroy; Joe Conlon (Mr Song and Dance); Nick Grennell; the brave Fr Brian Darcy; Fran and Red Hurley; Frances Boardman; Sadie Cuffe; Kay Lynch; Belinda Murphy; Frank McNamara and Theresa Lowe; Andy O'Callaghan, Clodagh, Sheenagh and Kate; Gabriel Byrne; Gay Byrne & Kathleen Watkins; Alan (Gaiety Theatre) McQuillan; John, and the entire McColgan family; Geraldine O'Callaghan (love her to bits and back!); Wagner; Gilda Turner; Mary McEvoy; Maria Blayney; Sorcha Furlong; John Sullivan; Derry Glen; David Downes (Celtic Woman MD genius); Earl Gill; Chris Keneavy; Jim Doherty and Ann, Joan and Tony Kenny; the legendary Billie Barry; Frank Sheerin and Catherine; Johnny and Joey Morrison; Judge Anne Watkins; Elizabeth Maher; Lord Henry and Lady Iona Mountcharles; Larry Bass and family; Billy McGrath and family; Phillip Kampff and family; Noel (too funny) V. Ginnity; Pat Reilly (No.1 session singer); Rita 'Blossom' Bizedenhaut Madigan; Paul O'Kelly (backgammon pal); Rick O'Daniel and Scott Sublet (Indiana cowboys USA); Shirley Andreuchetti; Simon Delaney; Mickey Higgy, (Michael Higgins and Steven); Noel Pearson; Helen and Katie Jane Goldin; Michael Early; my darling Brendan and Eileen Grace and all the bunnies and grandbunnies; Elvis Presley (thanks for the cool ring Elvis!); Margaret Milner and all my lovely Kerry cousins; Michelle King; Mike and Noelle Dalton; Grace Cleary and Cassie.

Les Davies – showjumper and welder extraordinaire; Jimmy "Guitar legend" Smith – what a f***ing ridiculous talent!

Una Crawford O'Brien; Eileen Gibbons; Janet Phillips; Laura Kelly; Ellen McElroy, Grace Dunne; Gavin Lamb-Murphy; Mary Coughlan; Mary (Crystal Swing) Burke; Geraldine Plunkett.

Hilda Fay; Honor Heffernan; Daniel O'Donnell; Dickie Rock; Lucy Kennedy; Michelle Mais (Maisie); Pamela Keely; Paul Foxy Martin; Phil Sterling; Rebecca Stephanie Olive and Jimmy Barry; Ronan Collins; Derek Davies; Noel Pearson; Steve (brilliant) Blount; Theresa Rocca; Julian Benson; Gail Kaneswarren; Vivienne Connolly; Shane (Rugby) Byrne; The divine 'Seoiges'; Ryan Tubridy; Joe Duffy (LOVE that man); Craig Doyle (should be a law against being that handsome and sexy); Bláthnaid Ní Chofaigh; Nuala Carey; Peter Andre; Barney (yes the purple one), Dustin the Turkey ... whatever! Richie Hayes; Brian Ormond; Jass and Mick, and, of course, the gorgeous Ciara Ormond.

The irrepressible Brendan O'Connor and Sarah Cadden, and their darling daughters; Barry Egan (who always 'gets' me!); Ciara Dwyer (and no I don't call you O'Dwyer!); Miriam O'Callaghan; Dana; Mary McEvoy; Alan Hughes and Karl Broderick; Dave Kavanagh; Kohlin Harris (keep up the good work chef); the brilliant Bill Hughes; Colm Keogh (amazing Irish dance partner); great, great talent Des Allen; marvellous broadcasters, Pat Kenny and Vincent Browne; the *Indo's* Mary O'Sullivan; great British choreographer, Brian Rogers; the bright and beautiful Olivia Tracey; Gerry Walsh (super actor); Derry Power; Sil Fox; Brendan O'Carroll; Jonathan Ryan; Bill Golding; Pat Egan; Tony O'Connor; Don Irwin; Johnny McGuigan; great young actresses Claire Birmingham; Maud Johnston; Anne Doyle 'melti instramuntalist' (private joke); Gerry O'Connor and his brilliant son Doc; dancer turned successful Donal Shiels and of course the divine Pat Moylan.

Anita Notaro; Mick Quinn; Jim Bartley, Noelle Brown, Geraldine McLaughlin (stay strong Ger!); Cha and Mya and Cork hero and gentleman, Michael Twomey; Frank Kelly; Des Keogh. Jackie McGrath and the wonderful Alan and Lisa. The gifted young actress Eleanor Byrne and smashing Mom Rita. The totally amazing Vavasseurs, Adrienne, Sophie, Dr Claudine, Alex and Conor, Phil and Barry Connolly and the fantastic Craig and Victoria.

Roseleen Bouktilla and the brilliant young actor Adam. Rebecca Smith, Sheila and the amazingly talented Daniel Allwell. The amazing Rosie and Catherine Watson; Terry Neason; John Kavanagh; Áine Ní Mhúirí; Ben Barnes; the delightful "Byrne" girls, Crona and Susie; Jimmy (gifted musician) Smith; Jonathan Ryan; Helen Jordan; Claire Ivory; Lorna, Adele and Darren Dempsey; Natasha May; super musical director; Eugene McCarthy; Seanna Woods.

'De 3 KAHLEANS' ... Aileen Pringle, Karen Black, Joan Lee, Jenny Newman, amazing session singers. Not forgetting "token Kahlean" Tommy Moore.

The wonderful Carolan Boys; (Jack, Ben and Niall, and the divine Jack and Myles Roynane. Barry O'Connell; Conor and Aengus McAnally; Maureen Cairnduff; Sharon Brown; Dec and the exquisite brown boys Alex, Matthew and Dudley, Áine Lane, Anne Doyle (fine young actresses). Likewise, the beautiful Ms Fiona Byrne. The extraordinarily super Spollen family, especially Marina, Gillian, and Steven. Also, the great McCartney kids. My 'teddy bear', Megan Frances, and of course Sarah Jane; Sinead and Agnes.

The divine Mick Devine (chauffeur to the REAL big stars); Andrew Lynford (brilliant British director ... short fuse!); Alan Stanford (the rolls Brendan..); Michael Grennell; Grace and Cassie; Angeline Ball; Lisa Lambe; Susan McFadden; Stuart O'Connor; Niamh Flanagan; Hilda Fay; Rebecca Smith; Johnny McGuigan; Don Irwin; Tom Flanagan, (best floor managers in TV); Tony O'Connor (wardrobe RTÉ); Earl Gill; Mavis Ascott (the greatest theatre director of my life).

Chris Keneavy (gifted pianist); Des Moore (BRAVO Des ... LOL); Desi Reynolds; Paul McAteer; Des Lacey; Noel Guthrie; Greg and Andrew Boland; Bill Summerville Large; John D'Ardis; Johnny Tate; Paddy Gibbons; Johnny, Susan and Maureen Ward; Sonny Knowles (how long would you say that hall is Sonny?); Des Smyth; and all the Murphys of the Stillorgan Bowl.

R.I.P. my darling friends ...

Gerry Ryan; Perry Como (and I love you so!); Mo Po (Maureen Potter); Jonathan Philbin Bowman; Dermot Morgan; Bernadette Greevy; Tom Dunphy (love always); my dear friend and world talent, Dory Previn; Joe Dolan; David Kelly; Ann Bushnell (Annie B); Uncle Chris, Auntie Meta, and Colin Bailey; Marjorie Courtney; Eithne McGuinness; Annie Cuffe; Fred O'Donovan; Paul Goldin; Vic McNamara (The strangers); Aiden Grennell; Dick Hill (best TV boss ever); Tom Murphy (brilliant young actor taken too soon); Mickey (Big 8) O'Neill; Noel Kelehan; Phyllis O'Brien (great dancer); Tommy and Phil Ellis; Dara O'Broin (RTÉ floor manager); Mick Lally; the beautiful Katie O'Callaghan; Kathleen Doohan (my tutor); Paddy Murphy; Lil Keogh; Chris Vavasseur; Theresa O'Dwyer; Fr Hubert Condron; Ray McAnally; Aengus Fanning; Beryl Fagan; Eugene Lambert; Bill Fuller; Bill La Russo (owner of our favourite 'watering hole' in Vegas – the Flame); my beautiful young acting student Daniel Maher; Jim White (my brilliant dancer and friend); Dr Maurice Neligan Snr; Sam and Madge McCoubrey (thanks for all the great tea, sandwiches and good old 'Mayo' advice during rehearsals in Wilfred Tce. Madge!) Life long, self-confessed 'Life president of my fan club', the wonderful and brave-to-the-end, Violet Tully.

Albert Healy; Paddy and Carmel Sullivan; Hal Roach, Tom McGrath (RTÉ); Ronnie Drew and Barney McKenna; Charles Mitchell (my greatest fan ever ... his words); Fran O'Toole; Brian McCoy; Paul Ashford (Miami/Stepaside); Maud Gonne's film maker son; Podger (The saxy) Reynolds; Frank Walsh (yes Louise, your Frank!); Jim and Deirdre Murtagh; Alice Cleary; RTÉ's Áine O'Connor; Kevin Marron; Pat (Sands); John Feeney; Tony Kavanagh (my great drummer); Jack O'Donoghue (Thunderbirds); Brendan Kearney (bank manager); my darling Uncle Jack, a slip of a lad at 96; As I go to print, I had to take dearest friend and life-long stage manager Yvette Hally, off the 'stage manager' list and sadly name her in this one.

And most importantly, Maeve Binchy from whom I learned my love of the English language.

My Profound Love and Thanks to the Gay Community of Ireland ...

For your love and support (not to mention countless impeccable impersonations of me throughout the years) the Sacred Heart Lamps under my pic ... Ha!! One of my all time favourite gigs was THAT night in the George.

Your 'pink pounds' spent in to all my shows have bought many a pair of FAB pink shoes for me and my gals ... LOL!

Love you all with all my heart and soul!

Stay strong and proud y'all

And remember ... *'Nil illegitimi carborundum ...'* ('Don't let the bastards grind you down!')

You rock ! x

Dear Santa,

Can you feel free to leave the following men under my tree (not all at once you understand ... space them out over a few years please!)

John Suchet - marry me please? At least let's have dinner?

Laurence Llewelyn Bowen (yum yum); Alan Titchmarsh - all from other walks of life, and Classic FM, my No. 1 radio station on the planet.

Vladimir Ashkanazy; Keith Duffy; Bon Jovi; Adam Clayton; George McMahon; Adam (from the late great OTT); Richard Dawkins No. 1 brain on the planet; Stephen Fry; Terry Wogan; Dara Ó Briain; Dr Zahi Hawass (Egyptologist); Jonathan Ross; John Bowman; Liam Neeson; Gabriel Byrne; Fr Brian D'Arcy; Sgt Larry Byrne (The Bridewell); Greg Feith NTSB; Dr Maurice Neligan Jnr; Dr Joel Christianson; Eddie Macken; Peter Collins (sports god!); Craig Doyle; the two stunningly beautiful 6ft Turks that live in Knocklyon – Ne Kadar kalamği düsünüyorsunuz çok güzel canimlar?

And most importantly ...

My two babies who passed to another world without me knowing them or them knowing me ... we will meet again little ones … Mama promises. XXX

And to my animals ...

All my beloved dogs, cats, ponies, horses, birdies, fish, and wonderful furry companions who have sadly left my life, we will all meet up again over the bridge, I promise … and hey mutties, we will have endless time together playing ball down at the dodder. I love and thank you for your unquestioning, unconditional love, true friendship, life-saving kindness and devotion. I have loved you all passionately.